The Reminiscences of Charlotte Lady Wake

Lucy Wake

BIBLIOLIFE

The Reminiscences of
Charlotte, Lady Wake

EDITED BY

LUCY WAKE

SECOND IMPRESSION

William Blackwood and Sons
Edinburgh and London
1909

PREFACE.

CHARLOTTE, LADY WAKE, whose reminiscences are contained in this volume, began her life with the last century. Born on June 9, 1800, the second daughter of Craufurd Tait of Harviestoun and of Susan, daughter of Sir Ilay Campbell of Succoth, she was named Charlotte Murdoch after her father's mother, one of the Murdochs of Cumlodden. Of her young days she retained the liveliest impressions, and in the earliest of the 'Reminiscences' that follow there will be found a very graphic and amusing and often touching description of life in Scotland and of Edinburgh society in the beginning of the nineteenth century.

In 1822 she became the wife of Charles Wake, son of Sir William Wake of Courteenhall, Northamptonshire, whom he succeeded in 1847. Her marriage brought her to live in Derbyshire, Worcestershire, and Northamptonshire, and with her husband she travelled much on the Continent in the days before railroads. Here also, as in Edinburgh and at Harviestoun, she laid up a store of experience to be drawn upon later for these recollections, which, as will be seen, are particularly vivid of the Revolution of 1830, during which she was close to Paris.

It was at Pitsford, Northamptonshire, where she resided after her husband's death in 1864 until her own on March 31, 1888, that Lady Wake wrote these 'Reminiscences,' with which she has incorporated some by her brother Archibald, afterwards Archbishop of Canterbury. She began them originally—little thinking she would survive one eleven years younger than herself—as a record of his early years, and a few of them were included in his 'Life.' Like him and her eldest brother, Sheriff Tait, Lady Wake possessed force of character and intellectual ability, and to the end of a long life, which had been lived in four reigns and had witnessed the jubilee celebrations of two sovereigns, she preserved her great interest in affairs, both public and private, in the world around her. Her conversation, like her writing, was always most entertaining, and even in her extreme old age visitors were constantly coming for a chat with the charming and picturesque old lady who, to a wide acquaintance and vivid impression of the past, added a keen appreciation of the present.

CONTENTS.

viii Contents.

CHAPTER XIV.

. CHAPTER XV.

CHAPTER XVI.

CHAPTER XVII.

CHAPTER XVIII.

CHAPTER XIX.

CHAPTER XX.

CHAPTER XXI.

ILLUSTRATIONS.

THE REMINISCENCES OF
CHARLOTTE, LADY WAKE.

CHAPTER I.

FOREFATHERS OF THE TAITS—FAMILY HOME IN PARK PLACE.

Two hundred years ago there dwelt in Aberdeenshire
a family, valued for their worth, the Taits of Ludquharn,
of the class that used to be known in Scotland by the
name of "Bonnet Lairds," honest men living on their
own farms, and wearing the broad blue "bonnet" that
marked the simplicity of rural and patriarchal lives
far removed from the fashions and customs of the
towns.

Tait is an old Norwegian name signifying love and
affection, and some interesting legends are given of the
origin of the family in the eighth chapter of Ferguson's
'English Surnames,' legends full of romance which,
though we cannot stop to dwell on them, will delight
those readers who love tales of mythical kings and
heroes of doubtful existence.

The Taits of whom we write were said to be a junior
branch of a family well known in Peeblesshire, the Taits

A

of Pirn, and probably this is true.[1]   We find in them
that blending of education and refinement with inde-
pendence of spirit that tells of gentle blood.

In the churchyard of Longside, Aberdeenshire, there
is this inscription on their family tomb—" Under this
stone are interred the ashes of William Tait of Ludquharn, and of Agnes Clerk, his wife.   He died in the
year of human salvation 1725, aged 57, and she died
in 1739, aged 70."   This William Tait left several
grandsons, some of whose fortunes we can trace.   The
life and death of one are thus touchingly recorded in
the faithful family annals of the churchyard—

"To the memory of George Tait of Red Bog, who after
having lived 48 years, in the fear of God and the love of all
men, was, on the 30th May 1757, killed by the fall of a
stack of timber at Peterhead, justly lamented by his friends
and sincerely regretted by all who knew him."

This George Tait left one son, who, made desolate
by the sudden death of his father while yet a little
child, was received into his more prosperous cousin's
family, and by him and his wife brought up with their
own son at Harviestoun, and his prospects in life as
actively forwarded as though he had been their own.
This kindness was never forgotten, and bore most unexpected fruit long after they had passed from life's
busy scenes.   Another grandson became an English
clergyman, rector of Normington in Rutlandshire.

The eldest grandson was grandfather of the Archbishop, John Tait, of whom there is in the family a
beautiful portrait by Raeburn, which well depicts the
calm good sense and manly benevolence which he
inherited from the Blue Bonnets of Aberdeenshire.

[1] To the family of the Taits of Pirn John Tait's descent was traced, and
he was set down as one of its cadets when he applied at the Herald's
College for his proper coat of arms.

JOHN TAIT OF HARVIESTOUN.
From the Painting by Sir Henry Raeburn.

Though more than one knightly branch was quickly grafted on the parent stem, we must not lose sight of these good men whose records are only in the church-yard. Their descendant John followed out with distinguished success the career marked out for him by his father as Writer to the Signet. While very young he was received into the office of one of the most distinguished of the profession, Ronald Craufurd, whose talents and social qualities caused his society to be courted and prized in the first circles in Edinburgh, then really the capital of Scotland, London not having yet drawn from it those families who congregated there to rob the winter months of their gloom. Among them Ronald Craufurd was a universal favourite. His daughter and only child married the Earl of Dumfries. He appears to have shown much friendly kindness to young John Tait, whose attachment to him continued to the day of his death, when he succeeded to his business, and to the confidence of many of his distinguished employers.

John Tait married a young lady of the singular name of Charles Murdoch. She was so called after Prince Charlie, the hero of Scottish ballads and the idol of Scottish imagination. In the cause of this last of the Stuarts her family had suffered much. She was related to many of the best families in Scotland, and, according to a pedigree carefully compiled by one of the Cochrane family some fifty years ago, was descended from Robert Bruce, King of Scotland. She was a very pretty woman with a highly cultivated mind, and of so independent a spirit that with the work of her hands she supported her widowed mother, who had been left in the deepest poverty. Nor was this a singular instance; there were many of the far-descended daughters of families ruined by their devotion to the

Stuart cause, who in like manner supported their mothers and themselves; and it tells well for the good sense and good feeling of the Scottish society of that day that they were always regarded as equals by the ladies who employed them. There was a deep sympathy for all who had suffered in the cause of the beloved Prince Charlie, who had the misery of carrying into exile the grievous knowledge that his gallant but rash attempt to reconquer the throne of his fathers, with no source of help but the romantic chivalry of his countrymen, had brought ruin, death, and desolation on all who were devoted to him.

His fair and feminine namesake Charles Murdoch, becoming the wife of the young John Tait, was happy in his affection and in the culture of the mind of their only son Craufurd, who had been named in grateful remembrance of the kind and influential friend who had so beneficially forwarded his father's interests, the head of the firm John Tait was received into.

Till the time of this marriage the family, like many others in the north of Scotland, had been Episcopalians, and it was her influence that drew her husband into the Established Church of Scotland, involving the consequence of her son being brought up as a Presbyterian.

But the mother imparted also to her son much of the poetry of her own mind, and a love for the many traditions of her ancestry, one of the most interesting of which was the origin of her family, commemorated by the three ravens, each pierced with an arrow, which formed their armorial bearings. According to the tradition that had come down from father to son, there dwelt upon a high peak in Galloway, in the time of the perilous wanderings and escapes of Robert Bruce, a widow known by the name of the Widow of the Peak. The king had been forced with his followers to seek for refuge, like David of old, among the rocks and fastnesses of the wilderness, and for many weeks had always been traced and his hiding-place discovered by the singular pertinacity of three ravens, which perpetually followed and hovered over the little band. Vain had been every effort to bring them down, till the Bruce came to the neighbourhood of the Widow of the Peak, whose sons, celebrated marksmen, at once joined him, and with their arrows brought down the traitorous ravens. The king grate-fully rewarded them, and the youngest of the three, Murdoch, was the ancestor of the family that bore his name, the Murdochs of Cumlodden; the king having bestowed the lands adjoining their original home upon the brothers, who had gallantly adhered to his cause, fighting bravely for him till his enemies were overcome and the English driven from the land.

The descendants of the Widow of the Peak inherited the same dauntless spirit, and I shall afterwards refer to a young daughter of the line who in much later days showed herself worthy of her name.

Craufurd Tait's mother died when he was only sixteen, but his boyhood had been too deeply impressed with the poetry of her mind for its influence ever to pass away. Perhaps it would have been better if his father's quiet good sense had rather been the prevailing element in the formation of his character.

The family home in Edinburgh was, at the end of the eighteenth century, in Park Place,[1] a bright, sunny batch of houses looking over their own gardens at the back towards the Castle Hill and the beautiful

---

[1] The houses in Park Place have been pulled down to make way for the new buildings of the University of Edinburgh. A bust of Archbishop Tait has been placed in a niche in the wall to mark his birthplace.

building called Heriot's Hospital, across the Meadows,
then a public walk full of fine trees. It was next
door to the house of Sir Ilay Campbell, then Lord
President of the Supreme Court of Scotland, a man
as much beloved for the straightforward simplicity
of his character as respected for his talents and
legal knowledge. His wife was in her day a celebrated beauty, and this, with a ready wit and unusual
ability, gave her much influence with the political
men of the time.

Before her marriage "bonnie Susie Murray" was a
popular toast, and with the young men of the day,
in their convivial meetings, it was a favourite witticism
to add, "We will drink to bonnie Susie Murray in
spite of her teeth," alluding both to the young lady's
well-known determined spirit and to the fact that
her teeth were not so pearl-white as they ought to
have been to match with her brilliantly fair complexion. Her father was Archibald Murray, Lord
Henderland, a judge in the Court of Session, and
her mother the daughter of Lord William Hay, son
of the Marquess of Tweeddale.

Their house was the resort of the most agreeable
society in Edinburgh; the kindliness of its owner
sought out and brought together the rising young men
of his own profession, while the more worldly spirit of
the lady drew together the world of fashion.

The then celebrated Duchess of Gordon was one' of
her intimate friends,—perhaps associates would be a
better word, for friendship could scarcely have existed
between two such spirits. There was just sufficient
similarity in their talents and their tastes to make
them suitable to each other, for the formidable duchess
had the reputation of fairly overriding all who would
submit to her; decidedly bonnie Susie Murray was not

to be overridden by any one. Through her veins ran a
fiery flood, and if she was a star in the world of fashion,
to her children she was rather a portentous meteor, for
their orbit was not hers; and her sudden appearances
when she used to flash down upon them from her house
in town to their sea-bathing quarters, where they were
regularly sent both for their health and that they might
be out of the way, filled their young hearts more with
dismay than with filial delight. Often in after years
they have described the trembling with which they
used to hear the rustling of her silk dress in the passages
approaching their schoolroom door. These visits might
almost be called domiciliary visits, so keen was the
search into all wrong-doing, so swift and sure the
punishment that descended upon a convicted culprit.
If the mother was severe, the father was invariably
kind. His nature was to be indulgent to the young.

The early love which in their youth had sprung up
between this ill-matched but truly united pair continued
to extreme old age. They must have known each other
well, for their respective families inhabited apartments
in one of those enormous piles of buildings[1] which
formed the best houses in earlier times in the old town
of Edinburgh.

Story after story—more properly, in the speech of
the day, flat upon flat—rose up into the skies, each one
spacious and commodious, and one common stair connected all the apartments together. The tide of fashion
has rolled from them; dingy, dark, and of evil odour
now, such of them as still exist are inhabited by every
degree of the lower classes, and for the convenience of
their present inhabitants they are now subdivided into

---

[1] *Vide* the account given in the Caldwell Papers of David Hume the
historian drinking tea with Mrs Campbell of Succoth, the mother of Sir
Ilay Campbell, in one of these flats.

all manner of apartments, but many still retain in the ceilings and chimney - pieces traces of their former magnificence. When the tastes of the families who inhabited them were congenial, these enormous houses contained the elements of a most pleasant form of social life.

In the days of courtship nothing could have been more charming; but there were inconveniences attending this jumble of families of different habits, as Sir Ilay afterwards found, his first married home being still in St James' Court. He used to relate that he was often sadly disturbed in his studies by the violent commotions that took place exactly over his head. As the stairs mounted higher, the pretensions of the occupants of the flats went down in the opposite scale, and the apartment overhead belonged to Dr Spence, whose wife was not of the most peaceable disposition. The thunders of Jove were a trifle to the uproar that shook the ceiling when this lady was more than usually irate, and once, when Sir Ilay was deep in the preparation of a difficult case, his cogitations were disturbed by a strange stamping above, accompanied by showers of dislodged plaster. He looked up, and lo! after a furious thump, down came a large displacement, and a very tidy-looking leg and foot with a little high-heeled shoe appeared through the ceiling. Mrs Spence had stamped too hard.

It was in one of these houses in the quarter that was called St James' Court, looking over the beautiful slope where the town of Edinburgh now stands, that the young Campbell of Succoth became devoted to the beautiful Susan Murray of Henderland. His own father was a Writer to the Signet, and brought up his eldest son as an advocate in the Scottish courts of law. His mother, Ellen Wallace, was the heiress

SIR ILAY CAMPBELL OF SUCCOTH.

of Ellersley, the family property of William Wallace the famous Scottish patriot, the representative of whose family she was, being in straight descent from his brother : the hero himself had no child.

They were early married, and his success at the Scottish bar was rapid ; he was successively the Lord Advocate and Lord President of the Courts of Scotland. Perhaps some tender recollections of his own youth and early love led him to encourage the attachment that grew up between one of his younger daughters and the son of his next-door neighbour.

Susan Campbell, fair and gentle, inheriting his most lovable disposition and much of her mother's beauty without any of her temper, at eighteen years of age became the wife of Craufurd Tait.

Few still live who remember the father and mother of the Archbishop of Canterbury, for his mother died young and his father did not live to be a really old man. It is impossible now to look at his picture without being attracted by his clever face and broad benevolent brow. The smile that is still there seems to say, "The pains I took in forming the mind of my youngest boy have not been lost. He is all I foresaw he would be ; whatever other plans of mine have failed, those made for him have been successful."

Poor father! he did not live to see them realised, and many cares gathered round his declining years ; but through the clouds the welfare of his children shone as a cheering light, and chiefly, indeed above all, the success of his youngest son, as, step by step, he followed out the path he in his own mind had marked for him, and for which he carefully trained him.

The earliest and most distinct remembrance I have of my mother is of her being seated on the sofa of the little drawing-room. It is the more indelibly impressed on my remembrance because of the scene that there took place some ten years afterwards. But the future is hid in mercy from us, and there was nothing then to mar the perfect enjoyment of mother and child : the child sat at her feet on a little stool, making a picture from the flowers in her gown by pricking them with a pin upon a piece of writing-paper she had given her. I remember it well, for she laid her hand upon my head and in a low voice repeated Cowper's beautiful lines in his address to his mother's picture. All this became afterwards more distinct from this poem being an especial favourite with my father, whom I often heard repeat it in detached lines, and never without that early picture rising in my mind.

.

CHAPTER II.

A FEW years before this time, in 1800, our grand-father, John Tait, had died at Harviestoun: the old man had been as happy in the tender care of the young wife of his only son as though she had been his own child. It was a misfortune that he did not live longer, for his calm good sense was a safer guide to his son than his own erratic genius.

He left to him the estate of Harviestoun with a tolerably good house, and besides this a beautiful property on the shores of Loch Fyne, which he had named Cumlodden after the family place of the Murdochs, his wife being the representative of that ancient family. His son Craufurd threw himself with ardour into the improvements his imaginative mind already saw transforming the habits and lives of the Highlanders, their actual condition alternating between listless lounging during the summer and daring activity in the herring season, when the lochs were covered with their fishing-boats. They dwelt in houses scarcely deserving the name, the smoke escaping as it could through the doors; and the half-naked children and women, though picturesque in the highest degree, made up a population it was

impossible for the new laird to see without longing
to raise them into something more worthy of the
paradise of scenery amidst which they dwelt. He
accordingly devised a new order of things, building
a series of charming cottages, each having a little
garden and four acres of land attached to it. Instead
of the midden before the door, borders of roses and
mignonette were to delight both eye and nose ; but
alas ! gardens require culture, and roses will not bloom
unless they are carefully tended. The Highlanders
cared nothing for flowers, very little for the profit
and convenience which the croft of four acres was
intended to produce, and they especially detested
the steady labour by which alone it could have been
made profitable.

Had the laird and his family resided at Cumlodden,
something might, perhaps, have been done by influence
and example ; but there being no good house on the
property, beyond a few holiday weeks spent in a
better sort of farm, they never could be there, and
the ideal village which was to have worked such
wonders vanished like a dream, leaving nothing
behind but dilapidated buildings,' broken fences, and
a confused wilderness of thistles asserting their
native right as lords of the soil over the prostrate
roses ; and a still worse result, the necessity of settling
the innumerable bills the scheme had entailed. Donald
returned well satisfied to his lounge and his fishing-
nets, and Meg, his wife, to her usual labours in and
out of the smoke ; while the disappointed proprietor
turned his attention to the more hopeful capabilities
at Harviestoun, where all things speedily shone out
in the glow of his enthusiasm. The old house rapidly
grew, and though within the house of Harviestoun
was charming, with every possible convenience, the

exterior bears traces of the stiff regularity of the
taste of the times. But the improvements that
succeeded each other in rapid succession quite changed
the face of the country. The highroad ran too near
the house—it was moved as though by magic half
a mile lower; clusters of poor mean-looking cottages
occupied ground too near the back of the house—they
disappeared. The cost of the removal of this village
may be estimated by the fact that most of the cottages
were feus or perpetual leases, and therefore had to be
bought from the proprietors at their own prices. I
only remember a straggler here and there; a lovely
garden took their place, laid out by our father with
Milton's description of the garden of Eden for his
guide. Yes, it is true, and surely there never was
a flower-garden like thàt which the idea produced.
Of great extent, it enclosed the lower part of the glen
and mountain at the foot of which it lay, one of the
Ochill range. A dell of lovely green turf led down
from the wilder glen right through the garden, and,
leaping from the rocks above, a bright and noisy burn
danced merrily on through its entire length, speeding
on through ferns and wild-flowers, when it suddenly
disappeared. Some hundred yards below, it as
suddenly emerged with a bound from a cave, falling
over a little ridge of rocks into a small pool which
formed the delight of the children of the family. In
summer the little creatures, very lightly clad, used
to plunge into this basin, leaning their naked shoulders
against the low ridge of rock till the checked stream
rose over their heads like a Queen Mary's ruff.

Some five-and-twenty years later an elderly gentleman approached me in a drawing-room in London,
and asking to be introduced to me, said, " The last
time I saw you, you were one of the little naiads

dancing and splashing in the pool below the cave at Harviestoun; the Ochills in the background, the group of children in and out of the water making it fly in every direction! Never can I forget the scene, that, hot, weary, and dusty as I was, arriving from a walking tour, seemed to me the perfection of beauty." His words brought back the whole party, and I at once remembered his arrival and knew his name to be Craufurd.

Certainly there could not have been a happier family: the father thoroughly enjoyed the society of his children, and seeing all his dreams of picturesque beauty brought into tangible form, had no misgivings as to the expense which attended the gratification of his tastes. It never crossed the imagination of his wife that he could be wrong, and thus improvement after improvement followed each other in rapid succession.

Many things that are now common in the way of agricultural inventions were early seen at Harviestoun, the product of his active brain, including machinery for chopping and steaming all manner of food for cattle, and the spit at the kitchen fire turned by the pressure of water from a branch of the mountain stream. The poultry-houses were the marvel of the whole countryside: story upon story of most comfortable chambers rose one above the other, reached by a flight of little stairs made of bars, up which the various inhabitants ascended with the utmost decorum, the cocks conducting their hens to the highest story, well furnished with comfortable nests; the turkey cocks and their ladies in like manner taking possession of their apartment on the second floor; while the geese and ducks waddled well satisfied into their proper places in the lowest room. Naturally people were slow to believe

CRAUFURD TAIT OF HARVIESTOUN.

that all this really took place. Once in the midst of
an absorbing argument, Craufurd Tait was suddenly
astonished by his brother-in-law Lord Succoth starting off in a race towards the poultry-house, where he
stood agape watching the ascent of a large old turkey
cock. "Well, if I had not seen him I never could have
believed that bubbly-jock [1] would ever have done such
a thing," was his speech as he quietly turned back and
took up the broken thread of the argument. It was
not probable that any circumstance would have been
suffered to interrupt it altogether, for, brilliant in conversation though our father was, and full of amusing
anecdotes, he was, it must be confessed, unconscionably
fond of argument, and never if he could possibly help
it would he let his adversary go without either convincing him or acknowledging himself convinced.

One evening when his wife's cousin, Murray of
Henderland, as fond of argument as himself, had after
a long discussion taken refuge in bed and was just
sinking to sleep, the curtains of his bed were suddenly
drawn back, and the voice of his host startled him
back to life with, "Do you not see, William, that it is
perfectly clear that if so-and-so had been, such-and-
such must be the result," &c., &c.

It was a part of my father's creed that family
affection was in itself a religion, and as such, would
accompany each child as it grew up, a constant protection from evil ; and there is no doubt that he acted
upon that principle, for there could not be a happier
home than ours. Our schoolroom troubles vanished
in the influence of his bright genial temperament, and
the over-strict observances of the Scottish Sabbaths
were tempered into happy Sundays when he was at
home. We children were allowed at all times when

[1] *Scotticè*, a turkey cock.

in the country great freedom in our rambles. We had learned early to take care of ourselves, and when once emancipated from the actual nursery we roved at will, wading in the burn, climbing the rocks, and finding for ourselves lovely glades, making secret haunts among them that filled our very souls with joy. The God of Nature taught us by His works.

Once—I never shall forget it—I had got separated from my constant companion, my brother Jemmie, and forcing my way through tangled bushes, I found myself upon the top of a sunlit brae : shaded by the trees, bright with spring flowers, I threw myself amongst them, looking up into the blue skies. A lark was singing above my head ; up and up it went as though it would reach the light fleecy clouds, and its song seemed to fall round me as a shower of music : " How beautiful it all is, and God made all these things, so beautiful, so happy ! He cannot be the terrible God I have read and heard about. He must be full of love and kindness, or why should He have made all these lovely flowers and all these happy things." For the bees were humming about, and the butterflies chased each other in a sort of merry dance through the soft air, quite near the moss on which I lay. How long this lasted I do not know ; I was so happy that I could not move, and then and there it was revealed to my childish heart that the awful God of the Old Testament whom I had dreaded was indeed the loving Father of all creation, and that we were His children. Never has the lesson He thus taught me on " the Canty Knowe," for that was the name of the place, faded from my memory. It has been a ray of sunlight through many a gloomy sky in after days, and the rejoicing song of the lark has fallen again from heaven as a hymn of praise, for on that day I had learned that God is Love.

The summers and autumns were passed at Harviestoun; each November saw the families reassembled in Edinburgh. There were only four houses in Park Place. The first and largest in the row was Sir Ilay's, the second was ours, and No. 3 was in those early days inhabited by Sir William Honyman, Lord Armadale, one of the judges of the Court of Session, deriving this last title, as our uncle, Lord Succoth, did his, from being a judge. The Honymans were great friends of the three families among whom they dwelt, and had a number of boys who were mixed up in all our brothers' games. One of the younger succeeded to his father, and was well known afterwards as Sir Ord Honyman, colonel of the Grenadier Guards, but he had had an elder brother of whom there was told a story I remember well. It was in the days when all sorts of abuses were permitted that could forward the advancement of those whose position in life could command it, and it was customary to purchase commissions for the new-born babies of families of distinction, their rank progressing as opportunities afforded. This had been done for the eldest son of the house of Honyman, and one morning a gentleman, who had called very early to procure a private interview with Lord Armadale, being requested to wait a few minutes, could not but overhear Lady Honyman calling from her bedroom door, "Jean, what's the matter? What's all that crying in the nursery?" And the answer, "Oh, my leddy, there's naething the matter; it's only the Major greeting for his parritch."

In the fourth house lived our uncle, Lord Succoth. We were almost all one family; I was too young at

B

that time to remember more than the salient points
of our life, and a very principal one was our lady
grandmother in the next house. She had early become quite childish, and almost entirely kept to her
own apartments, where it was our great delight to
visit her,—not that we ever imagined she was fond
of us, but it was a sight to see the beautiful old lady,
with a complexion of lilies and roses, not a line on
her fair face, seated in her arm-chair beautifully
dressed in stiff dark silk and clear white muslin.
Her intellect, overworked, had become weakened, and
it was a strange sight to those who had known her
an eager politician, active in every intrigue of the
time, a beauty and a wit, to see her sitting there
with the novel 'Amelia' in her hand : I do not remember ever seeing her with another book, except
that every night a large Bible was placed open before
her. No trace remained of her former talent, but, de-
spite her taste for fashionable and extravagant society,
she had always been a very careful woman with regard to money, and of this very evident traces remained ; for well I remember her sufferings on the
annual return of Hansel Monday, on which morning,
according to immemorial custom in Scotland, her
chamber was invaded by all her grandchildren coming
for their hansels. She used to receive us sitting up
in her bed with very evident ill-will ; she would try to
put us off with a sixpence each, then one of our
aunts would say, " No, no, leddy, it must be a
shilling apiece ; and this is a big boy, he must have
half-a-crown." Almost a shriek of dismay, and exclamations of dissent considerably stronger than the
ladies of our time would dream of using, accompanied
the laughing attack made upon her steel-beaded purse
(I see it now) for a five-shilling piece for her eldest

grandson. But she was always conquered, for each year she was induced to give us what we considered our due, though we quite understood it was not a little against her will; and this was she, the very rustle of whose silk used to make her childrens' hearts quail within them. Nevertheless, I have found among the old papers a most motherly letter written to one of her little girls, entering into all the child's feelings and amusements; therefore I feel sure there was mingled with the stern discipline of the times the usual tenderness of a mother's heart.

It is best to be always kind. In turn we must depend upon each other, and truly in the days of her weakness the leddy was watched over by her children with the most tender care. To the last hour of her life her husband was devoted to her, and it was touching to observe, as even we children did, the change that came over her look and manner as he entered the room, the courtly grace with which she always half rose to receive him, the kind smiles that passed between them, the gentle cheerful tones of his voice as he spoke to her. When memory had failed her for all things else, it was still fresh and ready for every little observance connected with him, and nothing could ever induce her to go to bed till she had assured herself that the President's pillows were all right. Dear old man! I seem to see him now with his silk stockings to his knee and the bright buckles of his shoes, his dress of faultless neatness, and his wig that seemed a part of himself. His figure seems to connect our earliest days with the happy years of after life, always the same with his bright kind face, remarkable for a frowning brow with a very smiling mouth, which gave him a peculiar look of thoughtfulness and kindly good-humour.

Nothing surprised us more than to read in Lord Cockburn's 'Memorials of his Time' that the expression of Sir Ilay Campbell's face was hard. Those who knew him well at home could never have thought so. Children are excellent judges of countenance, and the pleasant and heart-warming vision of him that stretches so far back and has lasted so long must be a truthful impression.

It never occurred to any of us that his wig was not *bonâ fide* part of himself, till some years after this time that most mischievous urchin Henry Murray,[1] in a fit of uncontrollable fun, pulled it off. Words can never express the horror of the profanation, as well as astonishment at the deed, which filled our souls : it is a wonder that the urchin was not sacrificed on the spot by our boys. He owed his safety, I do believe, to the unmitigated astonishment that rooted the whole juvenile party to the spot. Sir Ilay's momentary look of disturbance subsided into his usual kind smile, and with a slight shake of the head at the offender he quietly replaced his wig and resumed his newspaper. Young Murray came from behind the arm-chair looking rather foolish at the sudden sobering effect his joke had produced on the noisy and merry circle of playfellows.

When Lord Advocate, Sir Ilay had been obliged constantly to attend Parliament in London, and his only unmarried daughter, Mary Frances, accompanied him. She was the one of his six daughters who was most admired, but her beauty in no way resembled her mother's, for she was a lovely brunette with teeth of pearl, and moss-roses on her cheeks. The literary reputation Edinburgh enjoyed during her youth drew to it many distinguished young Englishmen, and both

---

[1] The younger son of the Earl of Dunmore.

at home and in London she enjoyed all the advantages of what is called the best society. When her mother's powers failed, she became the head of her father's establishment and added much to the attractions of his house.

It may seem strange that the handsomest of Sir Ilay's daughters was the only one unmarried, but the reason was stranger still, and her escape from an unhappy match was a very narrow one. She had insisted on engaging herself to a very handsome man, ' spite of warnings that he was both bad tempered and too fond of money. She determined to disprove the latter accusation by having her fortune settled entirely on herself, and preparations for the marriage were carried on up to the arrival of the bridegroom the day before that fixed for the wedding. Riding with his *fiancée* that afternoon, he tried to gain her consent to a change in the marriage settlements, and when she held to the proof of his disinterestedness he displayed so violent a temper that on her return to the house she confided to one of her sisters that she dared not marry him nor dared she tell him so.

The evening passed as usual on such occasions, but on the wedding morning great was the commotion when it was found that no bride was forthcoming! After all had retired the previous night, a carriage had quietly driven away, and the terrified bride had eloped with her sister to the safe hiding of a house at some miles' distance.

She never married, but in course of time the disappointed bridegroom consoled himself with a wife whose force of character must have equalled his own. So great was his dislike to paying the smallest sum that she took upon herself the management of the whole establishment, garden and stables included; and report has it that once a year, having cleared the house of all visitors, she shut herself up with him in his library, braving his wrath till she had extorted from him a sufficient sum for the whole year's expenditure.

It was always with the greatest delight that we children returned in the spring to Harviestoun, which in 1810 was the scene of what appeared to us a magnificent military spectacle. It was the day of the Jubilee when George III. had reigned fifty years, and great was the enthusiasm and delight with which we manufactured an immense decoration, with a splendid G. R. in the centre, to be suspended over the turrets at the front door of the house. The Clackmannanshire Yeomanry, of which our father was the commander, wheeled and curveted round the house, fighting sham battles and performing the most warlike feats. Great was our admiration of our father mounted on one of the grey carriage horses, most magnificent in our eyes with his helmet, on which was a silver thistle and the motto, translated for us, " For our country and our firesides." The whole land had been excited into a frenzy of loyalty and patriotism by Buonaparte's threatened invasion, and though our love for the king was a real feeling, our hatred of the French was more real still. A grand dinner was laid out in the entrance-hall for the occasion, and there the gentlemen of the neighbourhood dined with the troopers, and we heard with delight the speeches and the hurraing. Besides the military ardour of the Yeomanry, which we the better appreciated in that we fully understood it was to be our safeguard against the French if they landed, there was a quieter witness close at hand of their having been daily expected, in the shape of an immense caravan (it would now be called an omnibus), which

had been built by our father's orders for the purpose
of carrying us off to the other side of the hills
when the French fleet should appear in the Firth of
Forth. We thought the escape to the mountains
would have been great fun, and we rather grudged,
as time went on, that it had nothing better to do
than to perform the peaceful duty of carrying us all
to church on rainy days.

CHAPTER III.

THE summers and autumns spent at Harviestoun
were a time of delight.   Yet we liked our winters
in Edinburgh.

I remember, I remember—and oh, how long ago it
seems!—the happy family group that used to gather
round my father's breakfast-table in the dear old house
in Park Place.   Breakfast was my father's favourite
time, and a good hour he always made it last; every
child except the babies, and the two poor boys who had
been previously hurried off to the High School, was
present, and much we enjoyed it, for we heard the
newspapers read and the particulars of the war de-
scanted on.   Buonaparte was then in the full career of
his victories, and the impression made upon our minds
was so strong that to this hour I can remember the
words of some of his "Moniteurs."

No plea of business was suffered to shorten this
delightful hour; our mother would sometimes slyly
attempt to carry on some favourite piece of needlework,
but she was always detected, for my father was so
hearty a lover of books he could never believe in the
attractions of needlework,—scarcely of the pencil; and

so she sat while between at least half a dozen cups of
tea the newspapers were fully discussed, as well as
every subject of interest of the time, visitors who
knew his habits often dropping in to breakfast with us.
Besides himself, the only other very intellectual member
of the family was our Aunt Campbell, the wife of Lord
Succoth, and very delightful to some of us were the
hours spent in her house. I'm afraid there was an
especial charm to us in the greater laxity of her
manner of keeping Sunday : she used to give us pencils
and paper as a fit amusement for the day, which in the
stricter *régime* of our own home was considered altogether wrong. Our family was Presbyterian, altogether
Kirk of Scotland ; Aunt Campbell was Episcopalian,
and brought up her children accordingly. On looking
back I am bound to acknowledge that in those days
there was very little religion in the Episcopalian house,
much more in our own, though it was a serious mistake
making Sunday irksome to the children, who were of
too lively a character to be content with reading grave
books which they could not understand. Yet we could
not but receive abiding religious impressions from our
own gentle mother : each night when she saw her little
ones in bed she would bend over us whispering the
well-remembered verse—

> " This night I lay me down to sleep,
> And give my soul to Christ to keep,—
> Sleep I now or wake I never,
> I give my soul to Christ for ever."

It became so fixed a habit with us all, that in after
years it was most touching to hear our soldier brother
tell that he never, even when sleeping under arms on
the ground, forgot to repeat this prayer.

About this time Sir Ilay resigned his public employ-

ments and retired to Garscube, his country place, in
which till now he had spent the summers only, and
then began that patriarchal life which ministered to
the happiness of so many. His son, Lord Succoth,
then removed from No. 4 to No. 1, his father's house
in Park Place.

In 1811 a trouble came into our own house. The
youngest of our family was a dear little black-eyed boy,
Ilay Campbell by name, the plaything of the house.
One night he was restless and ill. In the morning it
was found that in the course of that night one limb
had been completely paralysed; the medical men said
it was in consequence of cutting his teeth. Our poor
mother was grievously distressed, she could not bear to
think of the child's blighted life, for to her mind the
restoration of the withered limb seemed impossible : the
misfortune made too deep an impression on her and
cast a shadow forwards.

Shortly after this we were enjoined to be very
still, for that our mother was ill. The cause was soon
made clear to us by the arrival of the old nurse, in
whose presence we always took a mysterious pleasure :
she had visited us about every two years, telling us
she had brought us a new little brother or sister,—
sometimes she had found it among the cabbage-beds,
sometimes below a rose-bush. Whatever she chose to
say we believed, for, while her short reign lasted,
her power was absolute. By her permission alone
we could see our mother, or make whispering visits
to the new baby's apartment, close to her. Accordingly, on the 21st of December 1811, we perfectly
understood why we were to have a holiday, on the
usual condition of being very quiet, but we observed
in the days that immediately followed that something
unusual had happened. There was some mystery in

the house, for there were grave looks and shakings of
the head, not only among the servants but also among
the lady friends who came and went. There was not
the usual gladsome tone in all that was said, though
we were kept at too great a distance to hear the
words spoken. At length, with the connivance of the
old nurse, after some days I crept into my mother's
room, and through the darkened light saw her in
earnest conversation with the family doctor, George
Bell. She had been crying, and he was comforting
her with hopeful words. He said, "You have been
thinking too much of poor little Campbell's leg, but
I hope we shall be able to set all this to rights;"
then catching sight of me, as though glad of a diver-
sion, he lifted me up and placed me on the bed.
My mother gently kissed me but told me not to
stay, so I passed at once into her dressing-room,
from which was heard the wailing voice of the new-
born baby, and for the first time I saw my little
brother. He lay on the old nurse's lap making a
complaining noise; and no wonder, for, poor little
thing, instead of the lovely little feet that it had
always been our delight to kiss when a new baby
was brought among us, the nurse showed me a mass
of bandages. He was born club-footed!

Certainly the circumstances of his birth did not
promise the noble career of usefulness with which God
has blessed him, and, had he been born in lower life,
or had his parents been either careless or faint-hearted,
he must have remained a cripple all his days, for his
poor little feet were found to be completely doubled
inwards; however, the assurance was given that there
was good hope that they could in time be brought
to a proper shape. "In time," alas! it was over
these words my poor mother wept, for she knew that

they expressed a suffering infancy, and a childhood
debarred from childhood's active enjoyment. She was
full of faith and love, and perhaps God whispered to
her heart that by those very means He would best
form her child for the work He destined for him; for
when she left her room to rejoin the little circle, that
never felt right when she was absent, she brought
with her her usual gentle cheerfulness, and the only
outward sign of the misfortune was that the baby
Archie was fondled and spoken of with an inexpres-
sible tenderness. She was the most submissive of
women, and so she found rest to the disquietude of
her heart: she knew her husband to be the most
energetic of men, and, thoroughly believing in him,
she felt assured that all that could be done would
be done.

Many were the visits the baby received before he
was a month old, in the little apartment in which
the old nurse held her court; but his first appearance
in public—that is to say, his christening—was the
event to which we, the younger branches of the
family, looked forward with the greatest interest.
At length the day (the 10th of February 1812)
arrived. Our mother was sufficiently recovered to
receive her friends, and the usual little circle was
gathered round her; while all her children except the
eldest, who had returned to Harrow after the Christmas holidays, dressed in their best, gazed with a little
more than the usual amount of watchfulness on the
well-remembered ceremony which added a new member
to the visible Church of Christ, and a new name in
the chorus of voices that already filled their nursery.
The mysterious large china bowl occupied once again
its conspicuous place in the drawing-room, making the
centre of the solemn group where the father held up

his infant, Archibald Campbell, to receive his baptism
from the hands of the friendly minister of the old
Church of St Giles, Dr Thomas MacKnight, who had
come once more to perform his loving office. The
gentle mother and the seven brothers and sisters encircled him : the newly named Archibald Campbell was
a lovely baby, his long robes hid the poor little feet,
and if there was any difference in the welcome given
to him from that which greeted those who had come
before him, it was only that it was even more tender
and loving, and, as our mother passed her treasure
from friend to friend, admiring smiles saluted him
and soothed the distress she had hid away in her
heart.

And thus she returned to the daily duties of her
life, bringing back with her the quiet influence that
had in her family all the effect of an absolute rule.
On looking back to her character there shines out
this remarkable difference between her and other
women, that no one ever saw her in the slighest
bustle or fuss of any kind, nor can any one remember
her voice raised in anger. Her memory comes back
with a sort of moonlight radiance. Clouds in her daily
life there must have been, but she passed through
them all. brightening them to others, and by them
herself undimmed.

I love to remember her kneeling in the large white
old-fashioned chair which belonged to her bedroom.
Often she retired there for private prayer, and among
the memories of earliest childhood her figure shines
out as in a picture, kneeling upon the cushion of the
high-backed chair, her earnest face lifted up to God,
but she never prayed aloud; it was only while we
were very little children that she did not mind the
presence of one of us when she carried her distresses

to the Comforter. Everything she did was so quietly done that, though we saw when we were at Harviestoun that she always kept in her bedroom a little bunch of daisies carefully tended in a glass of water, not one of us knew till long afterwards that she gathered them from our little brother Willie's grave, and thus treasured them for his sake; yet he had died so long ago that few of us had the slightest recollection of his birth, and he had lived but for six months. She must have gone to the grave quite alone in the early morning, for no one ever saw her there.

Dear mother! she was so purely and so innocently good! The modern language of what is called the religious world was unknown to her, but the true spirit of religion dwelt in her, and her left hand did not know what her right hand had done. Of her self-denying deeds of charity few were known till her death caused them to be missed, and I cannot remember ever to have heard her speak unkindly of a single human being. The religious books of her day did not bring forward the evangelical truths of all that Christ had done and is still doing for us, but she had the Word of God itself. I remember her sympathising in the remark made to her by a poor woman who was fond of reading, to whom she had lent a volume of Blair's sermons as a good book, when to her inquiry whether she had liked them she replied, "'Deed, leddy, no' that weel, for in a' that reading" (turning over a number of pages) "there's neither God nor Jesus Christ."

My mother's good-natured charity was so well understood by the poor around our country home, that some of them did not hesitate to encroach upon it. I remember her amusement at the answer made to her by a pensioner as to whether she would like best to have money or oatmeal given to her, " 'Deed, leddy," with a curtsey, " baith's best."

Many were the lingering superstitions of the place and time : a poor woman came in haste to beg linen rags for her child, who had been dreadfully burnt. They were immediately given, with everything that could be wanted, and the inquiry made, " How did it come about ? " " Oh ! leddy, the bairn never grew ony, and we thought she was a changeling ; and folks told us that if we put her in a creel,[1] and the creel on the lowe,[2] the fairies would come down the lum[3] and tak her awa' and gie me back my ain bairn ; but they never cam', and the poor wean was a'maist burnt."

This remembrance vividly brings back another : a great commotion in the passage leading into the house-keeper's room, into which my mother rapidly passed, and straight opposite, at the other door of the room, a very old woman staggering forward with the blood trickling down her face. I seem to see her now with the firelight full upon her, the great blood drops falling from her brow while she tottered with terror, anger, feebleness, and age. Poor Jean Duncan ! her story in these past times was a common one. She was old, infirm, and cross ; by most people supposed to be poor ; she lived alone, and steadily discouraged all visiting ; few had ever ventured over her threshold. It was plain to all the country round that she was a witch, and everything that went wrong within ten miles round was placed to her account, and this was the reckoning. Many a threat had been uttered that she should " be scored aboun the breath," the only real way of destroying her evil power ; and now Jim

[1] Creel = basket.   [2] Lowe = fire.   [3] Lum = chimney.

Christie's cow had unexpectedly run dry, so he had
caught the wretched old woman just about dark, and
drawing his knife right across her forehead, had indeed
scored her "aboun the breath." The horrid look of
poor Jean with the red light falling full upon her,
and the ashamed faces of a group of young men who
stood behind her as my mother spoke to them, are
indelibly impressed upon my memory, but of what
she said or did I know nothing.

Not long after this scene followed the final act
of poor old Jean's long and joyless life. She became
very ill, and it was evident that she was about to die.
Her nearest of kin was her nephew, John Drysdale,
our gardener. Most people thought that she was
poor, but he knew better; and he knew, moreover,
that he was her heir, and it was, according to the
custom of the times and place, his plain duty to watch
through the night by the corpse—yet it was a horrible
idea, for John was by no means assured that his aunt
was not a witch. It was fearful to think what might
take place now that she was dead; nevertheless, it
would have been considered extremely disreputable
to shrink from the duty, so he made up his mind, and
boldly took his place in the lonely cottage. It was
a cold winter's night, and John shivered as the hours
passed on. The fire on the hearth was burning low;
he could not let it die out, so he rose with an effort,
casting many a glance over his shoulder at the bed
while he heaped on the hearth lump after lump of
good coals that were piled in the corner. Soon a
bright fire blazed up the wide chimney, a genial
warmth filled the room, and the red light glimmered
over the white sheet that covered the bed. John
Drysdale's eyes were riveted upon the ridge formed
by the body of the dead woman that lay beneath

it; his very head began to swim, for it moved, yes, it moved, and slowly the rigid form raised itself upright. All that he had ever heard rushed upon his memory, and in one moment he was out of the house door running for his life.

It was not whisky on his part that had bewildered him; it was not Satan who had come to claim his own; it was the ruling passion of her life that had raised her from the dead. When he returned with some neighbours after the sun had well risen, behold the dead woman lay quite stiff between the heap of coals and the chimney corner, the tongs clasped in her right hand, and a piece of coal beside her that had evidently been dragged from off the fire. The truth was plain : poor Jean had been a thorough miser all her days; the unwonted warmth of a good fire had recalled her from the death - like stupor in which she had lain, and with returning life, the thought of the waste of her coals shot through her brain, and so her last chance of life was destroyed. When found she was quite dead, and was carried back to her shroud and her bed; but she lay alone the next night, for all her neighbours believed her momentary return to life to have been supernatural, and no consideration could tempt any one to risk the sight of another resurrection. Besides, who could say that on the third night she might not be carried off bodily! It would not be safe to interfere.

Certainly the superstition and credulity of the Scottish peasantry were at that time unbounded, and I am not sure that it was altogether confined to them. I cannot otherwise account for a somewhat remarkable process to which I had myself been sub-jected in the early years of my life. Having been born with marks of fruit on my face, which could not have added to its beauty, the medical men considered that they were caused by aneurism and required very decided treatment—an operation which must have left me scarred for life. The surgeons had been in the house, when, happily for me, my mother's heart failed her, and she sent them away with the promise that she would reconsider the subject, and if she could make up her mind to it, she would send for them again. There was another member of the family who also took the subject into consideration. Our then nurse, Effie, had arrived at a conclusion somewhat different from that of the doctors. She was convinced of the truth of the popular belief that a dead man's hand laid upon my cheek and brow would effectually remove the marks. This she expounded to my mother day and night, striving to wring from her permission to try. It was a shocking idea; nevertheless it was clear that besides the pain, the surgeon's knife must certainly leave a mark of its own, whereas the dead man's hand, if it did no good, could scarcely do any harm. So in the end, just after the annual migration of the family to Harviestoun had carried my mother safely out of the reach of science, she yielded her consent; but as a man could not be killed for the occasion, it was necessary to wait till some one died. An old man at last did die in one of the nearest cottages. I must have been taken there asleep, for no child would have forgotten it, had she been carried awake to the bed of the dead man and seen and felt his cold hand placed on her face; and I was old enough to have remembered it, for I have the most distinct recollection of being constantly stopped in our walks by the widow, who always examined my cheek in order to ascertain the state of her husband's body in the grave,—as the marks, she told my nurse (in my hearing, though at the time I did not understand it), would certainly fade away as he turned into dust. I doubt whether my father knew anything of this experiment till long after, but all parties were satisfied that, whatever the cause of the cure, the red marks faded away as I grew older, and in time disappeared. The nurse's conclusions on the matter were very decided. About the same time her marriage with the coachman made way for the introduction into the family of one who became a very important character in it — Betty Morton, whose name will never be forgotten by any of us. She lived with the Campbells of Dudingstone, and was a middle-aged woman when she came to us.

The baby of that period was a very long thin child, with a much more handsomely developed nose than usually belongs to babies in long clothes. He was always called by my father " the ancient warrior," and he looked the name to perfection, almost as well as he did after thirty years' service in India, a Queen's aide-de-camp and distinguished for gallant conduct in many a hard-fought battle, at the head of the Irregulars known by his own name, Tait's Horse. Well I remember his first combat when old enough to run about. On a summer evening, when the whole family was happy in one of those strolling rambles in which our father delighted, they were alarmed by cries of mingled rage and pain. At some distance a strange sight was to be seen—little Tommie in single combat with a gander. With merciless beak he held on to the arm of the child, who was thrashing him in self-defence with might and main. I can see them now, my mother running to the rescue. Poor Tommie; for many a day his arm bore the marks of the beak of his adversary, which had frightened him as never Afghan or Sikh has since had power to do. My father laughed heartily at the attack made upon his ancient warrior.

CHAPTER IV.

IN the summer of 1812 we were as usual gathered
together at Harviestoun. Never was there a place
better fitted for the enjoyment of a large family.
The house—in itself a treasure to children from the
many hiding-places in its turrets—stood on the slopes
at the foot of the Ochill Hills; behind it were glens
and waterfalls; through the park before it flowed the
river, "Winding Devon, crystal Devon," celebrated
by Burns, and furnishing the trout-fishing which gives
so much delight to men and boys.

Alas! the valley in which Harviestoun stands is
much changed. The railroad, ruthless and unsparing,
has passed through it, changing the course of the
Devon, and all along the valley the beauty of the
scene is now marred by the manufactories of Alva
and Tillicoultry, whose tall chimneys, vomiting clouds
of black smoke, tell of the increasing prosperity of
the country, but do not add to its beauty.

There are so many places of interest near, that
few weeks passed without expeditions to some of

them, and our father was never so happy as when
he carried off his children and his guests to enjoy
them.   Vain was all remonstrance from distracted
governess, "the children could not be educated amid
so many interruptions."   The answer was always
ready that " the best of all education was the appreciation of the beauties of nature," followed by the
advice that she should accompany her pupils.

From this time everything seems to become more
clear, and the visitors who came and went have left
more vivid impressions, — naturally so, for till now
we were children, and had made but little account of
any of them, unless indeed they, as Annie and Helen
Walker of Dalry, ministered to our own special enjoyment.   Gathered round them we had eagerly listened
to never-to-be-forgotten tales of fairy-land, of second-
sight, and all manner of bewitching lore.   Never were
there, never could there be, such story-tellers as these
two sisters.   It was one of these Walkers of Dalry
who had an experience that might well have ended
in a tragedy.   One day, while visiting in a very poor
part of Edinburgh, her attention was attracted by
sounds of distress in a house she was passing.   Her
knock at the door receiving no answer, but the moans
continuing, she gently opened it, and found a woman
lying on a bed evidently very ill.   She made no
attempt to answer the questions put to her, and
having done what little she could to relieve her, Miss
Walker left.   But she was haunted by the look of
intense distress and horror in the poor woman's dark
eyes, and she visited her again and again, reading
to her and trying to give her comfort.   Never a
word did the woman speak, but the ministrations
seemed to be received with pleasure mingled with
an expression of fear, and constant uneasy glances at

the door. So when one day an evil-looking man entered, and the sick woman was visibly agitated thereby, Miss Walker was surprised and relieved that he received her explanation of her presence with civility, and even offered to show her a shorter way back when she was ready to leave. He then passed into an inner room, and the sick woman, signing to her visitor to bend close, said to her in an eager vehement whisper which it gave her quite a shock to hear : " Go ! go at once, by the way you came in ! "

Soon after this all Edinburgh was excited by the celebrated trial of Burke and Hare, the criminals who decoyed and murdered their victims for the sake of what they gained by selling the bodies for dissection. Believing there might be a connection between them and the sick dumb woman, Miss Walker, not unaccompanied this time, sought her, but all trace of her had vanished. There seemed little doubt that the unfortunate woman had taken refuge in silence as an escape from her terrible position as wife of one of these murderers, a silence she had broken to save the life of one who was kind to her.[1]

This summer we had many visitors. One family we especially remember, because they brought with them a thread which was afterwards to be woven into the web of our family history, though this slender thread consisted but of the frequent mention of a name of which till then we had never heard. Where or how our father had become intimately acquainted with Lord Rothes, and began a friendship which has lasted into this the third generation, I do not know, but he, with Lady Rothes and their two daughters, were welcomed as friends and remained some time with us :

[1] This was a favourite story of Lady Wake's, but is here related from memory by the editor.

all thought him the most agreeable of men, and with us children he soon became an immense favourite. He was so full of anecdote, told his stories so well, and was so amused by our amusement, that at his special request we were allowed to attend the after-dinner dessert much earlier than was our custom, that we might hear his adventures while he was a boy and young man; and great was the excitement with which we listened to these tales of wonder, in which a certain Sir William Wake who had been his schoolfellow had had his full share, for they appeared to have vied with each other in all manner of mischief and practical jokes. This name speedily became associated in our minds with every species of fun and frolic,—we gave him, among ourselves, the title of the " Madcap English baronet,"—and little did we think how large a space he would one day occupy in my future life, when the Highland hills and the valley of Devon exchanged for the wooded parks in the agricultural district of Northamptonshire, a grey-headed, handsome old man, the very perfection of an old English gentleman, was to become the centre of a dear circle, delighting to recall the well-remembered frolics of his youth, and to talk of his schoolfellow and friend Leslie, the very Lord Rothes who was then filling our young imaginations with these stories. These links in life are very curious.

There was another visitor this summer who stands out in bold relief from the groups who came and went. From the habit I have mentioned of the children of the family being always admitted to the breakfast table, we had heard much of Sir Thomas Graham, afterwards Lord Lynedoch; of his having joined the army as a volunteer, like one of the knights of old, to soothe away his grief by filling up with the excitements of war the void left in his heart by the death of his wife, and of his deeds when there, bravest, it is said, of the brave. We had often heard him called a hero, and when we knew that he was to return one evening with our father from some public meeting, it was resolved in council that we would have a sight of him, though he had to leave early next morning. We decided to hide behind the drawing-room sofa when supposed to have gone to bed, and there we lay snugly ensconced, recalling all the vividly-coloured pictures we had seen in our story-books of heroes with hyacinthian locks, crowned with green laurels, with bright complexions and Roman noses. Great was our astonishment when, after a little bustle of arrival, a thin mild-looking old man entered the room with our father. Not that he was really old, for more than twenty years after that time he rode among the foremost with the Pytchley hounds, quite as much appreciated in Northamptonshire as he had been in Scotland for his heroism in the field. As one lives on one learns that there are all sorts of heroes.

Late in the autumn we returned to Edinburgh, our mother full of anxiety for her two youngest children. During the latter part of the summer she had been to visit her father, Sir Ilay Campbell, at Garscube; it was very seldom she ever left her family, but she sorely needed the change, to distract her thoughts from dwelling too sadly on her little cripples. On her return she brought back with her tidings of a newly recognised connection of the family, who had made his first appearance at Garscube and had been highly approved of. Our astonishment was great when we found that he was the son of the very madcap English baronet in whom, though we had never seen

him, we so much delighted,—young Charles Wake,
come down to Scotland with the Northamptonshire
militia, just of age, extremely good - looking, and as
full of fun as his father could desire. To our still
greater astonishment we were told that he was nearly
connected with ourselves, his mother, Mary Sitwell
of Renishaw, who had died at his birth, having been
the only sister of Frank Sitwell, our uncle by marriage.
We did not like Uncle Frank, but that was no reason
we should not like his nephew. He speedily arrived
at the Castle of Edinburgh in charge of French
prisoners, and at once took his place in our family as
prime favourite with old and young.

This was a golden era in our family history. We
were fast passing out of childhood, yet no cares had
come upon us, and we enjoyed every hour as fully as
though we had known the bright day would soon be
over. Young eyes seldom look for gathering clouds.
We made frequent visits with our new friend to the
Castle of Edinburgh, where the French prisoners were
the objects of unceasing interest. Accustomed as we
were to our stalwart countrymen, they appeared to us
so small, more like sickly old-looking boys than men,
and a weary monotonous life the poor fellows led. A
line of low buildings had been thrown up for their
accommodation ; in these they lived, at least in them
they slept, for they spent the hours of light in a large
sort of yard in front, a space enclosed by open palisades,
through which they could hold conversation with whomsoever they chose to talk to. Here they cooked their
food, of which, so far as we could see, they had abundance, while Englishmen and Scotchmen looked on
with astonishment at the various efforts of genius
which produced potage, ragout, bouilli, just as they
pleased, out of the simplest materials, carefully pre-

1

serving every bone, which they cleaned and polished
till they shone like ivory. Marvels of ingenuity were
produced from these : ladies' workboxes, card-cases,
fruit-knives, and above all, little women sitting spin-
ing industriously at their wheels,—in fact, the ivory
spinning-jenny, then much esteemed as an ingenious
toy, that showed the movement of the newly introduced looms in the factories ; all sorts of pretty things
grew under their hands, and were joyfully purchased
by the continually changing groups of visitors. This
sort of work, and the little excitement produced by
the sale of it, made some variety in the monotonous
hours, but far less than would have been the case
had not the customers been so very sorry for the poor
fellows who sold that there was no thought of
bargaining ; they looked gravely at them, and gave
them whatever they asked, so there was nothing
that could call the vivacity of the Frenchmen into
action ; their natural temperament caused them at
times to sing, but the song sounded sad and dreary ;
they moved about cold and miserable under the grey
December skies, on the top of that mountain of rock
on which the Castle of Edinburgh is built, having
at least the advantage of one of the finest views in
the world. They were far better off in summer, but
I fear that many of them never returned to their
sunny France. While looking at them we felt deeply
for them, but once down the Castle Hill in the genial
atmosphere of our own home, all sad thoughts were
dissipated. It was a particularly happy winter ; our
home circle had grown wider, and we enjoyed the new
element of fun brought into it by the cousin who was
not our cousin, though the nephew of our aunt. He
was a great favourite with both the heads of the
house ; with our father he had long political debates,

maintaining with all the ardour of twenty-one the Whig principles in which he had been educated; our mother's heart he stole away by his unusual love for children, especially manifested towards the universal pet, the youngest, who, delighted with his red coat and gilt buttons, in the most demonstrative manner returned his affectionate admiration. In this first year of his life began a friendship that never cooled, and one of the first words that little Archie spoke was an attempt to utter the name which he would always call out as soon as he appeared.

Spring as usual took us all back to Harviestoun, to scamper far and near on our ponies, to climb the hills, to rush down the glens, and to expend our gladness in every permitted manner; but our mother would now tell us that, being older, we must behave more like grown persons. Alas! we might no longer climb the trees—all that was over. Nevertheless new enjoyments were opened to us, and new ideas were fast flowing in.

From one cause and another—chiefly, I believe, because Walter Scott had suddenly awakened in English minds an intense curiosity about all things Scotch—English friends and English connections often appeared amongst us, and began to take their places in that which constituted our everyday lives; and it marks the period that an English lady, Miss Wake (whom we always called Aunt Charlotte, because she was Charles Wake's aunt), was the first person who brought among us any knowledge of what is, and I believe was then called, the Evangelical Church. Her nephew, whose knowledge of the kingdom of heaven brought to earth by the Son of God as Redeemer of a sin-struck world was then far ahead of ours, had given to our mother the four volumes of Cooper's Sermons, which interested her deeply and surprised her not a little. It almost alarmed her to think that the glad good news of salvation in Christ our Lord was indeed freely offered to all—it seemed almost too good to be safely accepted; but the more she read the statements contained in these four volumes, the more she dwelt upon them, and she could not but find them verified in the Book of books which had always been her greatest treasure and her constant guide. In Cooper's Sermons, though now they do not appear strongly doctrinal, there was just that supplied of the want of which in Blair's sermons the poor woman had complained to her: there was God and Jesus Christ in every page. Also about this time Hannah More's tracts had made their way into Scotland, and words cannot express the joy it was to us to find the stories they contained, and by carrying the religion of the Bible into the daily scenes of cottage life, they had shown to us religion itself under a new view, not only wearisome advice and still more wearisome reproof, but a Living Power. Still, had our mother gone through these tracts herself, it is very doubtful if she would have approved of the history of Dick White the postilion, of Mrs Jones the cottage cook, &c., as Sunday reading; but happily she took them upon trust, having perfect confidence in the recommendation that had brought them to the house. She was strict in carrying out in all things what she considered to be the plain directions of Scripture, but from them she drew no deductions, and it never occurred to her that they in any way affected the mutual relations of society so long as these did not cause association with known bad characters. She encouraged the little dancing-parties given to children, and regularly every winter gave one herself, in return for the invitations she

accepted from the parents of our companions, and
she, as well as our dear father, considered it quite
a part of our education that we should be taken to
the theatre when any first-rate actor came to Edinburgh : it would be well if all were conducted in the
manner of the little Edinburgh theatre, which was
then in the possession of the Siddons family, the man-
ager being Henry Siddons, the son of the celebrated
actress.   His own powers of acting were not great, but
his character was undoubted, and he and his charming
wife were held in high esteem.   She and her brother,
William Murray, played together in a style which,
though it never rose to the highest efforts of histrionic
art, yet was faultless in its way, and gave forth with
purity and truth many of those impressive lessons
in history and in feeling of which Shakespeare was
the great master, and of which the drama boasts so
many specimens.   Since from all time the mind of the
mass is easily reached and stirred by representations
which, seeing, they can comprehend, and by vivid and
poetic words expressing the feelings of characters whose
actions are carried out before them, would it not be
worthy of the attention of our rulers so to regulate it
that what is good and great should be brought before
them, bringing the history of their country actually
before the uneducated, and thus prevent them from
falling a prey to the wilful misrepresentations of news- ·
papers written purposely to mislead them ?

   The summer party at Harviestoun in 1813 was full
of gladness.   The riding and driving parties were
rendered more joyous by the English cousin having
his tilbury and horses with him, and more interesting
by having a great deal of sketching introduced.   Some
of the Garscube party joined ours, and many were
the expeditions made to the Cauldron Lynn, Castle

Campbell, and the summits of the various hills. , Our
father was in his element. Our mother was happier
on the subject of the two little ones, — both were
stronger, and in spite of their lameness as merry as
possible. She was the beloved centre of a happy
family circle, and though once or twice a shadow was
thrown over its brightness by her fainting in the
midst of us, no presentiment of evil found its way to
the mind of any one.

Her birthday and that of one of her boys was on
the 1st November, and also on that day was the
Harvest-Home, the Kirn of Scotland, when, after all
the crops, including what is called the black crop,[1] are
gathered in, there is a most joyful gathering of all
the workpeople and their families : every cotter, every
farmer, and the laird's whole family, old and young,
with all his visitors (care being always taken that on
that occasion there should be a goodly number of
these), are gathered in joyous assembly. This was
usual throughout Scotland, and in many places it is
still the custom. At Harviestoun the kirn always
took place in a very large building, a sort of barn
loft, at one end of which was one of the many agricultural machines in which the laird delighted, and
which for the evening was covered over with napery,[2]
and thus was transformed into a splendid buffet, on
which there was a profusion of everything that was
most esteemed in the way of refreshment by the class
of guests for whom it was prepared. Whisky toddy,
punch, cold and steaming hot, and mountains of short-
bread cake,[3] were the most favoured among the good

---

[1] Peas and beans, which are allowed to remain in the fields till quite black
[2] *I.e.*, linen tablecloth.
[3] One of the most excellent of Scottish cakes, only now beginning to be
known in England—thanks to the royal taste for all good Scottish dainties.

things provided for the occasion, and innumerable were the visits made to the buffet by the panting couples, who for a brief space broke away from the dance at the upper end. Fast and faster still, each foot kept that wonderful time, of which none who have not witnessed real Scottish dancing can form the faintest idea. It is a wild enthusiasm that almost seems like a regulated delirium, while every limb answers to the marvellous music of the Scottish reel and Highland strathspey. Feet stamping, fingers snapping, eyes as it were on fire, heads thrown back, while shouts mark the crisis of the dance,—it must have been seen to be imagined. Great was the admiring astonishment of the English guests, intense the delight of the young ones. The young ladies danced with the shepherds and the various working-men belonging to the estate, and the gentlemen with the country lasses, till all were so tired that they were obliged to withdraw. The steward was bound to remain till the kirn was closed, and to see that the whisky-drinking was not prolonged to an excess that would have been full of danger to the well-filled granaries in which it had been held.

A few days after this harvest-home the family returned to Park Place. On the 20th of this month was the twenty-second birthday of the young Englishman who had been received into the family; many were the little gifts he received, and it was a happy evening they all spent together. It was nearly the last. The Northamptonshire militia had been ordered home. Peace had come, and there were no more French prisoners to guard.

December brought bitter frost and early snow, but little we cared for that; were not the Christmas holidays at hand, and all the delights of Christmas-

MRS CRAUFURD TAIT.

time? We looked forward to New Year's Day, and above all to Hansel Monday—that great day among Scottish children, the first Monday of the New Year. This year it would be on the 3rd January (1814), and we should give and receive our New Year's gifts. Already we were busied in our preparations, manufacturing, painting, and cutting out, with hearts full of glad anticipation. The 1st of January came ; winter, real storm winter, was without, but in our home all was warmth and happiness. Monday the 3rd, the much desired Monday, came, and the house rang with the glad voices of children. In the early morning we crowded round our mother's bed and received from her hands our New Year's gifts.

In one hour all was ended. We were motherless.

The over-taxed heart had given way, and she lay dead upon the sofa on the very spot where I had first remembered her ; two scenes, the beginning and the end, so intricately blended that it is impossible to recall the one without the other.

CHAPTER V.

January 1814.—Dark and dreary were the days that
settled down on Park Place. The lovely mother whose
gentle presence had been felt everywhere, consoling
every trouble, smoothing every difficulty, and by a
very few words righting every wrong, had been
carried away from her children, and they crept about
the house with a fearful consciousness that the snow
which all day long darkened the air was falling upon
her grave. More than half a century has passed since
then, yet as I write the hush of the house returns to
me, broken by the murmur of voices in a room near
our own where a conclave of mother's especial friends,
including her two sisters, consulted over the difficult
question, "What was to be done for the best with
the nine children [1] thus suddenly thrown upon their
father?"

[1] John, born 11th February 1796, afterwards Sheriff of Clackmannan, then
of Perth ; died 1877.
Susan Murray, born 2nd March 1797 (Lady Sitwell) ; died 1880.
James Campbell, born 29th October 1798, Writer to the Signet ; died 1879.
Charlotte Murdoch, born 9th June 1800 (Lady Wake) ; died 1888
Anna Mary (Marion), born 15th February 1804 (Mrs Wildman) ; died 1879.

Our father! . . . Oh! how well I remember his constant pacing up and down, the look of care and grief that had altogether changed his countenance, and the knowledge, which I know not how came to us, that, besides the sorrow of his loss, there was something more that caused him perplexity and trouble. While she was by his side there was a sunshine over him that brightened all, but now that light was gone, disturbing facts stood out in their real shape, and he had to acknowledge to himself that, misled by his sanguine temperament, he had embarked in and even carried through enterprises which, though they benefited many, had ruined himself.

His taste for the beautiful had been freely indulged, he had created a paradise, and while she, his Eve, lived to enjoy and adorn it, he had never taken himself to account for the sums expended upon it; but the shock of her sudden removal had shattered the enchanted world in which he had lived, and he stood face to face with the appalling fact of an overwhelming debt. Children though we were, these things came to be understood by us. Half sentences, uttered by the friends who consulted over our destinies, expressive of thankfulness that our mother had never known it, and the measures taken to meet the coming difficulties, had from the first roused our attention. Everything was out of joint. One era was ended, another was beginning, and all the uncertainty of the unknown was before us.

The establishment was quickly reduced, the grey

Thomas Forsyth, born 20th August 1805 ; Commanded Indian Irregulars, known as Tait's Horse ; died 1859.
Craufurd, born 9th September 1807 ; died 1828.
Ilay Campbell, born 1st June 1809 ; died 1821.
Archibald Campbell, born 21st December 1811, Archbishop of Canterbury ; died 3rd December 1882.

carriage-horses, not sold, but sent into the country to be useful on the farm, and the dear old coachman whom we had known all our lives was going away. The parting scene was characteristic,—he came into the drawing-room, where we sat expecting him; we were all in tears, he and we, and many kind words were spoken between us. At length to my sister he said, "Weel, fare ye well, Miss, and I hope ye'll live to drive your own coach and four"; then patting my head he added, "A pair will do for you, Miss Chattie." The two nurses, Betty Morton and Mary Russell, and one man-servant, George Watt, who was in the house before we were born, one housemaid and a cook, were all that remained; with so large a family these were necessary, and it showed their attachment that without the least difficulty they dispensed with the subordinates to which they had been accustomed, each willingly doing the whole work. In a short time the governess was gone, and my younger sister and myself were for a short time sent to school, very much troubled in mind at the prospect of a life so very different from that to which we had been accustomed; but we spent every Saturday at home, and this kept up our spirits. And so time passed on, wearily and drearily, as the first year after the loss of a mother must ever do.

The constant care that Archie required endeared him to us all. In a short time he became a well-grown child, beautiful in countenance, with a touching look of appeal that went straight to the heart. He was naturally more lame than Campbell, who had but one limb affected, but both brothers were unable for the usual climbing and racing of boys of their age; and it was a touching sight to see them all in all to each other, while yet a complete contrast,—for

Campbell had bright black eyes and dark hair, his face rippling all over with fun, while Archie, blue-eyed and fair-haired, with the expression of an angel, seemed to watch the lively movements of his brother as though they were a necessary part of his existence. Very early, as though in a prophetic spirit, his father gave him the name of "Little Bishop," having from his babyhood destined him for the Church in his own mind. Whether from any internal feeling, or simply from always having heard this, I know not, but the child fully adopted the idea, and grew up for his future destiny carrying with him the thoughts and habits proper to it. I well remember that when any of the more riotous part of the family forgot that Sunday should be spent in a different manner from other days, little Archie's voice of appeal would be heard in childish protest, " Whisht! it's the Sabbath." His nurse, Betty Morton, was a truly religious woman, and took care that the day was, in her nursery at least, a day of quiet. There was a large old family Bible full of pictures, very old and very quaint, as may be supposed from the dedication being to Catharine Parr : it was our unfailing delight, and caused each child to be fully versed in every character and circumstance recorded in Holy Writ. Some of its pictures were indeed perplexing, — such as the re-building of Jerusalem, represented by a beautiful young queen surrounded by her handmaidens, who were attiring her with all manner of splendours; and another, in which our Lord's precept against pride of heart expressed in the words, " Why beholdest thou the mote that is in thy brother's eye, but considerest not the beam that is in thine own eye?" was illustrated by a beam as large as the cross rafter of a roof sticking out of a man's eye.

Every summer the boys were taken to Harviestoun by our father, but the first three autumns after our mother's death were spent by the two younger ones under their nurse Betty's care, superintended by the ladies of the family, at Garscadden, a strange, weird old house, the occasional home of our youngest aunt, Mrs Dalzell Colquhoun, in which she received the overflowings of Garscube, which was only three miles distant, when Sir Ilay's hospitality filled it beyond its powers. The quaint rooms and pictures, the old-fashioned landing-place on the second storey reached by outside stairs, above all the wonderful turreted gateway at the entrance of the old avenue, with hideous faces that gaped and grinned from every corner, could never be forgotten by any child, and, indeed, is the first distinct recollection of the little Archie. This old lodge, the pond embosomed in trees, and the curious old-fashioned gardens, made a paradise for children ; and here he first learned the charms of country life, until he was considered old enough to join his father and elder brothers at Harviestoun.

The wild free life at Harviestoun was considered not to be fit for young ladies, which we much regretted ; but we soon learned to value the home we found with our grandfather at Garscube, as indeed we well might, for it contained every element of enjoyment, Sir Ilay living as one of the patriarchs of old, surrounded by his children and his children's children, and exercising a good hospitality to rich and poor. His fortune was large, and he spent it, not in ostentatious display, but in contributing to the happiness of every one who came within his influence. His youngest daughter, Mary Campbell, still extremely handsome, was at the head of his establishment, and a more charming lady of the house can scarcely be imagined : at all times she dressed beautifully, but we always knew when company was expected, by the diamond side of the watch she habitually wore being turned outwards. Two other aunts, both widows, lived with their father,—the elder, Mrs Sitwell, had her two daughters with her, and Garscube was their permanent home ; the younger, Mrs Dalzell Colquhoun, was the life possessor of Garscadden. Her husband had died very early of paralysis, probably inheriting a weakened constitution from his father, who was one of the hard livers of his time, when the country gentlemen were in the habit of meeting at some country inn, or "change-house" as it was then called, for the express purpose of a drinking-bout. The last occasion on which the old laird attended the usual meeting at Luckie Baillie's, one of his neighbours, looking to the chair on which he had been a long time silent and very pale, gave a nudge to the man next to him, saying, "Garscadden looks unco gash." "Weel he may !" was the reply ; "he's been wi' his Maker thae twa hours, but I wad say naething to disturb the company." [1]

This in every way shocking fact may give an idea of what was possible, though happily not universal, not much above a hundred years from the time in which we are living. The silver whistle which was used instead of a bell in this very change-house passed into the possession of our family at the death of our aunt, the widow of the laird's son, and bears the date, with the inscription "Hurrah for Luckie Baillie !"

These men must have been contemporaries of Sir Ilay's, one of the most temperate of men. His house was the natural resort of most of the talent of the country, and visitors from England were without end.

---

[1] Here, it is believed, we find the original of Galt's story in 'The Last of the Lairds' (chap. III.)—ED.

It is perhaps worth while noticing one party which I particularly remember, that of Mrs Apreece, at that time a celebrated blue - stocking, escorted by Sir Humphry Davy, whom she shortly afterwards married, and several other English gentlemen, all more or less distinguished. She found the conversation of our good aunts rather flat, during the prolonged sittings in the dining-room after the departure of the ladies : she felt herself aggrieved that even Sir Ilay's excellent wine could prove a stronger attraction than herself ; and much amused were we of the younger faction of the house at her various manœuvres to shorten the period of separation, taking no notice whatever of Aunt Mary's graceful bows from the head of the table ; but our delight knew no bounds when one evening, driven to desperation by the gentlemen tarrying even longer than usual, we saw her actually possess herself of the dinner-bell and ring it loudly at the dining-room door. There was no misunderstanding that hint. It is scarcely necessary to add that Sir Humphry's marriage took place shortly : what chance had he or any man at the hands of a lady of such determined will ?

Many of the members of the Scottish bar, young and old (always those on circuit), were frequent visitors, and also a class which was rarely found in houses of that calibre, the ministers of the Scottish Church. To these Sir Ilay paid the most marked attention ; and very dear to their hearts he was, as indeed he might well be, for he, while President of the Courts of Scotland, had caused their stipends to be raised to a certain mark below which they could not under any circumstances be reduced.

It is no wonder we were happy, for Sir Ilay delighted to see us so, and he never would allow us to be scolded for any of our many misdemeanours,

gravely telling our aunts they should have taken
better care. Never but once did we see him angry,
and that once is worthy of record. It was on a still
summer evening, when the band of young cousins, boys
and girls (for it was vacation time), of ages varying
from sixteen to twenty, set forth on our usual ramble
up the Kelvinside through the wooded walks to the
bower where we generally held joyous rendezvous : on
this evening the subject that entirely occupied us was
Miss O'Neill's acting. She was then in the zenith of
her beauty and glory. We had seen her in her most
celebrated characters, and enthusiastic each for the
one we most appreciated, from discussion we rose to
declamation, giving in the grandest manner the tragic
scenes in "Isabella" and in "Belvidera." Shriek after
shriek, such as those hapless heroines had uttered
in the delirium of grief and terror, resounded down
the valley, the Kelvin flowing from us to the house.
The discussion finished, we wended our way quietly
home, and stood paralysed when, looking down from
the top of the bank, we beheld the whole household
rushing forward, headed by Sir Ilay himself with
one of my aunts in close attendance, running faster
than he had ever been seen to run before, grooms and
stable-boys with ropes and poles, men-servants and
women-servants, hurrying on if possible to save our
lives, none of them doubting that we had all fallen
into Lynn Jowl.[1]

The greeting we received may be imagined, especially
as our other aunt lay insensible on the drawing-room
floor, having recognised the voice of her daughter
in the shrieks of Isabella.

The society of cousins that gathered each autumn
at Garscube had been enlarged by the adoption into

---

[1] Properly Lynn Dhiaoul, or the Devil's Lynn, a dangerous pool in which
many a life has been lost.

the circle of two members of the family from England.
One was Charles Wake, our old friend and our mother's
especial favourite, with whom, while yet children, we
girls had been more than half in love. He had affronted
us all by, at two and twenty, marrying his own
cousin on the English side, Mary Alice Sitwell, and
now returned to us a widower of twenty-three, as
handsome as ever, but with a changed and perhaps
more dangerous interest; no longer full of fun and
frolic, but softened and saddened by the sorrow that
had fallen upon him. The early death of his young
wife seemed to have added a shade of romance to
every thought connected with him, and though at
the time of her marriage I had looked upon her,
without ever having seen her, as an interloper, for
the very good reason that he had been used to call
me his little wife, yet, as she was dead, I heartily
forgave her, and felt a tenderness for her memory.
One autumn after another he returned to Garscube.
I was still in the schoolroom, but my eldest sister
Susan, our cousins Mary Amelia Sitwell and Madeline
Connell, each the eldest daughter in her own branch
of the family, had been introduced into society, and so
pretty were these three cousins that they received the
name of the three Graces. Of course the girl in the
schoolroom was in the background; but Charles Wake
had no idea of her being made a Cinderella, and became her avowed champion, for which she was deeply
grateful. A sketch was made of her standing on a
pedestal in a shabby dress darning her stockings, and
underneath, the inscription, "The Venus de Wakici."
The other new member of the family from England was
Sir George Sitwell, who had been at Garscube while
a boy of sixteen with his stepmother, the Dowager
Lady Sitwell, and now returned, nearly twenty, with

his friend Henry Heathcote, youngest brother of Sir Gilbert Heathcote, who afterwards became Lord Aveland, to shoot in the Highlands. They remained with us some little time, long enough to get rid of the shyness which had afflicted them on their first initiation as members of our enchanted circle; they were to return to it on their way back from the Highlands to Cambridge, and they did, but poor Sir George reappeared in evil plight. He had met with an accident on the moors which, by being entirely neglected, had become most serious. It was impossible that he could keep that term at Cambridge, so his friend had to return without him, but except for the inconvenience of being lame, he was not much to be pitied : it was many weeks before he could travel, and meanwhile he was nursed and petted by the whole party, the girls taking it by turns, with the help of a boy from the garden, to draw him about in a sort of light bath-chair, for he could not put his foot to the ground. Under these circumstances it was not surprising that the young baronet was in no great haste to be pronounced fit to travel, and when the time of parting did come, it was very evident he would soon return.

NOTE.

This round-robin letter to the absent eldest brother, by whose family it is now produced, gives a vivid description of the home circle in those days.—Ed.

GARSCUBE, *September* 18*th*, 1816.

MY DEAR JOHN,—I am much obliged to you for your very amusing letter, which was the more welcome as it was quite unexpected. I feared that you would only write to the eldest ones.

We are glad to hear you have again found Maclean. It would have been a great annoyance to be separated from your travelling companion in a foreign country.

I should like much to be present at a confab between you and Monsieur Biermam. Do you remember a conversation at Oakfield, between Stonefield and Deaf Keith? I should think you must be in a predicament something resembling theirs, as neither the one nor the other could discover what they meant.

Sir George Sitwell has returned to Garscube in rather a disabled state, poor fellow. He has been much astonished by the Scotch moutons. He thinks that even though they are at home they still retain their resemblance to lions.

Susan is at present teaching Mr Heathcote to dance in the drawing-room We allege that she is taking all this pains in hopes of a handsome dashing partner at the October balls. She is, however, mistaken there, for though handsome Heathcote must always be, he never could be dashing, or I am much mistaken. We have surnamed him the Bishop on account of his gravity.

Papa is at Bute just now. We have never seen him since he left us, but we hope that he will soon be here, as we are impatient to see him again.

Poor Mary Ann and the Connells are to set off from this to-morrow for school. They are in great distress, poor animals. I pity them with the same sincerity that I congratulate myself on my being safely fixed at home.

All insist on having a share of this letter, so I must conclude, however unwillingly. . . . Archy and the rest of the boys and girls are in good health. . . Mary Ann will give you the loves. — I remain, my dearest John, your most affectionate sister, CHARLOTTE MURDOCH TAIT.

. . . .

MY DEAREST JOHN,—I received your letter to-day when I came over from Garscadden, and was delighted to hear that you had met with Maclean again.

I suppose you will be at Geneva when you receive this. It is to be a joint epistle from all of us. . . . You ask us to tell you all our news, but there is very little at present.

I take it for granted you know Sir George Sitwell and Mr Heathcote are here just now. The Duke and Duchess of Montrose are to be here to-morrow, which all the cousins think a great misfortune, as there can be no fun. I am going back to Miss Potts to-morrow with the Connells. Mr and Miss Julia Walker are also here, so there are a nice number for dancing.

Did you like the German theatres, and what were the plays?
. . . Bell is in good health and misses you very much in the
dairy exploits. . . .

All my aunts, cousins, brothers, and sisters join with me in
best love,—and believe me, your very affectionate sister,

MARIANNE TAIT.

MY DEAREST JOHN,—We expect your next letter to be from
Geneva, where I trust, my dear John, you will receive my
letters. The postmasters must be a terrible set, when you
have not got one of our letters, but my hope is that you will
find them awaiting your arrival. If you do not I shall be
much provoked that my witty and sensible letters have all
been to no purpose, for I don't suppose that any person would
be much edified excepting yourself.

Since I wrote to you last we received accounts of poor Mrs
Wake's death. Poor Wake is as well as he can be expected to
be after such a dreadful misfortune. They were a very happy
couple, and only 24 years of age, both of them. . . .

Poor Sir George Sitwell at the time that it happened was
confined with a sprain he had got on the moors, at Perth, not
able to move   He recovered so far as to be able to come here
about a week ago, and Mr Heathcote. Poor Sir George is of
course in very bad spirits. I think he is a very fine lad, and
so is Heathcote—the latter I like the best. He is very much
like his brother; very handsome but very shy. I have been very
busy teaching him to dance, which he could not till he came
here   But I assure you he is a very apt scholar, and I think
under *my* tuition he will make his début at the October meeting
with great éclat! I am thinking that when all other trades
fail I shall succeed very well in this scientific profession.

You did not know how useful your sister is. . . . I have
also been teaching him to play "Miss Tait's favourite" and
"Lord Portmocks' delight," with which he is quite delighted.

We have really been getting delightful fun, much better
than we thought we could possibly have got without my dear
Johnnies, Tait, and Campbell. . . . When the two lads first
came we got no fun, as Sir G.'s spirits were very bad, and we
were all very sorry about Wake. . . . Charlotte has taken in
Mr Walker of Dalry, and Mr Dunlop, the History of fiction, as
the French countess, which she does capitally. . . . We have had
dancing several evenings . . . and last night we had such an
excellent game at "Blind man's buff." . . . My aunts, papa, and
Uncle Connell all joined us, and I do not think I ever got such
fun. . . . Poor Sir George cannot walk, so he was only able to

look on; but Heathcote is a famous runner, there was no possibility of catching him. In the forenoon, if it is wet, we play at tigg up and down the stairs, and if it is fine we yoke Sir William Broke's *coach* and drive Sir George, who cannot walk. He has a capital equipage drawn by six fine ponies, all different colours—some pink, some blue, and all colours.

Yesterday we set off on an expedition to the wood near Mrs Peters at the quarry. We took provisions of all sorts, which we devoured with great eagerness, after pulling by turns for several miles.

Heathcote and James went out to shoot a few days since, and brought in more than ever you did, *mon cher mouton*. . . . They have gone out again to-day, and Sir G. and Marion (Mary) are going out in the gig, and I am going to ride by them. . . . Heathcote killed every day almost, when he was in the Highlands, 35 brace of grouse. What do you think of that, sir? . . . He heard yesterday from his brother, who is at Dresden.

The Duke and Duchess of Montrose and Lady Lucy were here for a day and night lately. The Duke is very pleasant and so is Lady Lucy, but I think the Duchess is very stiff.

Papa arrived here two days ago. He had been at Bute for several days. Poor man, he is still very blind (Old Bussie means the Marquis—not poor papa). He is rather better, but not materially.

Before the Englishers came we used to read our old friend Shakespeare in the forenoon. . . . Poor Julia Walker left us with a very heavy heart on Thursday last. She was very sorry to go, poor girl. She is a very fine good-humoured lassie. I found out when she was here that she stood in the greatest awe of you, and was very frightened for you. I tried in vain to persuade her that you were not a terrific person, and she was always astonished at my ecstatic delight when a letter came from you.

We are very uneasy about not hearing from the Succoths since they left Dover. We heard of them, however, through a very extraordinary channel.

Aunt Sitwell had a letter from her most amiable son, Frank Sitwell. It began "Madam" and ended just "Frank Sitwell," without "Yours" or anything of the sort. He is at Chantilly, and the Campbells had passed through, but fortunately had not seen him, as I think he seems perfectly mad. . . . He regrets extremely not having had an opportunity of shooting Lord Succoth; therefore, my dearest John, I entreat you not to attempt seeing him, as he will certainly, if he can, shoot you.

You must excuse this dreadful scrawl, as I am writing in the library with Charlotte, Sir G., and Madeline romping about me and making a dreadful noise.

I have some hope of Mary Sitwell going into Edinburg with me for the October meeting—I mean the races. . . . Kean is to be down, and there are to be balls and concerts. . . . I wish my dearest doggie was with us, we would get such excellent fun.

I had a letter from Mary Ann Cameron two or three days ago. She is to be there, and Donald is to be down. Heathcote is to be there also, so that we shall, I hope, get delightful fun; though I shall miss you and my dear other Jockie very much indeed. I daresay you will think us a pack of old fools romping at such a rate.

I must once more thank you for writing so often; pray continue to do so. God bless you, my dearest fellow. . . .

. . . .

September 24th.

MY DEAR JOHN,—Yesterday Mary, Madeline Connell, and Sir George went in the gig, while Jemmie, Heathcote, and I rode to the Knockie Muir to see that view of Loch Lomond. We had a most delightful ride, and got excellent fun, trying to make the Englishers admire the views, which they were determined not to do, to torment us. We had beautiful nags. I rode the old chestnut, and Jimmy a *cart horse.* Heathcote's made ours look very woeful indeed, as it is a very beautiful horse.

We are going into Edinburg, I am sorry to say, about the first of October. I shall be very sorry to leave this, though not so sorry as usual, as my darling grandpapa, aunties, and cousins are to be in Edinburg next winter. I shall not know myself without you when I first go to town.

I shall leave the rest of this for papa in case he has something to say to you. Pray, my dear John, write very soon. —Believe me, my dearest brother, your ever most sincerely attached, S. M. TAIT.

. . . .

Grandpapa desires his kind love to you, and bids me say that he approves of your journals very much, and hopes you will continue them. . . . He bids me say that when you see the Succoths he wishes you to tell them that he has not heard one word from any of them since they left England, and he thinks that the letters must have miscarried some way or other. How happy you will be to see them! . . . The

Governor, tell them, arrived in good health, but not in such good spirits, poor body.

. . . .

23rd.

We have just received your kind letter. We were much entertained with your adventure at the play-house. I have no doubt but you passed for some grand monsieur or other.

Papa sends his very kind love to you. He goes to-morrow.

We are all going a famous riding expedition to-day, and we had a delightful one on Saturday. It was the best thing you ever saw—Jemmie's exhibition as "Landlord" when the Duke and Duchess were here. He seemed in a terrible funk when he said, "May I give your Grace some mutton?" . . . Stewart Derbyshire was here, and we had famous fun with him and Sir Ilay, who, when he was introduced to him, laughed excessively. The truth was that he thought he was some of us dressed up, as there has been a great deal of that sort of thing going on.

. . . .

Monday morning, 23rd of Sept. 1816.

MY DEAR JOHN,—Susan is in such a hurry when she once begins a letter to you that she never tells us till it is finished, and therefore I am now obliged to content myself with the crossing.

There have been very few people here this year compared with the usual quantity. I think nobody has stayed here more than a day but Julia Walker, Dr Hope, and Stewart Derbyshire. But what people were here I had always to officiate to in the office of landlord. . . .

The Duke and Duchess of Montrose came here to dinner last Thursday, and went away the next morning. You may be sure I made a laughable appearance at the foot of the table. I could almost have wished myself in your place for an hour or two. Not but that I should not like to change places with you altogether, but more particularly for that time.

I suppose Susan or Charlotte have told you that Sir George Sitwell and Heathcote's youngest brother are here just now. I was the only unfortunate culprit of the male gender left here to entertain them, as George Campbell left this for Fife last week, and Arthur Connell did not arrive here till yesterpay; but now with his assistance I hope to get on better.

Heathy and I went out shooting twice. He shot two birds,

and I wounded mortally other three; and I flatter myself that I have now turned a good shot, for, as we were returning home, we fired off our guns at a fence two or three times quite close to it; and every time Heathy's carried out the piece, and yours scarcely made the lead-drops stick in the wood. Now, sir, I hope it is evident that I am not such a bad shot as you before thought me, and as I thought myself.

We are all going to Edinburg in a short time. We intend to honour Kean, races, and the balls by our company. Mary Sitwell is to come out then. After that week is over I believe Susan is going to Tilliecoultry, and I to Mr Mylnes at Dollar.

Charles Mackenzie is still in Glasgow. My father has been here for three days. He left Bute the other day. . . . The Marquis' eyes are little or no better. . . . My apprenticeship is as you left it—notwithstanding the united efforts of Sir Ilay and Lord Succoth, Uncle Connell, Aunt Mary, Aunt Colquhoun, and all.

Have you ever had reason to use your pistols yet ? I almost think I should be inclined to use them against the postmasters for telling you such cursed crammers.

Your letter which arrived here yesterday was much admired, as all the sentences you addressed to the children were so well adapted to amuse them.

Stewart Derbyshire has come to Scotland and is perhaps going into the 42nd. It was very amusing to hear Aunt Colquhoun and he talk about it. She said they would not admit him as being an Englishman, and he said they were always too happy to get an English officer.

We had such a nice game at Blind Harry the other night. Aunt Mary, Aunt Colquhoun, Uncle Connell, and Papa all played. The latter leapt over Sir George, who was lying on the side-board, and lighted on his knees on the carpet. We all thought he had broken both legs,—which would have been rather ridiculous to have done at Blind Harry,—but he was not the least hurt.

Sir Ilay has built an addition to the house here. It is just a story added to the wing next the stables. It has a very ugly appearance, and is more like a cottage built on the top of a wall than anything else. I hope grandpapa won't happen to see this remark, as he is much pleased with it.

Tom is going to get a tooth pulled to-day, poor wretch. I smell the agreeable fumes of breakfast coming from the dining-room to the drawing-room where I am sitting, and as it is a nasty, cold, raw, damp morning, just one suited to make one hungry, I must bid you adieu.—Believe me, your affectionate brother, JAMES CAMPBELL TAIT.

E

Lady Wake, referring to the annual visit of the Duke and Duchess of Montrose, wrote : " It was, by the young ones, always looked upon as rather a formidable visitation, the Duchess being as stiff as an old-fashioned brocade. Year after year we were in turn named to her in answer to her inquiries, and year after year she looked and listened as if she had never seen or heard of us before. Of course young Lord Graham made himself agreeable, and his father was at all times most genial and pleasant. One day just after dinner, according to custom, the child of the house came in to dessert, and little Ramsay Campbell happened to enter during one of those pauses which sometimes occur. The child's attention was at once riveted by the Duchess's figure, sitting silent and bolt upright on her chair. He stole up to her on tiptoe, and placing one little foot on the bar of the neighbouring chair, and bringing his hand smartly down on her shoulder, he shouted a loud Bo! in her ear. It was evident he had doubted whether she was alive. The Duke, who sat opposite, went into convulsions of laughter, while the Duchess recovered herself as best she could, and poor Aunt Mary quickly gave the signal for the ladies' departure. The Duchess for ever after went by the name of ' Duchess Bo,' a sobriquet hailed with delight some years after across the Tweed by some who knew her well."

CHAPTER VI.

THAT winter, Lord Succoth and his family having gone
to Rome, Sir Ilay moved into his old home, the large
corner house in Park Place : we were in our father's
house once more, reunited with our father and our
brothers. The three cousins went much into society :
Aunt Mary, still a beauty, was their chaperone,—a
fitting one for the three Graces,—and very much they
were all admired. Sir Ilay had his large dinner-
parties, and we a few quiet ones, at which I well
remember Sir Walter Scott among other distinguished
men. The authorship of the Waverley Novels was
then a pretty generally known secret, but an un-
acknowledged one ; and on his arrival one evening for
dinner, my eldest sister, the youthful shy hostess,
begging her father to " hasten down because Walter
Scott was come," was overcome with confusion on
turning to find that the guest whose name she had
used with familiarity as an author's must have over-
heard her.

We had much enjoyment from the supper-parties of

our cousin, John Murray (afterwards Lord Murray), at which habitually assembled all the talent among the Whigs, and where we met Jeffrey, Horner, Lockhart, and other lights of the age. John Murray was then one of the distinguished writers in the 'Edinburgh Review,' and shortly afterwards became Lord Advocate of Scotland. His mother, our great-aunt, was very kind to us, and always invited us, even me, to these reunions, which we were not likely to forget. I remember my secret surprise, knowing the men to be of first-rate talent, at hearing how much of their conversation was generally devoted to the discussion of wines and other material subjects.

Altogether this winter in Edinburgh was very pleasant: we were happy with our father and our brothers. Susan, our eldest sister, strove all she could to supply a mother's place to the little ones. Poor girl, she had enough to do to maintain anything like order among so lively a party, the manner of education at the High School causing the schoolboys to be much at home. The garden behind the house was their principal playground, to which they invited their favourite companions, always including the cousins from the next house; of these Ramsay, the youngest, as lively as a child as he was quiet in after years, was Archie's especial companion. Without the steady and loving help of the nurse, Susan could not have managed them at all. Betty Morton held her own in the rather unruly community, keeping the peace among them in a determined manner, and in her own peculiar dialect terminating many a dispute, for the boys inherited their father's love of argument, with, "Gae wa' wi' ye, wi' yer clavers; ye wad arguy-barguy a cat de'd."

Spring came; again the family dispersed, the girls returning to Garscube with Sir Ilay and his family.

Almost immediately the English cousin, Sir George
Sitwell, reappeared, with no trace left of his accident
which had detained him so long in the autumn, except
for the tender recollection he had retained for the
eldest of his nurses, my sister Susan, for whom it
was evident he cherished something more than gratitude; and it was no wonder he fell in love with
her, for she was an unusually pretty girl. It may
easily be imagined what an interesting amusement
it was to the junior members of the family to watch
the progress of this love-affair, especially as the wooer
was the shyest of the shy; and though it would have
been difficult to have mistaken his object, "never a
word did he say." But he could write, and it was
no matter of surprise that a few posts after his
departure brought a modest entreaty from the bash-
ful lover that she would tell him when he might
hope to call her his own.

The marriage of the eldest of our house, transferring
her to England, naturally produced a change to the
motherless juniors of the family; and for this reason
it is dwelt upon, as it probably was the originating
cause of much that followed in their after history,
Renishaw, the family place of the Sitwells, very much
taking the place of Garscube after good old Sir Ilay's
death at the age of ninety had changed the face of
affairs in Scotland. Our eldest brother had passed
this year, so eventful to the little party at Garscube,
at Geneva, having been sent there ostensibly for the
purpose of finishing his education after leaving Edinburgh College, by the study of modern language,
but really and truly to get him out of the way of
the loveliest of the three Graces, his cousin Mary
Sitwell,—there having existed, young as they both
were, a professed attachment between them from

their earliest years. He was allowed to return to
Garscube for his sister's wedding, which was fixed
for the first of June (1818). A Scottish is so very
different from an English wedding, that it is worth
while to give a few lines to the subject. That the
old house was fuller than it could possibly hold would
happen on either side of the border, but the necessity
for this is aggravated in Scotland by the fact that a
Presbyterian marriage permitting no assembling in
the church, all the guests, many coming from a long
distance, must be received in the house itself. A very
pretty sight it was when on the appointed day the
family in all its branches was assembled in the
drawing - room; by far the greater part in the first
bloom of youth, but the centre of all was the dear
old grandfather, who had been the friend and benefactor of almost every one in the room. It is true
that such of us as still possessed fathers and mothers
were glad enough to know that they were there, but
there was not one who did not feel that Sir Ilay was
the patriarch of the whole company, and accordingly
watched his every look and word as he moved about
among us, and went forward to receive his granddaughter the bride, who, having quietly entered with
her two young bridesmaids, was at once led by him
into the middle of the room, where she and her
bridegroom plighted their troth, and promised to be
faithful, loving, and true to their lives' end, their
hands being joined by the good old minister of the
parish, who had known us all from our early childhood. But no ring was placed on the bride's hand
at the time of the marriage,—that was done after
it was over, simply by the bridegroom apart. The
joining of hands was followed first by a simple, earnest
extempore prayer, all remaining standing, and then

by a somewhat heavy address to the young couple, exhorting them to fulfil their duties to each other and to set a good example in the place where they were to dwell. Then all was over except the cutting of the cake and the departure of the young couple amid a shower of shoes, and a household of rejoicing friends to celebrate the occasion; taking with them the bride's sister, who according to the custom of the times accompanied them during the wedding tour, to her own exceeding delight, just escaped from the schoolroom, for the complete holiday of a glorious month in the wild Highlands. Whatever it was to them, to her it was enchantment, for never had I been so free and so happy.

In the autumn the young couple departed for Renishaw, the family place in Derbyshire, taking with them this time Mary Sitwell, the other brides-maid. Her presence added greatly to the brilliancy of the young *ménage*. All boys and girls together, they had a most amusing time of it; the most frolic-some of them all was Lord Ashley (the present Lord Shaftesbury), then reading for Oxford with his cousin, the Rev. Frederick Ricketts, rector of the parish. The late Duke of Devonshire, then quite a young man, lived in bachelor state at Chatsworth, and much increased the gaiety of the place.

Meantime, things went on in Scotland much as usual, but never can I forget one day in November (1817). We were a happy family party, young and old, assembled round the dining-table at Garscube. The post had arrived just as we sat down, and all were in a great hurry for the opening of the news-paper, which was expected to announce the fulfilment of the country's hope in the birth of an heir to the crown.

Oh! what can I say that would describe the shock when the broad black edges of the newspaper disclosed in large dreadful letters the words, "Death of the Princess Charlotte of Wales and of her infant son, stillborn."

Nothing indeed can be said that could convey an idea of the thrill of grief and horror that ran through us. The possibility of such an event never seemed to have entered the mind of any one; and to us the idea of the young Princess Charlotte had been brought very near from our childhood by the constant letters which had passed between her and our governess. We had seemed able to trace her through what might almost be called the captivity of her childhood and girlhood, and now that at last she was happy, for her to be thus cut off was almost too much for us to bear.

We had almost idolised the picture our imaginations had drawn of her, and now we vividly pictured the scene at Claremont, where with her little babe she lay still and cold.

We could think and talk of nothing else. I well remember that next day, while visiting a cottage where lived an old woman of 105 years of age who had been the mother of a family in the "45" and a tremendous Jacobite, we told her of what had happened, expecting her to feel some interest in that which was filling our hearts. She did not understand whom we were talking about, her only remark being, "Aweel! since Prince Charlie didna get his ain, I kent there maun be a king in the land, but I didna care and didna ken wha it might be."

Charles Wake had spent the greater part of the summer in Scotland, partly at Garscube, partly in Park Place, the tie between him and the little Archie much strengthened by the gift of a writing-desk, which the Archbishop of Canterbury still has in his possession, having, as he lately told me, never forgòtten his pride and delight on becoming the proprietor of a real man's writing-desk. How far away and yet how distinct all this seems!—the pale, fair little boy with his books and the precious desk, sitting at his own particular little table, is still before me.

This year passed away, and the summer brought back the young married pair on their first visit to Scotland. In Edinburgh their first child was born,[1] and shortly after it was decided that I was to accompany them back to England. They took a circuitous route to Renishaw, making visits by the way, one especially to old Mr Parke at Highfield near Liverpool, Sir George Sitwell's maternal grandfather, who made a deep impression on my sister and myself as a live specimen of a class we had often seen in pictures and read of in story-books. A hale, hearty old man, round in body and full in face, with a large waistcoat, cheery voice, and countenance beaming with benevolence, not much of polish but a great deal of kindness in his welcome. His son, Lord Wensleydale, was then a rising barrister. England and Scotland, and almost everything and every person in them, were wholly different from each other in that far-back time, and you might have searched from Tweed to John o' Groat's House without finding, either among the old lairds or among the merchants of Glasgow (which was to Scotland what Liverpool is to England), anything at all resembling this merry-hearted old man, both a laird and a merchant, having made a large fortune in Liverpool, and become the proprietor of the house and lands of Highfield. As

[1] Alice, afterwards Viscountess Combermere.

thoroughly English was his pretty old wife, with neat white lace and muslin caps, and bright-coloured dresses—so different from our old Scottish ladies, who were universally dressed in black or very dark-coloured silks.

The circuitous route to Derbyshire brought the party to Cheltenham, where we were joined at once by Charles Wake, and where we tried to see as much of an English watering-place as we could in two days. It was the fashion then to attend sales, for they drew together the society of the place, and we went to a very large one that was then going on ; and the young wife taking a fancy to a handsome volume with beautiful engravings that was handed round, whispered to her husband that she would like to have it. He caught the eye of the salesman and nodded, and was pleased to find it immediately knocked down to him ; not so pleased when it was handed to him with the words, "Sixty guineas ; it is yours, sir. ' *Le Musée Napoléon*,' in forty volumes." Poor Sir George had been brought up in economical principles, and sixty guineas was rather a shock to give for a book he had not dreamed of wanting ! However, his wife was delighted, and it proved an important purchase, for it contained first-rate engravings of all the pictures and statues in the Louvre (with an account of each) as Napoleon had made it when he had robbed all Europe, excepting England, to fill it with treasures of art. Many an improving and delightful hour was spent over it, and the Archbishop has often said that that lucky accidental purchase had been of the greatest use to him, when afterwards visiting the various picture-galleries in the different capitals to which they were restored.

After leaving Cheltenham, Renishaw was soon

reached : we found there a rejoicing party, for it was the beginning of the vacation, and the kindest of sisters and most good-natured of brothers-in-law had gathered a happy party from Scotland, — our own four young brothers, Tom, "the ancient warrior," Craufurd, Campbell, and the little Archie, and a cousin, James Campbell. Under charge of the two nurses of our childhood, Betty and Mary Russell, they had been put on board a smack at Leith, which was then the established sea conveyance before the day of steamers. A dead calm had come on, and seven days and eight nights had passed before they reached Hull, in hungry plight, for provisions had fallen short. They had then a farther voyage up the Humber to Gainsborough, from which they posted to Renishaw. How different from the mode of travelling now !

Renishaw was a charming place. The house had passed through the hands of many proprietors while in the direct line of the Sitwells. It was small, none of them being rich, till an accident happened which changed the fortunes of the family. The last heir of the Sitwells, a fair blue - eyed boy of about sixteen, as represented by his picture, was drowned, it is not known how, in a piece of water on the property called Foxendam, and the place passed through the female line into the hands of the grand-father of Sir George, our brother-in-law. His name was Hurt, but on his succession he took that of Sitwell. He had made a great deal of money as a proprietor of ironworks, and added considerably to the house, which, as he found it, was but the centre of the building as it now stands. His son, born before his father's succession, had been christened Sitwell, and becoming the first baronet, as Sir Sitwell Sitwell he greatly enlarged the property and the house; but through the splendid apartments wanders the ghost (it is said) of the drowned heir, discontented with the change.

A few days after our arrival the rector of the parish and his wife accepted an invitation to dinner, and it would be difficult to express my amazement when, "Mr and Mrs Ricketts" being announced, there entered, instead of what we were accustomed to see in our own native land, an exceedingly fashionably-dressed little woman and a very handsome well-dressed young man, the one giving the tips of her fingers and the other a most graceful bow in acknow-ledgment of the cordial reception of the young lady of the house. A more complete contrast to the minister and his wife so well known at the time throughout Scotland could not well be imagined. It is well known that the birth of many of the ministers of the Scottish Church is the same in degree as that of their rural parishioners, above whom they are only raised in rank by their sacred profession, while in the English Church there is no rank that is not represented. In this especial instance the Rev. Frederick Ricketts was the nephew of Lord Liverpool the Prime Minister, and his wife niece of the then Earl of Shaftesbury, whose eldest son, Lord Ashley, had just left the rectory for Oxford. A magnificently handsome youth he then was, as full of fun and frolic as he now is of all deeds of charity and loving-kindness.

What my thoughts were when the plans for the Doncaster races were settled that evening it would be impossible to describe. The opening day, the best of the races, called the St Leger, in those days was always fixed for the Monday; therefore to be in time it was the established custom that all the

families from a distance should arrive on the Sunday
afternoon or evening; and this was supposed to be
so completely a matter of necessity that no one
dreamed of avoiding it. So after morning church
and luncheon the Renishaw party set off; a very
magnificent turn-out it was,—a beautiful barouche
with four handsome bay horses, and two more exactly
to match with outriders. Dr More, the vicar of
St Pancras (Sir George's uncle by marriage), inside
with two ladies, the rector of the parish with Sir
George on the coach-box.

What may have been the private thoughts of two
sisters carefully educated in the Presbyterian Church,
which in those days scarcely sanctioned a summer's
evening walk on the Sabbath, may easily be con-
jectured; and the sights and sounds when, after a
twenty miles' drive, we entered the city of Doncaster,
were not calculated to make us more easy in our
minds. The crowds in the streets, the various equipages similar to our own attempting to force their
way amidst jostling horsemen, the swearing of the
men, the rearing of the horses, the confusion increased
by a large black hearse and several mourning coaches
stopped by the crowds on their way through the town,
a numerous drove of oxen in the same predicament
with their white horns rushing hither and thither
among the vociferating multitude, the incessant ringing of the church bells for the races, and enormous
placards with " PREPARE TO MEET THY GOD " in
gigantic letters meeting the eye at every turn,
altogether formed a scene that now after more than
half a century has passed seems as fresh and as
astounding as though it had been but yesterday.

Happily these things cannot now be: the good
sense and good taste of the country have coincided

with the deeper feeling of those who abhorred the
desecration of God's appointed day of rest, and, together with the efforts of those men whose solemn
protests were made in the awful words of the placards,
have been sufficiently powerful to change the order
of these races. Now no family dreams of making
their entrance into Doncaster on a Sunday: the St
Leger is run on a Tuesday. A greater sense of
decency, there is no doubt, prevails in the land.

To such unaccustomed eyes as ours the race-course,
with its glittering equipages, the beautiful horses, the
splendours of the stand, the excitement of the races
themselves, gave the whole thing the appearance of
a magic scene. But an impression that never departed
was made by one little episode that took place close
to us. Early in the morning of the first day we had
made the acquaintance of a charming young couple
who had been but a few weeks married, and who
seemed radiant with happiness. On that same day
the favourite "Antonio" — I shall never forget his
name, — whom every one expected to win, was "no-
where." The gentlemen generally had betted heavily
upon him, and the excitement was as a storm,—the
stamping of feet over our heads was terrific. Very
near me I saw the young husband as one possessed;
his agitation was so great that men crowded round
him to hide him from his wife, and to hurry him out of
her sight altogether. I heard people saying to each
other that he had lost in that race a sum of money
that would cripple them for years; and when the next
day, after a cloudy morning the sun suddenly shone out,
I heard the young wife say, with a sad unconsciousness
of the evil that had befallen her, "Oh, I am so glad
the day is clearing, for William was so bad all night,
and has such a bad headache this morning, and looks

so pale, that I am thankful the day will be fine, for yesterday there must have been thunder in the air." Poor young thing! probably like myself she had never been on a race-course before. I had never heard much about races, but the impression made by this first introduction was never effaced.

At that time the Doncaster races were considered the best in the world, and thousands came from all parts to attend them. And so little was the objection then felt to them that the Archbishop of York was himself present—not, however, in state, but on horseback—with some of his friends. The spirit of the time and place pervaded even the boys' amusements, for they had donkey-races, with regular lines enclosed with ropes, under the direction of Sir George.

CHAPTER VII.

THE holiday months of August and September too soon
passed away, and the elder boys returned to Scotland
under the charge of Mary Russell, who though second
in authority was dear and precious as her superior
Betty. The two little brothers, Camie (*i.e.*, Campbell)
and Archie, remained at Renishaw with Betty. Why?
Because their elder sister, still a mother to her motherless little brothers, had persuaded her kind-hearted
husband to propose and carry out a plan, on the after
success of which hinged the whole life of the Archbishop. Happy woman to have a husband who would
so readily yield to her wishes! A letter was written
to our father setting forth the fame of two men who in
Lancashire had performed wonders in cases of lameness,
and strongly representing the truth, every day becoming more painfully evident, that time and the
means already used had done little or nothing towards
the restoration of either of the boys; that Camie's
whole limb was neither in power nor in growth in
any proportion to the other limb or to the rest of
the body; and that little Archie, beautiful child as

he was, remained deformed in his feet, and exceedingly lame. If their father would only give his permission that the trial should be made, Sir George would at his own expense take them down to Whitworth in Lancashire, and establish them there under the care of their nurse, the never-failing Betty, and from time to time they should come to Renishaw, when it could be ascertained if they were gaining benefit from the process.

Surely it was a sort of inspiration that suggested this; for these Whitworth doctors were men of no education, and by all the regulars of the medical and surgical profession were looked upon as nothing but quacks, though there was no question of the wonderful cures they had performed. Strange to say, our father had no misgivings, and at once consented. The following week the good-natured young baronet, with his two brothers-in-law and their nurse, posted to Whitworth, a distance of sixty miles, causing a great sensation in the little town, scarcely more than a village, where a gentleman's carriage was rarely seen. After making the best arrangements in his power, he left them there and returned home.

And now the best thing I can do is to introduce in this place the details I took down in March 1871 from the lips of the Archbishop when we spent the winter together on the Riviera. We had been talking of our early days, I questioning him of those things I had either forgotten or never known; for he had wished me to give in writing an account of those years at home, both before and after his birth, the memory of which was fast fading away as one after another of the family circle disappeared from life. He said in reply: " I must give you myself the history of my life in my seventh year at Whitworth, for no one else can

do so. No one living knows anything about it. Camie
and myself, with dear old Betty, lived in the 'Red
Lion,' a common public-house, but the best in the place.
Our sitting-room was the back parlour of the house,
with a sanded floor, adjoining the bar; our bedroom
a garret upstairs. In one large bed I slept with
Betty, Camie in a smaller one close to it. We soon
made acquaintance with the men who habitually fre-
quented the house, Jim o' Dick's and Tom o' Simon's
(their names being simply their christian names
attached to their fathers'), the manners and customs
of the district being too simple to admit of a universal
use of family names among the working-classes. The
skittle-ground and the tap-room were our places of conversation, yet I do not remember much evil; probably
we were too young to understand or observe it, and
certainly Betty kept a watchful look-out over us. One
great subject of interest was, I remember, the courtship
carried on by young Lomax, the son of a farmer in the
neighbourhood, who was paying his addresses to Betty
Lord, the daughter of the fat old landlady of the 'Red
Lion.' This was full of interest to us. We went to
the doctor's every day early (for the very good reason
that after nine every morning he began to get drunk)
to have the tin boots in which he kept our legs encased
properly arranged, and the progress of the cure attended
to. These tin boots hurt us very much, and I have
often marvelled how we were able to hobble about in
them, as we did all day long, except the short time
Camie had lessons from the village schoolmaster and
read Latin with the clergyman of the parish, Mr
Porter. I cannot recollect ever doing anything in
the way of lessons during the nine months I was
there. I have been told since that I had writing
lessons from this schoolmaster, but either I have for-

gotten it or he has confused me with my brother. I
do not remember even reading story-books, but I used
to wander about with all sorts of mysterious thoughts,
making plays to myself out of them, and fighting all
sorts of imaginary enemies with my stick or whatever
I could lay my hands upon. Camie and I amused ourselves very well, and dear old Betty was very kind to
us, helping us in every way she could think of. During
the nights we were distressed by the tin boots, in which
we were obliged to sleep, but by degrees we got accustomed to them. There was scarcely any one approaching to lady or gentleman in the place, which was full of
invalids of the lower middle classes, chiefly with real
or supposed cases of cancer or stiffened limbs, for the
management and cure of which the Whitworth doctors
were famous. Their name was Taylor. One of them
kept what he called a pack of hounds, which were of
course a continual source of amusement. He went out
with them after he had seen his patients in the early
morning, and in the evening when the sport was over
spent the hours in drinking till bed-time, from the
effects of which he had barely recovered in the morning. They had a nephew, a much more respectable
character, who, as I have since heard, successfully
carried on their practice after their death. This
was the mode of life of both the Taylors, and yet
to these men, under Providence, we owed our
restoration to the perfect use of our limbs. Probably
my brother, dear Camie's case was more difficult than
mine, for though much deformed in shape, my feet
were possessed of each bone and muscle in full vigour ;
therefore they had only, as it were, to be formed into
their proper natural shape by continual gentle force,
the force that comes from constant pressure, whereas
Campbell's limb had from paralysis while yet a baby

been weakened to that degree that its growth had
never kept pace with the rest of his body; yet by
the strange exceptional treatment of these men it
was perfectly restored, and at the end of a year his
lameness gradually wore off. The time we spent at
Whitworth was broken by a visit of some weeks to
Renishaw."

This is word for word the Archbishop's own account
of the strange episode in his life without which his
after destiny must have been completely different.
He says that he cannot recollect learning anything,
nor even amusing himself with story-books, while at
Whitworth; nevertheless I know that a short time
after this he could read very well, for during their
holiday time at Renishaw he and dear Camie used
to have some sort of lessons in my room every day.
They might have had a wiser teacher, for with the
want of judgment of a young girl I gave them the
books I was most fond of myself, and was greatly
disgusted to find they could not be appreciated. I
still possess the copy of Milman's beautiful poem "The
Fall of Jerusalem," in which the passage beginning
with "Tears had been shed o'er thee, by holier eyes
than mine, the Son of Man foresaw thy fall and wept,"
is all blurred and blotted with dear little Archie's own
tears, caused, not because he was stupid, but because
his sister, who was old enough to have known better,
was silly. When Dean Milman, years after, had become the Bishop of London's intimate friend, he was
much amused by being told of this first association
of his name and works.

The spring of the year 1819 Sir George and Lady
Sitwell had passed in London, having taken me with
them; it was the first season of the whole party, and
we went a good deal into society. I cannot say I

liked it, nor I think did they very much. The amusements did not seem half as real as those we had been used to. It was a great consolation to me that Charles Wake was there, bringing with him part of our early life; but a girl's existence at that time in London was a sort of honourable captivity, there were so many impossibilities for ladies then which do not now exist. We were for about two months in Thomas' Hotel in Berkeley Square, and, as may be imagined, made many acquaintances, scarce one of whom is now alive. I believe that my sister was nearly as glad as I was to return to Renishaw; but we did not remain long there, very soon after our return setting out for Scotland. After some charming weeks at Garscube we settled ourselves in the British Hotel till a house was found for Lady Sitwell's second confinement, and it was while in the hotel that I first made acquaintance with Lord Ashley, of whom I had heard so much at Renishaw. I thought him the handsomest young man I had ever seen: he was very tall, and his countenance radiant with youthful brightness. He had come down to Scotland with his cousin, George Howard, afterwards Lord Morpeth and Earl of Carlisle, whom he was very anxious to make as intimate with his friends as he was himself, but Mr Howard was, besides being naturally shy, quite a stranger, and did not see the pleasure or advantage of this; and I remember being infinitely amused by the manner in which the introduction was effected. We heard a sort of laughing scuffle at the drawing-room door, which was suddenly thrown open from the outside, and he was projected head foremost into the midst of us like a battering-ram, while Lord Ashley shouted out, "Enter the Honourable George Howard." Of course after this there was an end of all shyness: it must be remembered that neither of them was twenty years of age.

And now we were once more in constant association with my father and brothers. The two younger boys had remained long enough in England to be at Reni-shaw when the news arrived of the birth of the son and heir at Edinburgh; great were the rejoicings of the tenantry, and Betty celebrated the occasion by firing off a pistol! Having received all the benefit that the Whitworth doctors could accomplish they returned to Edinburgh, and the business of education was from this time regularly carried on. It was in Mr Ramsay's day-school that Archie began his career, working hard, and a great favourite with the masters, for whatever he did, he did it with all his might. He and Campbell were as happy together as it was possible for them to be, gradually finding themselves able to join in the amusements of other boys—a new life to them. The gardens at the back of Park Place resounded with their noise and fun on the half-holi-days which the school allowed. They had built a cabin in the far corner where the walls joined, in which they held high festival, and, under the general-ship of their brother Tom, who still retained his style and title of "the ancient warrior," the boys lost and won many a victory in those gardens: the only wonder was that they were not really killed.

In the autumn of that year the little brothers for the first time accompanied their father to Harvies-toun, as they continued to do for many successive autumns; for though the establishment there had long been broken up, an old family servant continued to reside in the house, and Betty always accompanied her charge, together with George Watt. The chief amusement was riding; wonderful was the number of ponies annually impressed into the service, and, mounted on the dear beautiful old Shetland called Lily (I suppose in contradiction to the fact that he was coal-black without one spot of white), which had been given to John, our eldest brother, when quite a child, Archie rode far and near.

Notwithstanding his many disappointments, our dear father took much delight in riding with his five or six boys around him through the extensive domain he had laid out with so much taste and skill. Though the improvements he so successfully carried out now brought no profit to him, the whole estate being in trust, they were yet a source of pleasure. He was a man of wonderful powers of mind, able to concentrate his thoughts upon subjects of literature, and taking a keen interest in the politics of the day, yet finding the greatest delight in conversing with his boys. He was in the habit of taking them long excursions, occupying from morning till night; on these occasions the little Archie rode upon a pad before his father upon Bessie Bell, the beautiful grey that used to be one of the carriage horses. One of the boys, Craufurd, very early showed great talent, and astonished even his father by the rapidity with which he acquired knowledge of all sorts. He was a remarkably handsome boy, full of strength and spirits, and it was he who naturally would have been selected from the group as the one who would distinguish himself in life—not the delicate little one, who looked rather like a flower to pass away in early spring; but God's ways are not as our ways. Craufurd was indeed to be sealed with his own seal, but for an immortality not such as man bestows.

While this part of the family were enjoying this life of perfect freedom, we returned to Renishaw with the little son and heir, whose birth had nearly cost his mother her life. She was in consequence too delicate to nurse him, and a stout Scottish lass was, with her husband's consent, retained for his benefit, leaving her own baby behind. Sir George hastened home for September shooting, while we followed slowly. Towards the close of the last day's journey, as we neared the gates of the park at Renishaw, Sir George, who had been on the watch, suddenly appeared at the carriage door in a shooting suit covered with mud. " Ech! keep us," exclaimed the Scottish nurse, " there's a puir body an' he's daft!" In her short life she had never beheld an English sportsman, and her consternation was great when she found this was her master, whom she now saw for the first time.

And now the little heir had to be christened, and it was to be a splendid christening. The Duke of Devonshire (the great man of the neighbourhood, and really, in spite of politics, a family friend) was to be godfather, and was to bring a large party from Chatsworth. Guests from all quarters flocked to the place. The baby was to be christened in the morning of the next day, and in the evening was to be given a grand ball. It may be well imagined how · full of life and bustle was every corner.

It was a brilliant frost; there could be no hunting, and skating was the order of the day. The numerous party assembled round a large pond in the park, which was quickly covered with skaters, while a noisy laughing group looked on. Sir George, who was always most kind to me, proposed that he and one of his friends, Mr John Parker,[1] the son of a

---

[1] Afterwards the Right Honourable John Parker, Secretary to the Treasury.

neighbouring gentleman, should take me between
them, skating as they went. They assured me no
harm could happen, and I assented.

While George was buckling on my skates, Mr
Parker said he would take a round on the pond and
return for us. George shouted to him, " Don't go on
the north side, the ice has been broken there." I
suppose he did not hear, for off he darted in that very
direction. Stooping down as we both were, we did
not see him, but in another moment the air was filled
with shrieks, and we beheld men and women flying
up the banks from the pond; not a soul remained
upon the ice, while in a dark-looking part of it poor
Parker was rapidly disappearing. An impulse such
as sends an arrow from a bow sent me across the
ice to the rescue, while George's outcries of " Charlotte
Tait, you—fool, you—fool!" each time rising into a
still higher key, sounded in my ears; but—on reaching the hole, nothing was to be seen but a man's arm
and a hand grasping the empty air. I caught hold
of it, and in an instant was pulled into the water,
but did not let go my hold. To this moment I
remember the icy cold of the water over my chest.
He all but drowned me without being able to help
it; nevertheless I saved him, for the impetus that
had been given him by my pull enabled him to rise
so as to catch hold of the thick edge of the ice where
it had been broken, and in a few minutes the scattered
crowd had recovered from their sudden panic. There
was no want of help, and I was soon lifted out, and
found the cause of the scene, like a drowned rat,
beside me.

The whole thing had been too rapid to realise any
sense of danger, therefore I am grieved and ashamed
to say my first thought was not thankfulness for a

merciful preservation, as it well might and ought to
have been, but a most annoying feeling (occasioned
by the vain efforts the half-drowned man was making
to express his gratitude) that he couldn't but think
I had risked my life to save his for love of him, and
that he would feel himself bound to fall in love—or
pretend to—with me; so that the first use I made of
my voice, when recovered from the choking gasps of
returning breath, was to assure him that he need not
thank me, for I would have done the same for the
least groom in the stable. This was ungracious, but
I believe it was the wisest thing that could have been
done under the circumstances. My second thought
was that I had spoilt my pelisse and would be well
scolded, and it was not till I felt the icy cold of my
dripping clothes that the third thought came — of
thankfulness to God.

The week of gaiety at Renishaw thus begun went
on, and was very successful. The little babe had
been very ill, so ill that the very morning of his
christening there had been fears for his being able
to go through the ceremony of his baptism; but he
got better, and, all over costly lace, was brought into
the drawing-room to have the words murmured over
him, in his name "renouncing the pomps and vanity
of the world, that he would not follow nor be led by
them." And, indeed, though at that time surrounded
by them all, I do not think that Reresby Sitwell, who
then received his name, was in after life led by them.

The ball in the evening was brilliant. My first
partner I felt quite proud of, he being a double first-
class man, young Charles Wood (now Lord Halifax),
introduced to me by Hurt Sitwell.

Some of the guests remained, others came. It was
a festal week, and I well remember hearing that

eleven hundred pounds was spent upon the celebration of this christening; also I remember quite as well hearing the baby, when grown to be a man, greatly regret that the money had not been kept for him till then, when he would have been very glad of it. Babies as a rule are not grateful in after years for such doings; but nothing could be more pleasant to his relatives than the honours paid to this particular infant, and, as may be easily imagined, in a houseful of the description of young people that were there assembled, much that was amusing and much that was interesting took place. A good novel or two might very well be written without any aid from fiction. The name of the "Diving Belle" clung to me in those old Renishaw days.

CHAPTER VIII.

CAMPBELL'S DEATH — ARCHIE WITH HIS FATHER — GRIZZEL
COCHRANE — LADY OF REDCASTLE — GEORGE TAIT'S GRAND-
SONS AND THEIR LEGACY—ARCHIE AT THE HIGH SCHOOL—
MARION AND BETTY ABROAD.

ALAS! a great sorrow was preparing for us all. But
chiefly for little Archie, for it brought to him the loss
of the companion of his life, bound to him by more than
the ordinary ties of brotherly love. Debarred by the
same cause from the active sports of childhood, Campbell and Archie had been all in all to each other, but
now by God's decree they were to be parted, to meet
no more till time should be at an end. Little Campbell,
from his earliest years, had set his heart upon going
to sea. He was, with his bright black eyes and quick
intelligent countenance, the very picture of a little
sailor, and he had been hard to convince that his
lameness made it impossible. When the hope of cure
had opened before him he had clung still to the idea,
and now that he found himself in possession of the use
of his limbs his joy was complete, when it was arranged
that he should be sent on board the training-ship at
Portsmouth to receive a proper naval education, as was
then required. This was in the beginning of the year
1821, and amid the joyful bustle of leaving school and
preparing for his new life there was little room for

fostering the grief of parting. Even Archie could not
but be glad for him, and had not yet realised what it
would be to live on without him ; but something deep
felt was stirring within Camie himself, and the two
nurses knew, though most probably the men of the
family did not, that each night before going to bed he
used to sit alone in one of the upper rooms, his elbows
on the table, his head between his hands, deeply intent
upon his book, and that book was God's Holy Word,
tears often gliding down his cheeks and falling upon
the pages. Was it that, now he was about to leave his
home, its sacred truths had acquired a new meaning,
that what had before been to him the histories and
lessons of a book had become living realities,—that
book which was to be his guide, his comfort, and his
guard when far away from home ? We only can know
what we do know, the inner life is ever hid from us ;
but to those who watch, the more plainly is it seen
that " God's purposes are ripening every hour."

A great alarm arose in the house, for the little Archie
was taken ill with scarlet fever : he had it severely but
favourably, and at the end of three weeks was nearly
well, though of course still confined to his room and
debarred all communication with his brothers. All
anxiety was over and there was a grand holiday,
Campbell's favourite friends and companions having
been invited to spend the day and dine in Park Place.
It was a sort of farewell *fête* to his schoolfellows, before
leaving Scotland to go to the training-ship at Portsmouth. The garden, with the hut before mentioned,
was that day the scene of much festivity, and in the
evening there was plenty of boyish fun.

When the hour for good-night came the playfellows
separated, each one returning to his home, many of
them thinking they also would like to exchange school

work for a sailor's life; and Campbell, flushed and excited, bade good-night to his father and his brothers (there were no sisters there), and left the dining-room to go to bed, but as he reached the door he turned round and said his throat was sore. Never more was he seen there, never again was his voice heard among them; before morning light scarlet fever in its most terrible form was upon him, delirium had entire possession of him, and on the third day the child left his home for his Father's kingdom. He had, before he went to bed, taken his Bible to the usual place, and had left his mark at those verses in St James' Epistle : "Go to now, ye that say, To-day or to-morrow we will go into such a city, and continue there a year, and buy and sell, and get gain: whereas ye know not what shall be on the morrow." How different was the morrow from that which had been anticipated when the garden was ringing with the glad voices of the boys. Camie lay dead, and Archie, still weak with the fever, had to be told that he had lost him.

Never shall I forget the arrival of the letter which brought the tidings. We were not used to sorrow then, and when I heard of Campbell's death, each day, each hour he had so lately spent among us rose vividly to mind, bringing a thousand cruel thoughts with them. Some are ingenious in self-torture, and it seemed to me now that I had not been half kind enough to the little boy I had loved so dearly. Of this we may be sure, that each impatient word, when it comes back as an echo from beyond the grave, will have a ring of unkindness in it; and when our love can be no longer spoken, it becomes so intense as to be but a regretful pain. Dear Camie! it is more than half a century since he left us, yet his bright black eyes and speaking face are vividly before me, and a sad pathetic look, half reproachful, which he turned upon me once as he let go my arm when I refused to take him with me a long walk to the village, because I thought that I could not bear his weight, only half restored as he then was, on his return to Renishaw from Whitworth. How often has that look come back to me, and how often have I wished that I had taken him with me, and not minded the weight! I wish it now after fifty years! The affections do not forget.

Paler than ever, Archie returned to his books, a sad and solitary child. As the months went on he gained but little strength, and those around him were pained to see him always, always reading. "Put away your book, dear, and go and play," was often said; but the reply was ever a sad shake of the head, with "I have no one to play with now." The autumn at Harviestoun was his best restorative, and now began that close friendship between the child and his father which certainly had the most beneficial effect upon his opening mind. Full of information, devotedly fond of reading, with a memory that retained everything he read, at the same time delighting in old family histories, traditions, and recollections, it is no wonder that, as the little Archie grew into boyhood and passed on into youth, his father was the companion and the friend in whose society he took the most delight.[1] From him he heard the simple story of his forefathers in the paternal line, who, though belonging to Aberdeenshire, had emigrated from the south. His grandfather's had been a peaceful career : the only

[1] All this respecting the Abp's intercourse with our father was given me by himself; he was very anxious to impress upon me how much he owed to his conversation, and also to the interest of those family histories.—C. M. WAKE.

warlike event in it was that in his youth he had been
present at the battle of Falkirk, having with a companion been drawn there by curiosity. There were
enough and to spare of wild romances in his father's
maternal line of Murdochs and Mackenzies, stretching back to the story of the "widow of the Peak" in
Galloway.

He was not likely to omit the daring deed of Grizzel
Cochrane (no further off than great-aunt to his own
mother). Her father having been concerned in
Argyle's rising in support of the Duke of Monmouth,
lay in the Tolbooth prison in Edinburgh awaiting
the warrant which was to consign him to a traitor's
grave. His daughter, a fair girl of eighteen, enthusi-
astically devoted to him, resolved to save him, and
having ascertained the time when the messenger who
carried all letters from England must pass a secluded
place well known to her, she disguised herself in man's
attire, hiding her luxuriant hair and shrouding her
girlish form in a horseman's cloak. Pistol in hand
she burst from a thicket, forcing her horse with so
sudden a shock against that of the courier, who was
carelessly riding on his way, that he was nearly
upset by the unexpected assault, and before he had
recovered from his surprise he found himself divested
of his letter-bags and helplessly gazing after the
robber, who had galloped off through bush and briar,
over hill and dale. Pursuit was useless, and crest-
fallen he slowly made his way to Edinburgh, in no
hurry to bring himself into trouble by the confession
of his misadventure. To his surprise he next day
found that the letter-bags had been safely deposited
in the proper official quarter, and as none at the
time knew that one paper had been abstracted, it
was long before any inquiries were made. Grizelda

made good use of the delay she had thus obtained. Preparations for escape and flight had been already all but completed. Another day and another night, and father and daughter were safe over the sea.

It was not till more than fifty years afterwards that this secret history transpired, which accounted for the disappearance of the Secretary of State's warrant for the execution of Sir John Cochrane. Grizelda afterwards became Mrs Kerr of Morriston, in Berwickshire. There is in the possession of my father's family an original picture of her at the age apparently of five- or six-and-twenty, fair-haired and blue-eyed, with a sort of innocent fearlessness of expression that well suits her story, to which reference is made by the addition of a large pistol hung up on a nail in the wall behind her. Probably she would not herself have permitted this, but long after her death it was introduced into her picture, that it might be known as her portrait, and the danger she encountered for her father's rescue remembered.[1]

Not less interesting, though far less romantic, was the story of the prudent Lady of Redcastle, who, finding that all her arguments could not prevail upon her husband to remain at home when the clans went out to support Prince Charlie, affected to agree with him that, however hopeless was the cause, he was yet obliged in honour to follow him to the field, especially as the Prince had sent word that he would sleep in Mackenzie's house the night before he marched to meet the Duke of Cumberland. He came, and there was an end of Mackenzie's hesitation. The winning manner and inspiring voice which had won the hearts of half Scotland banished all foreboding gloom, and the only question was how earliest to meet the clans gathering

[1] The original picture is now at Courteenhall.

for the battle of Culloden. The Lady, who had received the Prince with all the honours in her power, giving him the best she could, rose early in the morning herself to preside over their breakfast, which she took care should be excellent. She insisted upon waiting herself upon the Prince, who was indeed too much engrossed in the earnest conversation he was carrying on with the laird to observe that she herself was lifting the heavy kettle from the fire. It was no wonder that it was too much for her : her foot slipped, and stumbling forward, she emptied the boiling contents of her kettle into the jack-boot of her unfortunate husband. That he swore, and stamped the other leg with pain and rage, did little good. His agony was beyond expression. The boot had to be cut off; it might be a question whether he could ever mount again ; at all events, there was none as to the possibility of his getting into the saddle now, and the Prince was forced to depart without him. Culloden was lost, but the life and lands of Redcastle were saved. Not a Mackenzie belonging to him had been in the field, for they would not stir without their chief, and when the dreadful day of reckoning came there was no warrant of vengeance for them. It was long before the laird could again set his foot to the ground, but his children played about the house, none making them afraid, and the Lady kept her own secret as to the vow she had registered, that her husband should not rush upon destruction ; for her mind had long been made up that the best hope for Prince Charlie was that he should be helped to leave the country as soon as possible with safety.

These and many more such tales handed down in the Murdoch line were related in their rambles at Harviestoun and among the hills near Edinburgh ;

but it was equal pleasure to tell and to hear the
simple annals of their rural ancestors, the bonnet
lairds of Ludquharn in Aberdeenshire, who had supported and educated their families by their own industry. The story of one of the family having been
killed by the fall of a stack of timber in his own
woodyard never failed to interest the little boy.
Little did either father or son think, while they were
talking over these long-past times, that the kindness
shown to the orphan lad would after many days, like
the fruits of Egypt springing from the seed cast upon
the waters, produce an abundant harvest, and that
the little boy listening so eagerly to the story of the
man whose sudden death had left his only son penniless should one day be enriched by that very orphan.
Well brought up and cared for by his cousin, John
Tait, at Harviestoun, he lived to be the father of two
sons, who were also helped in life by the same liberal-
handed kinsman. They were men of retired habits,
little known beyond a very small circle of intimate
friends; the eldest son, George, was at the head of
the Edinburgh police, whom we children irreverently
denominated "George Tait the policeman"; the
younger, an officer in the navy, who early retired in
a fit of disgust, but reached the rank of yellow admiral.
They lived and died bachelors, and sixty years after
the death of their benefactor, left to the Archbishop
and his brothers a very large sum, with this touching
explanation in their will: "In remembrance of kindness received from their grandfather in our youth,
when we greatly needed it." To the Archbishop and
his brother James they left £20,000 each, and true
to their characters as Scotsmen, to the eldest brother
a still larger sum.

I need scarcely say that it was not only during one

year that all these conversations took place, in the
well-remembered walks which became the greatest
pleasure of his youth, nor how vividly he recalls the
various sorts of information his father then imparted
to him. During one of them he was introduced by
him to the celebrated Dugald Stewart, whose venerable
appearance máde a deep impression on him.

At the end of the vacation in the year 1820,
returning to Edinburgh with amended health he
devoted himself to working for the High School, in
which he had taken his place before Camie's death.
It was an established practice for the boys at the
High School to work with a tutor at home in preparation for the daily classes, but Archie had no such
assistance. His father's affairs becoming more and
more embarrassed, rendered it necessary to practise
the most rigid economy, and the faithful Betty was
his only help in learning his lessons. She used to
hold the Latin books close to her eyes, diligently
following each word as he repeated page after page.
"Aye, it maun be richt; it's just word for word, and
it sounds like it," was the encouragement he received;
and at times a sudden lowering of the book, with "Na,
na, it's no' that ava," would warn him when he was
wrong. Of one principal part of his education she
was thorough mistress; he could not have had one
better. She took care that he was out of bed early
in the morning, never permitting the slightest hesitation in the matter, and this was an important
point gained, for I doubt if, had he been left to himself, delicate as he was, the poor little fellow could
as resolutely have carried it out.

Nevertheless, for one winter and spring he was
deprived of even this assistance, for her services were
required by another member of the family. It was

necessary for the youngest sister Marion to spend a winter in Italy, and it was arranged that she should do so in the care of the old governess, Miss Potts, whom we have already mentioned as inspiring our childhood with so much awe, and with whom we had spent the first two years after our mother's death. She happened to be about to travel at the time. This was but a grim prospect for poor little Marion, and her joy was proportionately great when it was settled that our dear old Betty was to go also for the special purpose of taking care of her. She owed this great amelioration to the kindness of Sir Ilay : without it even sunny Italy with all its charms would have failed to please. But taking Betty was taking a part of home, and much amusement she derived from Betty's mode of managing and communicating with the Italians. In Rome, when assailed with the usual " Carita, signora, carita ; per l' amor di Dio, carita," she would turn upon the pursuing foe with "Gae wa' wi' ye, wi' yer clavers !" in a tongue unknown indeed but sufficiently intelligible, when given with all her natural energy, to discourage even a Roman beggar.

CHAPTER IX.

A LETTER returned to me in 1884 recalls so interesting a time that I cannot do better than give it. It was to my youngest sister, dated July 21st, 1821, and runs thus :—

"I send you my coronation ticket as I think you may like to see it, and pray treat it with due reverence, for some people actually paid fifty guineas for the same. I had quite given up all idea of having one, for owing to Aunt Hurt's being confined to bed, with a pulse at 120 and dreadfully ill, an application for one was not even thought of till a few days before the time, and then the difficulty, and consequently the favour, was so very great that we did not even attempt to ask. Judge of my surprise and delight when the day before *the* day one was sent to me! I discovered that the never-failing Colonel Percy had asked it as a personal favour or I could not have got it, for many a titled dame had failed. The newspapers will give you such a much better account of the whole scene than I can that I shall not even attempt to describe it, but only say that not Walter Scott's most glittering dreams, nor even the 'Arabian Nights' most splendid palace, can at all surpass the unrivalled magnificence of the Court of George IV. on his coronation day. I think

Queen Elizabeth's *fête* and pageant at Kenilworth will
give you the best idea of the whole. The dresses were
so magnificent that it was long before I could discover
those I knew. Every order had a distinct garb, and
each more splendid than the other. Lord Ashley was
in the dress of a royal page, which was the simplest
and the most numerous, as all the young noblemen
acted in that capacity. It was a scarlet tunic, flowing
blue sash, with white satin *et ceteras*, and silk stockings
(in the mode of the time) and high ruff. They were
so graceful !

"Sir Henry Fane, whom I knew at Bath, was
exactly in Leicester's white dress, with all his brother
Knights of the Bath. Young Lord, Bingham was the
very counterpart of Sir Walter Raleigh, in white satin,
slashed with pale blue and silver, and pale blue satin
mantle. He was with four others the king's own
pages. The peers in cloth of gold and silver. Un-
luckily, the king himself was the most absurd likeness
of a peacock, for when seated at the royal banquet
served before the throne his train, about a mile long
and full of golden stars upon a purple ground, was
spread high over the back of the throne, and the effect
was so like that of a peacock spreading his tail to
the sun every one present was struck with the absurd
resemblance While seated thus he was served by the
Duke of Devonshire and Lord Gwydyr on their knees,
both looking very graceful and the finest figures in
the world. The Duke of Devonshire looks very handsome—*at a distance.* Though it was full noon and a
bright lovely day 2000 tapers were lighted, and the
battle between the rays of the sun and the artificial
light had the most extraordinary effect, but added
much to the splendour of the scene ; the lustres looked
like immense clusters of stars hanging in the air. The

ceremony of throwing down the gauntlet was mag
nificent, and really brought back the olden times.   In
short, the eleventh century seemed shaking hands with
the nineteenth ; and the meeting was most amusing, for
John Bull could not always suppress his humour, and
sometimes even laughed outright at his transformation.
You might see a young courtier with high ruff, train,
and solemn gait suddenly take a spring across the hall,
laughing and flirting in modern fashion, then recollect-
ing himself, strut away like Burleigh himself.   But
when the king was present all was solemn gravity.
And if I lived for ever I could not forget the burst
of applause that rose like thunder after a silence of
hours, when the king appeared with the crown upon
his head.   We went between three and four in the
morning and got away at eight at night.   In all that
time I had but one sandwich and a glass of lemonade
and a little biscuit to keep me alive (sent by Lady
Willoughby, who had happily brought a small supply).
The fatigue was tremendous, and the pauses between
acts simply insupportable, but I amused myself with
watching my neighbours and those I knew. . . .
Hurt Sitwell and I in full court dress looked the
image of Sir Charles and Lady Grandison—such a
pair of figures !   Only fancy Queen Caroline's matchless impudence !   Twice she attempted to enter, and
such an uproar as she caused.   I only hoped she might
get in for the fun of it.   She forced her way into one
of the kitchens, where they coolly turned the key upon
her till all risk was over.   I could not have been
better placed for seeing the whole, for Lady Willoughby
de Eresby, as Hereditary Lord Chamberlain, had two
boxes in the gallery at the upper part of the hall
overlooking the whole,—one for her own family and
one for her friends, and we were in the latter."

There were many things not mentioned in this letter, very amusing and even of the greatest interest. I had been offered my choice of being present in the Abbey at the actual coronation, or in Westminster Hall where the banquet and all this pageant took place, but was advised to choose the latter. There were two or three incidents which deserve more particular mention.

In the performance of the ceremony of throwing the gauntlet, Dymoke, the Hereditary Champion of England, supported on either side by the Duke of Wellington and the Marquis of Anglesea, mounted on splendid-looking steeds caparisoned according to the times, paced up the entire length of the hall to the foot of the throne. When the glove was thrown a little bustle took place from our side, which was not explained till afterwards. This was, that from a group in the background a man had advanced to take up the glove. It was he who claimed to be the actual representative of the line of Stuart.[1] But the incident was not allowed to disturb the scene, for neither the champion nor his supporters even looked round, but commenced their difficult task of backing their horses to the entrance of the hall. Just then a man suddenly stepped up to the Duke and said something to him in a hurried whisper. What this whisper was soon came round to our box.

"Don't lay your hand on his quarters or he will lie down and die; he is the horse of Timur the Tartar."

No horses but those of Astley's circus could have been induced to go through that performance.

During our long waiting a pretty little episode diverted my attention. One of the younger sons of the Duke of Wellington had got separated from his elder brother, Lord Douro, a beautiful boy about

[1] Father of the so-called Duke of Albany, who died at Biarritz in 1881.

fourteen, magnificently attired in white satin, blue
velvet, and silver, with a plume of white ostrich
feathers fastened by a diamond aigrette into his
velvet cap.   After most anxious search, evidently
nearly reduced to weeping, he caught sight of him,
and it was touching to see how the elder brother
put his arm round him and comforted him.

Queen Caroline's attempt to enter was happily made
during a period when the king had retired to recover
from the fatigue of the coronation.   The silence of the
hall was suddenly broken by a clamour from without
and loud knocking at the great gates.   Those within
crowded down to the entrance, and amidst a great
nubbub and confusion cries of "The Queen! the
Queen!" resounded through the hall.   The commotion
caused was indescribable, and all our nerves were
strung to the highest pitch of expectation as to what
was about to happen.   Almost as suddenly as the
noise began it died away, and we were again left to
wait.

The Peers' Banquet was, of course, of magnificence in
keeping with the splendour of all around, and very
trying it was, hungry as we were, to look down on
the peers feasting.   The cruel case was that an
ample repast had been prepared in some chamber
behind for the occupants of all the boxes in the
gallery, but no one being told of it, it returned
untouched to the contractors who provided it.   This
was not known till afterwards, and the contractors
were then well blamed, as they deserved to be, for
taking no measures to show the way to it.

As the shades of evening began to gather, the
ceremonies being all over we had to reach our
carriages as best we could, and it was ten o'clock
before we reached home.

The panorama of life passes so quickly, few may know who Colonel Percy was and why he was thus able to procure me this great pleasure denied to so many others. Few at that time were better known, from the sadly interesting circumstances of his short career. A younger son of the Earl of Beverley, he was already a promising officer in a dragoon regiment when he was taken prisoner at the battle of Talavera. His sword and his parole being demanded, he flung down his sword, saying, "I will give you my word to escape if I can." This of course caused him considerable hardships as a prisoner before he reached his destination. His father being a *détenu*, lived in the same town as his son till the short-lived peace during Napoleon's detention at Elba liberated them both. When Napoleon's reappearance renewed the war, the Duke of Wellington, with whom he was a great favourite, chose him as one of his aides-de-camp, and at the close of the three days' battle of Waterloo entrusted him with the duty of carrying the news of the victory to England. After a few hours' rest he started early the next morning, with orders never to stop till he laid the French eagles with the Duke's despatch at the feet of George IV. (then Regent). From his landing at Dover the intelligence spread like wildfire, and as he dashed into London as fast as four horses could carry him, with the French eagles streaming out of each window, the excitement of the people amounted almost to madness. Arrived at Carlton House, behold! the Regent was not there, but dining with Mrs Boehm, a lady then well known in the fashionable world. One of the guests at that dinner-party related to me some years afterwards how the king, having risen from table with the whole party, was advancing in the centre of a semicircle through the wide-opened folding doors when a commotion was heard in the anteroom, and a young man in uniform, soiled and covered with dust, rushed forward with the eagles and despatches and fainted at the Regent's feet. . . . Thus poor Henry Percy accomplished his task, but paid dearly for it. The excitement and fatigue, prolonged through those dreadful three days at Houguemont and Waterloo, and the hurried journey to London, were too much for his young strength. The next day, while answering the questions of his friends, his sister, Lady Susan Percy, laying her hand on his sash, hastily drew it back; it was still wet with blood from Waterloo,— horrible evidence of the haste with which he had come. A few days afterwards he was laid low with a stroke of paralysis, and so was closed his military career. For though he remained in the army till the end of 1821 in the vain hope of recovery, he was never able to serve again. It was in this last year that I became very intimate with him.

CHAPTER X.

MY MARRIAGE TO CHARLES WAKE—THE EDINBURGH ACADEMY—
TOM'S DEPARTURE FOR INDIA—A WALK INTO ENGLAND—
ARCHIE'S FIRST VISIT TO BROUGHAM HALL—COLLEGE LIFE AT
GLASGOW—DR ROBERTSON.

EARLY in April 1822 I went down to Scotland to
make my farewell visit to my home before my marriage with Charles Wake, who in fact could scarcely
become more a son of the family than he had been
for years,—indeed, ever since the time of Archie's birth.
After a short time at Garscube with our grandfather,
I remained at Park Place till my father and brothers
were able to go with me to Harviestoun. During this
time I was particularly struck with the appearance of
the child Archie. There was something so touchingly
sad, so inexpressibly innocent in his whole look and
bearing, that he seemed to me as though destined for
a brief career in this rough world. His father had
given him the name of "the little Bishop," and his
friends having adopted it, he was more frequently
called by that name when speaking of him than by
any other; but to my mind he had more the semblance
of a little angel who was not intended long to remain
with us. Though full of thought and study he was
most exquisitely child-like. Often after these long
years his face and figure return to me as a picture,

when, coming out of the Old Greyfriars' Church one
Sunday afternoon, just as we were emerging from
the old archway, having dropped a bunch of flowers,
exclaiming, "Oh! I have lost my bouquet,"—"No,"
said little Archie, "here it is," holding up the psalm-
book he was carrying for me. The darling thought
it was the little book I had missed. We spent a very
happy time at Harviestoun riding about in all directions. I was mounted behind my eldest brother on
one of the old grey carriage horses, still a beauty, and
carrying us gallantly as we went from one old haunt
to another, glad to abridge the distances by this
expedient. It was a season enchanting in Scotland
when it is fine, the glens full of primroses and blue-
bells, and young peeping ferns just rising out of the
moss wherein they are loveliest, as we heard the
cuckoo on the 1st of May for the first time that
year. Full of glad anticipations were we, for John,
the eldest of us, was looking forward to his marriage
with Mary Sitwell, so long and so tenderly beloved:
we were thus to become double first cousins as well as
brother and sister, for our cousin Mary who was to
become his wife was first cousin also to Charles Wake,
who was to be my husband, and it was pleasant to
think that those we were about to marry were
associated with our earliest days of happiness while
we were yet children. The glens we were wandering
through, and the burns that ran sparkling through
them, were full of recollections of them, in that holiday
time before the troubles of life had visited us. We—
that is, my father, my brothers, and myself—did not
meet again for above two years. I had promised Sir
George and my sister that I would return to them
for my marriage, and thought myself obliged to keep
to it.

It was about this period that Archie, on his return to Edinburgh, had for a short time the advantage of private reading and instruction from Mr Craufurd Ramage, who took the most affectionate interest in his progress. He has often expressed how great was the help of these hours, regularly spent in learning to understand his work, to his onward progress. This was an important period in his education, for in it he left the High School and went to the Academy, then first inaugurated, Archdeacon Williams being the headmaster. To it the first-class families in Edinburgh all sent their sons, and it was greatly estimated by the principal men of the day who were distinguished for their talents — Jeffrey, Cockburn, Murray, Leonard Horner,—and all the Whig lights of the period took the deepest interest in the progress of the young ones educated there.

These first years of the existence of the Academy were its palmiest days, and great was the interest excited by every step taken in it. The yearly examination was made a great affair, attended not only by the talented but also by the fashionable world, and the distribution of the prizes was eagerly discussed as a subject of the highest importance. All this was exceedingly beneficial to the rising generation, stimulating them to exertion. By the Scottish system of living at home though carrying on their studies as in a public school, they were aware of the deep interest taken in their progress by their seniors, and therefore attached a far greater value to it themselves than do most boys in the great public schools in England. The young Archie Tait was soon distinguished by Archdeacon Williams, and the foundation of a lasting friendship was laid between them. With his whole heart he worked—too hard

indeed, for when I and my husband returned to Edinburgh two years afterwards we found him pale as a
little ghost; and when in January 1825 we were preparing for our journey home, and Archie was brought
to us in a sedan-chair to spend the last few days with
us in our hotel, never shall I forget the opening of
the chair when the men set it down in the entrance
hall, revealing by the light of the lamp above the
robust figures and brown weather-beaten faces of the
two porters in strong contrast with the pale little vision
within. He looked like a caged spirit; he was so
seriously ill that we put him immediately to bed.
After a week he was able to return to Park Place,
and not till after six weeks to his work.

Before our arrival the two long-settled cousin
marriages had taken place—that of our eldest brother
John to Mary Sitwell, niece of our mother and also the
niece of Lady Wake, my husband's mother; and that
of her sister, Anna Sitwell, to John Campbell, eldest
son of our uncle, Sir Archibald,—all the four being
grandchildren of Sir Ilay Campbell and first cousins.

We were, however, in time to be present at the
marriage of Sir Archibald's youngest daughter, Elizabeth, to the Earl of Leven and Melville. She was a
lovely girl, not yet nineteen; he was a post-captain
R.N., and thirty-six. He had been devoted to her
from her childhood, and had anxiously watched till
she had attained an age that warranted his gaining
her for his wife. The wedding took place in the
dining-room of No. 1 Park Place, and a very pretty
sight it was, with the usual assemblage of relatives,
including children, among the fairest of whom was
Archie.

The bride's father had retired from public life on
a pension, his plea for retirement being a growing

weakness of sight, which, it must be confessed, did not afterwards interfere with his enjoyment, so that it is not to be wondered at that many looked upon the whole thing as one of the Government jobs prevalent in those days. This opinion was amusingly expressed at an election in Glasgow, where a disturbance having taken place, there was a difficulty in ascertaining among the crowd who were the rioters, and Sir Archibald from the hustings, pointing to one man in particular, called out, "Take that man; I saw him." A voice immediately shouted in reply, "Ye see him! hoo can ye see him when ye get twa thoosand a-year for being blind?" That the Radical mob vehemently applauded this set-down to the Tory ex-judge may be readily believed.

Easter, 1873. Once again I have been in quiet intercourse with dear Archie, the Archbishop,—not this time as when in the same month two years ago we sat together out on the bowery terrace of the Villa Eleanore at Cannes, but in his beautiful library at Addington, and have been again able from himself to hear much of the early part of his life which I did not know. Now, as then, I cannot do better than give his own words.

"I remember well that on or about the 1st of September 1826 my father took James, Craufurd, and myself with him to accompany Tom during the first part of the journey which was to separate him from us, and was to be the beginning of his new life. He, my father, carried out his project in his own peculiar manner, embarking with us in the steamer from Newhaven, and suddenly determining to get on shore at Berwick, in the middle of the night, by means of a boat which accidentally put out with a

H

passenger. We slept at the 'Red Lion,' and the next day took a walk into England, crossing the bridge which joins the two countries. On the other side we met a gentleman with whom my father was very soon in conversation, obtaining from him as he always did all possible information of the surrounding country, traditionary and local. They were so mutually pleased with each other that an invitation was given and accepted to dinner, and on we walked, spending the intervening time very agreeably. Mr Robertson, our new acquaintance, was much taken with Craufurd, which greatly pleased my father, who was immensely proud of him. I remember the animated conversation of the evening, and the presence of a nice little girl, the daughter of the house. They had few visitors, living in a lonely situation, and the sudden arrival of three boys and their father, all full of life and energy, was quite an event, as I afterwards learned in the year 1868 when at Homburg a Lady Melville was introduced to me and immediately reminded me of every particular of that evening. 'I have always traced you,' she said, 'and am very glad to meet in the Bishop of London the little boy I remember so well as the youngest of that amusing party.' Next morning we separated, dear old Tom going to London, while we returned to Edinburgh. Only myself and James ever saw Tom again, but there was no thought of this : my father's sanguine mind never anticipated evil."

Thus took place the departure of the third son, he who from his infancy had been named "the ancient warrior," and, like "the little Bishop," lived to make the sobriquet a prophecy. It was the first flight from the nest, and deeply his father felt it, though the hopefulness of his nature always shed a sunlight glow upon the future, and in parting with his son he felt sure he would distinguish himself, as indeed he did. Few men of the period who knew anything of the affairs of India were not familiar with the name of "Tait's Horse," and there were fewer still of those who had been there themselves who did not know and love "the Colonel."

Of the brothers, Craufurd and Archie were still steadily pursuing their education. Archie rapidly passed from class to class, till at. the grand field-day, the final examination before he left the Academy, in the presence of a vast crowd of spectators, the pale slender boy was called to the front to receive no less than six of the foremost prizes, including the two medals intended to have distinguished two victors,—the medal for the first Greek scholar, and the gold medal for the head boy in all things in the Institution.

The enthusiasm excited by this unusual success in Edinburgh, where all knew each other, may easily be imagined, and the whole scene was inimitably described to us by Archie himself, who was a first-rate mimic, and in whom considerable powers of humour were beginning to develop.

After an extremely satisfactory examination of the lower class, in which each boy acquitted himself most creditably, Lord Cockburn,[1] calling forth that one who sat lowest of his form, and whose very ears were red with shame at the unenviable distinction, thus addressed the audience in the true Scottish accent, which by doubling and multiplying ,the vowels gives a quaint yet grave emphasis to each particular word :—

" Will it be believed that this boey is aactually the

[1] He did not become Lord Cockburn till after this period, though I have given him by anticipation the name by which he is most generally known.

veery laast of his claass, the veery loowest of the
school? If this manner of youth be the booby, what
must the dux be? what must be the merits of an
Institution whose lowest is thus so high?"

In his enthusiasm for the Academy, Lord Cockburn
forgot that the boy and his friends might not quite
enter into his feelings of admiring appreciation of him
who was "aactually the veery laast of his claass."
The proceedings wound up with an eloquent speech
accompanying the bestowal of the gold medal, at the
close of which he thus addressed the recipient, "Go
forth, young maan, and remember that wherever you
go the eyes of your country are upon you." He did
remember it through life, but he also remembered
the speech so thoroughly as to give it word for word
for the private entertainment of his sisters, always,
on reaching the climax, going head-over-heels, or
performing some other such boyish antic.

There is still a copy of the 'Courant' of the
2nd August 1827, in which there is a notice of this
examination of the Edinburgh Academy: ". . . The
other duxes were Master John Thomson Gordon,
Master Andrew Ramsay Campbell, Master William
Cousin, Master George R. Moncrieff, Master John
Wauchope."

In the same month Archie joined us in Derbyshire,
first visiting the Sitwells at Renishaw and then remaining with us a long time at Tapton Grove, greatly
adding to the enjoyment of our home circle. When
he left us it was to begin his studies in Glasgow
College; and on his way down to Scotland, having
received and accepted an invitation to Brougham Hall
from his father's old friend James Brougham, he arrived
at Penrith late on Saturday night by the mail, and
having slept at the inn, took a post-chaise, to use his

own words, " thinking myself a great man in doing so, and drove to Brougham Hall to breakfast, at which old Mrs Brougham presided. Henry Brougham, the future Chancellor, had, I believe, been expected, but did not come. The party consisted of James Brougham, Sir George Strickland, William Marshall, Apollo Hamilton, and myself. We spent the whole day in riding to Ullswater and back. Old Mrs Brougham, as all the world knows, was a splendid specimen of an old Scottish lady, and I daresay would have preferred to see the Sunday better spent under her son's auspices ; but she must have been accustomed to it, for in those days men of that school did not generally consider the seventh day as set apart for any other purpose than for relaxation, or for those occupations for which they had not time on the other six. There was this difference between Whigs and Tories,—the Tories acknowledged that it should be reverently kept but did not do it ; the Whigs utterly denied any such necessity."

Brougham Hall at this time was a small, comfortable, by no means ancient-looking, north-country squire's house. The ancient chapel, or what at least was afterwards declared to have been such, was then used by James Brougham as a store-house of agricultural implements ; and the Archbishop puzzled himself thirty years afterwards to trace the rooms which he remembered in his boyish days of the very respectable but modern-looking dwelling-house, lost as they are now in the venerable manor-house (which occupies the same site), with its baronial hall and highly decorated ancient chapel and grand library, all breathing an air of hoar antiquity, from the paintings of the Bayeux tapestry on the walls of the corridor down to the antique chairs on which the Barons de Brougham had sat from the time of the Conquest. Certainly these modern additions are a wonderful reproduction of the antique, and are worthy of Lord Campbell's story of the skull of Adam de Brougham! It is to the taste of William Brougham that all these additions are owing, and certainly the whole is admirably done. But to resume the Archbishop's own words :—

"I greatly enjoyed this short visit into the home of perhaps the most eminent man of his time ; and though I did not see him, I have never forgotten the impression made upon me by his mother, or the kindness of my father's old friend James Brougham. The uncomfortable feeling of the way in which Sunday was spent was the only drawback to my complete enjoyment. I believe it was on this first visit that my attention was attracted to a white Parsonage with bow windows and a little garden, on the road towards Shap Common, which for years was my ideal as the sort of parsonage in which I should be likely to spend my days, and during my fifty years that have since rolled on I have noted each time that I have passed along the road this house unchanged amidst the change of all things, calling up curious memories of the past. This first visit to Brougham has always remained a marked spot in my memory, and has become more remarkable now from my after connection with that part of the country as Dean of Carlisle. It was the first link of a connecting chain."

After this pleasant break in his journey to Glasgow his college life began. The studies of the young men were expected to be carried on by themselves during the long periods of the annual vacations, which in fact extended through one-half of each year, the college terms—more properly speaking, sessions—being only for six months. Many a youth from the working classes during the long summer vacation earned money by teaching in schools, sufficient to pay his way during the college winter term when the classes met again, living hard and straining every nerve to attain the desired end,—admission into the Scottish ministry. A life of self-denial begun in boyhood, and carried on through those years of early manhood which are so beset with temptation, must have had strong effect upon the character; but many sank beneath the attendant privations and constant strain upon the mind and brain, for these poor lads had no rest. The vacation only brought to them the exhausting labour of striving to educate the uneducated in the village schools.

I remember well a specimen of this class, poor Edward Macmurrough, a clever, shrewd Scotsman, the son of one of the workmen at Garscube, living in one of the lodges; but his health had given way under the overstrain, and he was dying. His languid face, his gentle touching voice and constant cough, are still present with me : none ever heard him complain; and his father and mother, tending him through the gradual decline which threw the shadow of death over their brightest hope, "to have a son in the ministry," never for a moment deceived either themselves or him : they knew he was dying, he knew it too, and their submission to the will of God was complete. " Patience had its perfect work," I remember it well ; the dying youth's education, and perhaps the very nature of his illness, had refined him, but his parents were of the very lowest order of the lowland Scottish peasantry, speaking the most unmusical west-country dialect.

Their son had sunk under the strife of intellect with the hardships of poverty ; but in the family inhabiting the other lodge a more robust nature had come off victorious, and was steadily rising into eminence. William Robertson and his wife were as handsome a pair as need be seen. Aristocratic in appearance, without the slightest touch of vulgarity either in manner or in accent, which was pure classic Scotch, they might have been of knightly race ; but whatever the antecedents of their family · may have been, they were now simple labourers, William Robertson having the out-of-doors work about the house of Garscube ; but his younger brother Archibald had, in the manner I have described, achieved an education, and had qualified himself in the University of St Andrews for the medical degree. He was a clever young doctor, and had been wise enough, instead of settling in some small country village, from which style of practice he would probably never have emerged, to take a wider range : he had become a naval surgeon, had sailed under distinguished officers, and soon reached the eminence he merited. In our young days at Garscube he was frequently a welcome guest at my grandfather's table, but had so little idea of being ashamed of the position of his family that he never could be prevailed upon to sleep in the house of Garscube, saying that he preferred during the short periods of his leave to live at his brother's house, which was the lodge of the east approach. I have often seen the one brother raking the leaves from under the dining-room window while the other was seated at Sir Ilay's table contributing greatly by his conversation and the variety of his information to the pleasure of the family party, who held him in high esteem.

It was at Garscube that my husband early became acquainted with him, and after my marriage, to my delighted surprise, I found him established in Northampton at the head of his profession, the family physician and valued friend of my father-in-law, Sir William Wake, and of all the principal families in the county. He owed his fortunate position to his own professional merit, having been vouched for by Captain Spencer, R.N., brother of the well-known Lord Althorp, with whom he had served, at whose recommendation he had come forward to fill the vacancy left in the county practice by the death of old Dr Kerr, the father or uncle, I am not sure which, of Lady Davy of blue-stocking memory, whom I have mentioned as Mrs Apreece, as visiting Garscube in company with Sir Humphry Davy before their marriage. Dr Robertson, being also well known to my husband, who had reported the high esteem in which he was held by those who had long known him in Scotland, had no difficulty in making his way with the different families in the neighbourhood, and very soon commanded the practice of the county. This is one of the many instances of the talent and perseverance by which many of the Scottish youths without the slightest assistance worked their way from the cottage fireside to the object of their ambition, whatever it might be.

CHAPTER XI.

TAPTON GROVE—BETTY AT GLASGOW—MISS BALFOUR'S FORTUNE
—SIR DANIEL SANDFORD AND GLASGOW PROFESSORS.

BUT all this is a digression, induced by the mention of
Glasgow College. Fortunately for the young Archie
Tait he had no such hardships to encounter, his vacations being, after some weeks with his father at home,
pleasantly spent with us at Tapton Grove, and with
the Sitwells at Renishaw, seven miles only dividing
the two places.

They were happy days! Archie was full of fun,
making us laugh by the unexpected turns of comic
humour which at that age was part of himself. Charles,
being of an eager temperament, when annoyed or excited would speak quick and loud, half frightening me,
when "Jupiter tonans," as Archie on these occasions
called him, burst upon the scene, and then in a stage
voice he would exclaim, "Vox faucibus hæsit," and
finish by a rapid dance round the room, singing the
words of an old Scottish ballad, "He's a terrible man,
John Tod, John Tod—he's a terrible man, John Tod";
never failing to end the scene by sending Charles and
myself into fits of laughter. We were all young then,
dear Archie was just passing out of boyhood; he and
I were personally so like each other that he used to
amuse himself by going into the nursery dressed up
in my riding-habit and hat, when not only were the

nurses and children deceived, but the baby used to put out her arms to " go to Mama."

The classes of the College again met in November, and then we lost the companionship so pleasant to us, for Archie had to return to his lodgings in the High Street immediately opposite the College gate. They were made as comfortable as circumstances permitted by the faithful Betty, who as soon as each term recommenced left her home in Park Place to become her boy's housekeeper and self-constituted guardian, for vigilantly she watched over his doings. The Principal of the College, Dr Macfarlane, whose residence was within its walls, often declared that the last light at midnight and the first in early morning to be seen was in the window of Archie Tait. Of this Betty took especial care, mercilessly pulling him from his bed at the exact hour he had intimated to her as that at which he had determined to get up. Such determinations are easily made, but they are seldom kept when left to the unaided powers of a young sleepy head finding much-needed rest on its pillow. She was equally strict as to the evening hours ; and when sometimes her boy, in company with his friend and old schoolfellow Henry Page, afterwards Page Selfe, would return somewhat later than she thought correct, her Scottish caution roused her into indignation against possible dissipation, and she received them with " Where hae ye been, ye ne'er-do-weels ? there's your books and your beds waiting ye ; come into the hoose and dinna waste your time in that gait," thus cutting short all further colloquy between the friends as they parted on the doorstep,—young Page going to the Professor's house where he boarded, and our Archie to his studies, in which, absurd though it may seem, the dear old woman was still a considerable help.

Garscube was within five miles of Glasgow, but great changes had taken place there. The dear old grandfather, Sir Ilay Campbell, had been gathered to his fathers about four years before this time, and was succeeded by his son, Lord Succoth, who retired from the bench and returned to his family name as Sir Archibald Campbell. We had thought the old house at Garscube perfection, but modern ideas travel fast, and he and Lady Campbell determined upon building to a great extent, having been assisted to this conclusion by having lately succeeded to a very large sum of money by a train of circumstances which are rather amusing. Lady Campbell was the youngest of a large family, the Balfours of Balbirnie; at the time of her marriage she was rich in beauty and in talent, but in nothing else, though her eldest brother was the proprietor of a large landed property in Fife. In the previous generation there were two brothers who had made enormous fortunes in India, which doubled, trebled in their hands, simply by never being spent. At the death of both, their sister, an old maiden lady, succeeded at once to their money and their habits. She lived in a small house with a small establishment, only seeing her family once a-year when she thought it proper to call them around her for a solemn dinner. They were waited upon by her ancient domestic, and at the very beginning of dinner she always thus addressed the party—

"Onybody for wine? Wha's for wine haud up their thumbs. Naebody for wine! John, tak' awa' the wine." Thus the solitary bottle remained unopened, for neither niece nor nephew dare incur her displeasure by signifying a desire for a glass.

It fell out at last that illness came upon her,— what would now be called influenza. After a week

or two intelligence of this reached one of her nephews,
who thought it would be right as well as wise to
look after the old lady. Finding on inquiry at her
house that she had seen no medical man, he sent for
the one of highest repute, and accompanied him to
her bedside. After due examination the physician,
drawing Mr Balfour aside, thus gave his opinion :—

"She is certainly very ill, but, as it is chiefly
from weakness, she may be brought round by gener-
ous diet and plenty of port wine : she will sink altogether unless she has three or four glasses of the
best port every day."

Suddenly he was interrupted by the bed curtains
being drawn sharply back and a thin querulous voice
calling out—

"Port wine! an' whaur's a puir body like me to
get port wine?"

Nothing would induce her to have it, and she
shortly died, without a will, leaving £840,000 to be
divided among seven nephews and nieces. With his
wife's share Sir Archibald was well able to turn
Garscube into a sort of palace; it was in process of
building when my brother Archie went to Glasgow
College, and they were living in the little inn across
the road, close to their own lodge gate, to superintend
the proceedings. They never forgot to invite him
each Saturday to spend the Sunday with them, and
very beneficial to him was the pleasant change, which
not only took him out of the crowded streets of
Glasgow, giving him fresh pure air, but substituted
the quiet of the country for the noise of the town.
The river Kelvin was then a clear rapid stream, and
its banks were full of beauty. They are so still, but
the various manufactories since established have altogether changed the scene which was so lovely in

the days of our youth : then it was the most charming place for a student to ramble in, reducing to order and bringing into shape the various thoughts and ideas which had crowded into his mind during the busy week.

And when the Campbells were absent he spent his Sundays very profitably in Glasgow, where he had the advantage of hearing such preachers as Dr Welsh,[1] Mr Smith of St George's, and occasionally Chalmers. The Evangelical party was then in its full vigour commanding the Established Church of Scotland, before the Disruption.

Of this period of my brother's life I can know nothing personally. As of the time of his childhood spent with the Whitworth doctors, it is only from himself that particulars of his life in Glasgow can be obtained. While we were beguiling a rainy day at Addington (in March 1874), and compensating ourselves for confinement to the house by an hour's walk up and down the spacious rooms on the ground floor, this is what he told me :—

"The man to whom I owe most during my time in Glasgow was Sir Daniel Sandford, Professor of Greek, who possessed in a wonderful degree the power of quickening into life the latent intellect of his pupils. To say that he inspired and kept alive the spirit of enthusiasm that stimulated a class of three hundred youths to press forward in their studies as in a race, is no slight testimony to the ability and character of the man. Many live who remember him, and no one who knew him can forget the extraordinary mix-

---

[1] Welsh, the biographer of Professor Thomas Brown, and well known as the Moderator of the Great Assembly, who, on the memorable day in May 1843, headed the exodus of the Free Church from St Andrew's to their temporary hall at Tanfield.—A. C. SWINTON.

ture of real genius with the singular weakness of desiring to be considered a first-rate man of fashion. To be a philosopher, a scholar, a fop, full of the affectations of a fine gentleman, was a strange blending; and he frequently gave offence by a sort of supercilious depreciation of the society of his fellow-professors, and of those with whom they gladly associated in Glasgow, which was full of rich merchants, more distinguished for their good dinners than for the perfection of their dress or manners.

"The desire to rise to the summit of the social scale, to lead in the senate of his country, was an ambition that sprung from both the strength and the weakness of his character, and he hoped to accomplish it by a *coup de main*. If he could succeed by a rapid dash in becoming a Member of Parliament, conscious of his powers he calculated upon so distinguishing himself in the House of Commons that his support would be sought by the Minister of the day, and he would thus obtain office and be enabled to hold his ground in London, where he trusted to become so distinguished that nothing would be impossible to him. A contested election was at hand. He collected together his forces of every description. He was returned, and rushed to the House of Commons, where was to be made the cast that would lose or win the game—for he could only afford the six months of the recess of the Glasgow College. During that time he, without resigning his Greek professorship, could devote all his thoughts and energies to politics. If he succeeded in obtaining office, these would become his objects in life; if he did not succeed, he would simply remain Professor of Greek. He made a brilliant speech, which was talked of at the time, but failed in producing any permanent impression. John Bull is not an impulsive

character. He is too slow in his paces to leap to
the conclusion that a new light suddenly appearing
must of necessity be transferred to the Cabinet; and
Sir Daniel's family circumstances did not permit his
giving the time necessary for his ability and usefulness
being tested. It was too dashing a stroke for success
in English political life,—more suited to a military
campaign in an enemy's country than to the warfare
in the House of Commons. So the hero returned,
not defeated, for he had experienced no overthrow,
yet unsuccessful, for he had not carried his point;
and it is no slight proof of the real force of his
character that he brought back to his work the same
active zeal as before, and that he never suffered dis-
appointment or regret to exert the slightest influence
over him." He maintained to the end of his career
his wonderful power over the minds of the successive
generations of youths who were by him stimulated
to exertion. The Archbishop never forgot the benefit
he derived from the impulse received from Sir Daniel
Sandford's energetic teaching.

My recollection of him is extremely vivid, but it is of
a lively and most mischievous boy, who, at the little
dances which it was the custom in Edinburgh for the
different families to give in turn, was the terror of
all the little girls—his great idea of fun being to run
down the outside of the line in which they were
standing up for a country dance, and untie every
sash as he passed! It is easy to picture the dismay
of all the little belles, and I know that in after life
I never heard his name mentioned (and he was often
spoken of as one of the cleverest men of his day)
without a sudden flash back of the ruined bouquets
of flowers lying at our feet, and our sashes falling
down over our dresses. How shocked he would have

been to think that he had ever been capable of such extreme want of gallantry even at twelve or fourteen!

Though Sir Daniel Sandford did not greatly appreciate the society in Glasgow, it had nevertheless considerable value in itself, and was of much use as a part of the training of such of the young men studying in the College as were of well-known families, for they were frequently invited to the dinner-parties of the city magnates. This early accustomed them, boys as in fact they were, to those habits of self-restraint which a life of too great ease led among themselves was by no means calculated to give. Besides, at the tables of these merchants all manner of subjects were constantly discussed with animation, —home politics, foreign politics, everything, in short, of interest at home and abroad,[1]—and this cultivated the habits of intelligent listening, and of being able to take part in the conversation of people much older than themselves.

The classes were generally extremely well conducted by the different professors. Buchanan was at that time Professor of Logic. Without any remarkable abilities, he managed to develop the minds of his pupils, not only through his series of lectures on logic and rhetoric, but also by perpetually requiring them to arrange their ideas in essays, which were read aloud in class, and listened to and commented on with great attention. The mathematical instruction was under the management of Jimmie Miller, a most amiable old man, but so absent as to be really unfitted for his work. The daily scenes in his class were only to be compared to Bedlam let loose.

"Here! let off these crackers," said Page to the Archbishop, who declined, leaving the honour of the

---

[1] They talked more of the excellence of the rum punch.—A. C. SWINTON.

I

fireworks to his friend and future connection. Down fell a pupil flat upon the ground, pretending to be dead. "What is the matter?" asked the terrified professor. "Mortuus est," was the reply.

Old Walker, Professor of Latin, was a very kind friend to my brother Archie, as was also Davidson, Professor of Law: to their houses he had continual access, and he was intimate with all their families. He was at Glasgow three years; during the first two his friends were principally Robert Abercromby, Johnson, Henry Page, who afterwards married his wife's sister, having changed his name to Selfe, and Morell Mackenzie, a very clever fellow. This last belonged to the class of students who came from a lower grade of life, examples of which I have before given: there were among them some remarkable men, such as Livingstone, whose life has been written, Halley, and Mackinley, who was, I believe, the son of a spirit dealer.

CHAPTER XII.

ARCHIE'S third year at Glasgow was saddened by misfortunes at home. The sky that had been gradually darkening there was now entirely overcast with a heavy cloud. Our father's affairs had come to a climax, and in order to pay his debts much actual property had to be sold, and the landed estates of Harviestoun and Castle Campbell were mortgaged to the Globe Insurance Company in order to produce a sum large enough to settle the whole amount. While these transactions were in process my father exchanged his home in Park Place for apartments lent him by the Duke of Hamilton in the Palace of Holyrood, in the royal precincts of which no man can be arrested for debt. It was some months before he returned to his family in Park Place : this in itself was very depressing, besides which much happened while he was there which threw a very sorrowful gloom over all the family. Before dwelling upon that, it is right, as well as interesting, to give an account of the benefits which he was the means of securing to the lands now passing out of his hands.

In what is called the estate of Castle Campbell, on the summit of a steep hill stood the ruined castle,

destroyed by fire long ago in one of the feudal wars
between the Grahames and the Campbells. It was
separated from the higher range surrounding it by
almost inaccessible glens, and was encircled by two
streams which, uniting into a broad brook, flowed in
one channel through the little town nestling at its
feet. These all retained their ancient names,—the
Castle of Gloom, the Hills of Sorrow, the burns of
Care and Grief, and the town of Dollar (Dolour).

How did they come by these names? They were
given by a daughter of one of the ancient kings of
Scotland in its barbaric time, who loved and was
beloved by a landless knight. To keep her safe, and
also to punish her, her father imprisoned her within
the castle, and there she might have remained till
now, had not a wild boar from the other side of the
mountains (no doubt a predatory chief) ravaged the
whole district, destroying everything before him.
After vain efforts to subdue and capture him, the
king, driven to desperation by the outcries of his
subjects and the lamentations of his daughter,—both
parties being convinced it was a judgment on his
cruelty,—proclaimed that he would bestow both the
castle and the lady upon whomsoever should overcome the boar. Fortune favours the brave,—that is
to say, they know how to make use of opportunities,
—and her knight slew the boar, wedded the princess,
and took possession of the castle. It is said he was
the knight Le Camille (whence the name Campbell),
but this is mythical. All this happened a very long
while ago,—it may be in the days of Fingal, for all
I know to the contrary,—but what belongs to more
modern days is certain.

Above a hundred years ago a child named MacNab
was left an orphan in the little town of Dollar, not

absolutely uncared for, for the neighbours were kind, and he was taught to read by the village schoolmaster, young Macorbry; but wearied of the sort of life, the child disappeared, having told his companions he was going away to make his fortune. For a little time his father's fellow-workmen talked about the orphan lad, and then he was forgotten.

Forty years afterwards the quiet of the village was disturbed by the unusual sight of a post-chaise driving up to the door of the little inn; from it descended a tall, good-looking man with intelligent countenance and hair sprinkled with grey; he had the dress and appearance of a gentleman, and as travellers frequently visited the old castle, though it was observed that he took no guide with him, he did not excite much curiosity. On his return to the village he walked straight to the schoolmaster's house and requested the old man to take a stroll with him about the village. Whether or not he revealed his connection with it is not known; if he did, Macorbry kept his secret. But this is certain, that expressing the deepest interest in Dollar and its inhabitants, he asked him what he thought would most benefit both. The schoolmaster said, " It wants a better school than this." That evening they parted.

Again some years passed away, when it was announced to my father, as the principal heritor, that the sum of £80,000 was left by the will of a Mr MacNab, a native of Dollar, for the benefit of the place, reference being made to the above-mentioned visit, but without distinctly stating in what way the money was to be employed. Then succeeded a long struggle as to what really would be the greatest benefit both to the place and to the country. It cannot be better stated than in a quotation from a note in a work by Rammage, of which the subject, strangely enough, is the present state of Italy. After stating the circumstances of the bequest, it runs thus :—

"The clergyman of the parish (the Rev. Mr Watson, an old man) proposed that it should be laid out in the erection and support of a gigantic poorhouse or hospital ; but this did not coincide with the enlightened views of Mr Craufurd Tait, a large proprietor in the parish, who believed that such an erection would tend to pauperise the district, and prove a curse rather than a blessing. He succeeded by steady opposition in the Court of Chancery in delaying the settlement of the question till the death of the clergyman, when by judicious appointment to the vacant charge, of which he was patron, he was able to carry out the noble design which he had originally proposed. To Mr Tait, therefore, Scotland is indebted for this celebrated institution ; he thus became as great a benefactor really as the donor of the money."

His scheme was entirely educational. He foresaw all the benefits which might be produced by this vast sum of money, which in the fourteen years' discussion had doubled itself, not only to the inhabitants at Dollar but to the country at large, by offering a first-class education at an extremely low rate for the sons of the many whose means did not enable them to educate their children for the liberal professions, according to their rank in life. To the inhabitants of the place and the district round, all the advantages of the institution were entirely free. Moreover, if any labourer's son possessed sufficient talent and a desire to fit himself for one of the learned professions—in short, to rise above his position in life,— every encouragement was offered to him and his parents. After he passed an examination to ascertain his capacities, an

annual sum was paid to his father while his education
was being carried on, equivalent to that which he
would have earned as a labourer. The benefits of
the institution were open to girls equally as to boys.
The Dollar institution soon attracted to, the valley
numbers of families to whom it was an object to
secure a complete education, both classical and modern.
The scheme was eminently successful, and extraordinary was the quickness with which it was carried out.
Always sowing, never for himself, always for others,
my father lived to see this ripen into fruit,—not indeed
to that maturity which it has now reached, but still
sufficiently to prove itself a widespread blessing to
those whose need is greatest: many a widowed
mother, for instance, rejoices in its benefits.

The traveller now looks down upon a charming scene,
—a noble building of Grecian architecture standing in
the midst of beautiful botanic gardens, the little town
of Dollar still picturesquely grouped on the banks of the
united streams of Care and Grief, pretty villas scattered
about upon the banks and braes, many of them the
professors' houses, and above, remaining in all its
desolate majesty, the Castle of Gloom, left untouched,
but more accessible—the spirited inhabitants of Dollar
having themselves planned and executed a wonderfully
beautiful approach through the rocky pass up the
mountain glen. What would have been the feelings
of the orphan boy, who, penniless and barefooted, left
Dollar so many years ago, could he have foreseen what
would be the result of his having gone to push his
fortune? Nothing whatever is known of his inter-
mediate history but the visit which has been detailed;
but we fear his life could not have been a happy one,
as he left neither wife nor child to benefit by the
hard-earned fruits of his industry, nor had he any

associations more tender than those of his orphaned childhood.

We will now return to Glasgow, where Archie was finishing the third year of his college life. He had studied hard; nevertheless, he owed his exhibition to Balliol to the circumstance of his being the nephew of Sir Archibald Campbell, who, as one of the principal proprietors in the neighbourhood, with a hospitable house, a cellar known for its wines, and an excellent cook, had, as a matter of course, an unquestioned influence with the professors of the college. There was no affectation of impartial judgment in settling the question. Sir Archibald invited all who had a voice in the matter to dine with him on a certain important day, and gave them a first-rate dinner. Archie was of the party. His youth entitled him to withdraw shortly after the ladies, leaving "the grave and reverend seniors to consult together over the unrivalled old port"; and probably before the party broke up all was settled, for in due time, that is to say immediately after, he was declared to have won the Balliol exhibition. In this present time of 1874 such proceedings would raise a storm of indignation, and convulse with horror the whole world of advocates for examinations, &c., &c., nor is it easy to set up any defence for the Glasgow College system, which had always so existed. Perhaps, however, this fact may weigh somewhat, that just as it then was it gave to the country such men as the celebrated Adam Smith, Lord Cranstoun, the first Lord Moncrieff, the eminent philosopher Sir William Hamilton, John Gibson Lockhart, and John Inglis, Justice-General, and the present Archbishop of Canterbury. Many very different characters, no doubt, perplexed and enraged the good Master of Balliol, Dr Jenkyns, who probably from this cause had, as I have heard, no love for the sons of John Snell (the founder of the Glasgow scholarships) sent to him in this easy offhand manner, but he certainly made amends for this by the warmth of his appreciation of those who brought credit to his college, which he was striving to raise above all others in Oxford.

Among the other advantages of the residence at Glasgow there was a debating society, formed by and for the students, where all sorts of questions, moral and political, were proposed for consideration and debate. In this there were many eager speakers— Swinton, Page (afterwards Selfe), Morell Mackenzie, and others—who thus early tried their wings, and acquired the habit of concentrating their thoughts and delivering them in clear and forcible language, thus preparing them for the wider arena of their after lives.

Before the close of the winter session it was necessary for Archie to matriculate at Oxford. And now I have once more the opportunity of writing from his own dictation.

"The day came when I must begin my university life, and from Scotland I went to matriculate. Well I remember the gloomy journey through the deep snow to Oxford, and my first impression of Balliol College, which looked like, as indeed all Oxford itself did at that hour, a city of the dead. I went there to reconnoitre as soon as I had arrived, and found not a soul moving, not a sign of life in the empty courts, all the inmates being out for their afternoon walk. I slept at the Angel Inn, and next morning repaired to Balliol at the hour Dr Jenkyns, the Head of the College, had by letter appointed. Not feeling in high feather, I waited in the rooms, so familiar after-

wards, for the dreaded interview in which my examination was to take place, and after a time Dr Jenkyns
appeared,—a little man, faultless in his academical
dress, with a manner that might be called finikin, and
speech to match, his words seeming to be clipped as
they left his lips. He received me with a somewhat
pompous kindness, saying, 'I will send for the Senior
Proctor,' a title which was intended to and did rather
overawe me, a freshman, not knowing that he meant
simply the Tutor of the College, who happened then to
hold that university office. Being summoned, he shortly
appeared in his black velvet sleeves. I was invited to
sit on a little sofa, and a book placed open in my hands.
It was Lucan, an author of whom I knew nothing, and
I was told to construe a passage that looked to me a
mass of difficulties. However, my wits did not forsake
me, and catching at the meaning of a few words, I saw
that it was an account of Cæsar in the boat between
Brundusium and Dyrrachium, and with the courage of
the hero himself, dashed through the difficulties, and
gave a rapid, and providentially a correct, translation
of Cæsar and his fortunes, &c., &c. The approbation
of the Master and the Proctor was very decided. In
his peculiarly clipped rather than polished English,
'And now, Mr Tait,' said Dr Jenkyns, 'allow me to
ask you with what view you have come here?' This
was rather a poser; I knew nothing of the man who
spoke or of his peculiarities, but by a happy inspiration
made reply, 'First, in order to study, and also I hope
to benefit by the society of the College.' I had hit
upon the very answer to please him, for he thought
nothing of a mere bookworm. A scholar, to win his
regard, must also be a man appreciating and appreciated by good society. 'Really, Mr Tait,' he said
with an approving smile, 'your answer is that of a

very sensible young man, and I am happy to welcome you to Balliol.' From that day forward I always
kept my place in the good books of the Master.
While this process had been going on, little Oakeley,
afterwards so kind a friend, limped in to have a look
at his future pupil. The next morning I went to
see Mr Ogilvie, who, with the Master, had been the
means of raising Balliol College to the eminence it
had attained. He was on the point of leaving to take
charge of Archbishop Howley's son at Rome, but still
expressed great interest in the young Scottish exhibi-
tioner, his friend Mr Veitch having mentioned me in
a favourable manner to him.

"My father, whose judgment in all matters connected with my education never failed him, had wisely
contrived to procure for me influential introductions to
many of the principal men in Oxford; and my journey
was so arranged that I was to spend a week in London
with Leonard Horner, who was not only the kindest
of friends, as he had long proved himself to be to
every one of us, but also a man whose talents and
character insured him the society of the literary men
of the day.

"I went up by steamer, and on board there were
Mr Ponsonby, and, returning from the moors, young
Adair, with his father Sir Robert. We naturally made
the sort of acquaintance one does under such circumstances, and were together below when the captain
summoned us on deck with, 'Now, gentlemen, come up
and you will see the finest sight in the world.' We
instantly followed him, and certainly it was a magnificent spectacle we beheld on entering the Thames
towards sunset. Ships from every quarter of the
world. All nations were represented. The river alive
with boats! Leaving the beautiful wooded slopes on

the river banks, we steamed into the jostling crowd of vessels of every size and every description. It was quite dark when we reached the pier, and it is a mystery to me how I ever found myself and my box after all the confusion of our landing at the Artichoke Stairs at Blackwall. For a moment I felt very desolate, alone for the first time in great London, but I attached myself to the companions of my voyage, who very kindly let me share with them the hackney coach that took them to their hotel in St James' Street, where I produced the address I had been given of Leonard Horner's house in Gower Street. They could throw no light upon the distance I had to go. They had never heard of Gower Street, and the only thing that had to be done was to take on the hackney coach, trusting to the better knowledge of the driver. The way seemed interminable, but at length I found myself in the hospitable home of my kind friends, with whom I was already intimate. Leonard Horner and his charming wife, with their daughters,[1] soon made me feel happy and at home. In the morning I was provided with the names of the places I ought to see, with all the necessary advice and directions, and in the next few days lionised London, even pushing my researches into the ball on the top of St Paul's, in a manner I never thought of again. I much enjoyed this week. I was but eighteen; nevertheless Leonard Horner treated me as a man, asking pleasant people to dinner, and introducing me to them. It was at his table I now first made acquaintance with Herman Merivale, afterwards my life-long friend, whose loss within the last few years I greatly deplore."

The business of matriculation being happily finished,

[1] Afterwards Lady Bunbury, Mrs Pertz, Mrs Lyall, and two younger wh have remained unmarried.

Archie, according to previous arrangement, set out to join us in Derbyshire, where time was bringing great changes to us. In the year 1829, the last year of his residence at Glasgow, while *he* was growing stronger and more manly every day, my husband's health suffered so much from suppressed gout, which affected his nerves and spirits, taking away all power of enjoyment, that it was decided we must leave the Grove, in which the air was too exciting and the life too quiet for him. We were to go abroad and remain on the other side of the Channel for some time. It was with painful regret I thought of leaving a home so suited to my taste. It was a long time before we could make up our minds that we must not remain; but clearly it was so, for each year my husband became more nervously averse to all society, even that of his most intimate friends.

Renishaw was at times full of company. In the Christmas season it was the scene of much gaiety; but it was then too much for him, and unfortunately my sister and her husband in the quiet season wished to be alone with their children. Therefore for him there was in reality no society. At all times he thought the change good for me, and insisted upon my going there when any gaiety was going on, but would not accompany me, and of course it was most painful to feel that he was alone at home while I was helping to entertain all sorts of gay people, myself exceedingly amused. There were frequently private theatricals which required much preparation, so that numbers of visitors often remained much longer than the usual "few days" in a country house. I remember that it was to what really might be called a congregation one Sunday evening that Archie preached his first sermon. The text was, "The wages of sin is death, but the gift of God is eternal life." He drew a vivid picture of the judgment-day, dwelling upon the opposite conditions of death and eternal life. I asked him why he had not also pointed out the difference between the "wages" and the "gift." He told me that he had written his sermon (and a very striking one it was) first and chosen the text most appropriate to it afterwards. This, his first essay in preaching, was listened to with profound attention. The scene returns to me now : the long low-roofed hall supported by pillars, the large old-fashioned fireplace with a heavy projecting chimney-piece over which was a picture of St Jerome and the lion, the brilliant light at the upper end near the fire, where sat the family and guests, the shadowy distance filled by the servants, who with Sir George's stable establishment were thirty in number, made altogether a striking picture. At the close, as we were dispersing, the future Archbishop of Canterbury whispered to me, " I thought I should have fainted when I discovered there was no Lord's Prayer in the book, I was in such a fright that I should break down."

He would have been not a little surprised could he then have had a vision of himself in St Paul's preaching to assembled thousands, and the breeze through the open windows lifting from before him the slender sheet of notepaper on which was jotted down the heads of his sermon, and wafting it through the church into the lap of the Duchess of Sutherland, while he calmly continued his discourse, in no way inconvenienced by the loss.

We had a great pleasure in the course of this summer — our last at the Grove. My dear father spent a considerable part of it with us, dividing his time between Renishaw and the Grove. He came to us when the Sitwells went down as usual to the Highlands for grouse-shooting, and very happy we were together. He was greatly saddened by dear Craufurd's death,[1] but was his old self again when fairly launched into an argument. Almost every subject was discussed between him and my husband; and I remember to this day some of his theories, often strenuously disputed by his opponent. One of these I have often thought of since, "that money could never be ill - spent." It might do mischief at the moment, encourage vice, and bring heavy responsibilities upon the spender, but in the long-run it was certain to find its way into the pockets of the right people—the butchers and bakers and workmen of all sorts,—and therefore it must promote trade and the wellbeing of men in general. To lock up money in a box was the only way of really preventing it being of general good. Our dear father certainly acted on his theory, for he never kept a shilling. In politics my father and my husband were supposed to be on opposite sides, but in fact the far-reaching schemes of the Tory were so much in advance of the Whig as to leave him far behind.

It was a great grief when the time for parting came. It would have been a greater had we known that we were never to meet again. In the winter of 1829-30 it was finally decided that we were to give up our home and cross the Channel; Archie was to join us a few weeks before we broke up our establishment on his way from Oxford, where he had been, as has been described, for matriculation, in the middle of the Glasgow session.

He found our whole party at Chatsworth, the Sitwells from Renishaw, and my husband and myself,

[1] Craufurd went to India in the autumn of 1827, but his health breaking down, he was obliged to return, and he died on the voyage home, 6th April 1828.

having accepted an invitation from the hospitable
Duke, who had desired us to leave a note 'for him
at the Grove with instructions to follow us there.
We found a large party, but it is so long since that
I forget who the guests were. One recollection, however, has never faded—that of Lady Blanche Howard,
the Duke's niece, a fair young creature of eighteen,
and her betrothed, young Cavendish, the son of Lord
Burlington and heir to the dukedom. He did not
look above twenty, though he must have been older,
as he was leaving Cambridge, where he had greatly
distinguished himself. He had brought with him a
friend, who came in all the glory of Senior Wrangler :
this was the afterwards celebrated Professor Airy.
That group remains in all its first freshness ; also, as
in a picture set in a brilliant framework of perfectly
dressed people, the Duke himself, still a young man,
at the head of the table with Lady Blanche on his
right hand, and placed just behind them Canova's
beautiful statue of Venus, as if on duty in attendance
on the banquet, the light so arranged as to fall in a
shower of radiance over her. During dinner a band
of music always played, for the atmosphere of sweet
sounds had an effect upon the Duke's defective hearing,
and enabled him to enjoy the pleasure of conversation.
Into this scene, out of the darkness and the snow,
Archie arrived late the first evening, not as a shy boy
but full of observation, modest and intelligent. I
remember that he made a favourable impression from
his perfect self-possession on finding himself thus
suddenly landed in the brilliantly lighted rooms of
Chatsworth among the assemblage of people, not one
of whom except ourselves he had ever seen before.

Very bright and very pleasant were those Chatsworth parties. How few remain of those who used

to assemble there! When I look now upon the venerable figure of Sir Augustus Clifford,[1] whose home then it almost was, I think that he more than any man must realise how the course of time sweeps ever onward, carrying on its tide those whose part is done, and bringing those who have still their part to do. Old peers are gone, their heirs are in their place: new ones are coming, but he is still the same,—not so upright, and very grey, but courteous and kind as ever.

It was shortly after Christmas, and the snow lay deep upon the ground. The fountains were frozen, but under glass there was a fairyland of flowers. The name of Paxton had not then been heard of, but he was *there* among the gardeners, his genius biding its time. When the party broke up the young Archie went on to Scotland to finish the winter term at Glasgow. In the month of May his studies there were ended, and he remained with his father, renewing the long walks in which they both delighted, and in which he gathered up stores of varied information, the habit of arranging them, and of reasoning from one point to another, of anticipating what *was* to be from what *had* been in the world's history.

[1] Usher of the Black Rod in the House of Lords.

CHAPTER XIII.

WE crossed over to France as had been determined, and established ourselves at Dieppe, arriving there in May, which with all its flowers is the loveliest month of the year in France. We found there the whole court of Charles X. He and his family were expected, but they did not come. It was very amusing to watch the different characters, so well and so distinctively known by public report, enjoying complete freedom from the masquerade of artificial life, and appearing to much greater advantage *au naturel:* the Prince de Léon was there, devoted to his wife and children, and that certainly was not the *rôle* he played in Paris. We made many pleasant acquaintances, both French and English; we were amused by a French lady, one of the pleasantest, who came to bid us adieu, and on our adding to our regrets an endeavour to persuade her to remain a little longer at Dieppe, she replied that she must return to her husband's property in the south of France, that she might have the benefit of the early vintage, for she always took a course of *bains au vin* in the early stages of the wines ! ! ! This gave us rather a new idéa of the flavour of French wines : it was, we were told, a favourite remedy in cases of constitutional weakness !

We enjoyed the sunshine, and admired the butterflies disporting themselves therein, all unconscious of the storm that was so speedily to disperse them. Yet it was gathering fast, and low mutterings told that it was coming. Through the medium of our French master we were soon made aware of the deep discontent of the nation with their rulers. It was a time when politics filled the minds of those who had any thought, for our own Reform Bill had just been brought forward, and the great wave of popular feeling rolled across the Channel and broke upon the shores of France, adding to the fermentation there. It was a bad sign that when the cannon announced a victory, and we inquired what was the cause of the flags and martial demonstrations in the streets, we were answered by shrugs of the shoulders and an apathetic " Oh ! quelque chose d'Algérie ! " so different from the eager excitement of the national appetite for *la gloire:* it was clear that nothing done by or for Charles X. could in the slightest degree rouse the enthusiasm of the people. The lessons of the French master being purposely chiefly devoted to conversation, we were during his hour made gradually so much aware of the expected overthrow that in one of our letters home we wrote, " If any dependence is to be placed upon what we hear is the general feeling of France, Charles X. cannot remain long upon the throne." It is just so we often believe without in any degree realising. Not the less astounded were we when our vague expectations suddenly became an established fact.

Leaving Dieppe we went leisurely on, spending a few days in Rouen, teeming with the interest of the old historic times, and a lovely and most peaceful Sunday at Mantes. Just before sunset we arrived, almost stifled with the heat and dust, at St Germain-en-Laye, from whence we intended in a few days to proceed to Paris on our way to Switzerland. No words can describe the lovely calm of that summer evening : after deciding on our quarters at the Hôtel d'Angleterre, we strolled to the terrace, taking the two elder boys (very small they were, yet able to enjoy) with us, and gazed with delight over the vineyards towards Paris, which, in the distance with Montmartre rising in front, bathed in the evening glow, looked dreamy and beautiful on that Monday night, the night that ushered in the memorable " trois jours." No murmur came upon the breeze, and the silver Seine flowed past us without bringing a whisper of the storm that had already gathered. We returned in the moonlight to the hotel ; crossed its garden to the Pavilion, a beautiful cottage embowered by acacia-trees, which we had taken for our nursery establishment ; saw our children safe in bed ; and then established ourselves in our pretty salon, well pleased with the prospect of at least one week of quiet enjoyment in the forest of St Germain. We had the hotel nearly all to ourselves that night. With the exception of a young couple on their wedding tour, there were no other occupants.

Next day, Tuesday, the heat was so intense that, our apartments in the hotel being like an oven, we spent the hours till evening under the bowery acacias, our children, as happy as birds, playing among them. It was a most silent day. All the world seemed to be asleep ; and even in the cool of the evening, when we wandered about the beautiful terrace, few people were to be seen. Two hours after sunset not a sound was to be heard but the constant call from the forest of the little chouette: we were speedily in our beds, as still as everything else. But very early in the morning a loud rap came to our door and our courier's voice was heard. In a moment my husband was with him in the salon; in two minutes he returned to tell me that extraordinary news had come down from Paris, that Charles X. had published three ordinances, which, as he briefly explained, were equivalent to our king having by his own will and pleasure abolished the liberty of the press, the Habeas Corpus Act, and the House of Commons; that intelligence of this had been sent from Paris to St Germain in the middle of the night. "Oh! if they are men," I exclaimed as I jumped out of bed, "they will never stand this." (I very presently wished they had been less of men, and perhaps would have been thankful if they had proved themselves old women.) "I do not believe they will stand it," was my husband's quiet reply; "you had better dress as fast as you can," and as he spoke he threw open the door into the salon. There was a confused noise surging through the house; from the open windows we saw a dense mass of people of every description. There was not the usual gesticulation or babble of voices, yet a sound as of earnest talk, and every face we looked upon was full of serious care.

The tidings from Paris explained the scene. On the evening of the previous Sunday Charles X. had published in the 'Moniteur' those ordinances which would have sent France backwards to the darkest days of despotism. Copies had been sent to the different officers of the State, who seemed purposely to have kept them back, so that on the Monday, instead of being in general circulation, it was difficult to obtain a 'Moniteur.' The astonishment was so

great that the evening of that day was chiefly passed
in the exchange of intelligence and of opinion among
all ranks. Tuesday morning found Paris seething with
preparation. As evening drew on the gathering storm
burst forth. The annihilation of the printing-presses
of the popular journals was, as it were, the conductor
which drew down the lightning in one vivid flash, and
then the tempest of the people's indignant wrath raged
through the entire capital, gathering intensity every
hour, as men of high repute joined themselves to the
avengers of the intolerable wrong. There is no need
to give here the history of that wonderful revolution,[1] which not only freed France from a besotted
tyranny but attracted towards her the admiration of
the world.

The details of the revolution raging in Paris came
rushing down to St Germain in every form, met by
corresponding intelligence from every part of France.
An English gentleman, Tarleton, arrived in the middle
of the day (Wednesday) from Rouen. As he passed
through, every shop was shut up, and the people were
turning out to fight : they speedily hanged the Préfet.
The uproar around us was beyond belief, and through
it the cannon in Paris were distinctly heard. In the
early morning there had been a sound of galloping
horse,—the Garde du Corps had been summoned for the
defence of the king. Towards evening many a horse
returned riderless, and a few with their riders stooping
over their necks, blood-stained, weary, and faint with

---

[1] Never was there a work of indignant resistance, defence, and retri-
bution carried out more heroically ; never was hard fighting more needful ;
and yet, though the passions of the multitude were roused to the utmost
frenzy, never was the sword more quickly sheathed when complete success
made its use no longer needed. Oh, why are the French so changed ?
who could have looked for a brood of communists such as have disgraced
and injured the country, to spring from the heroes of " les trois jours "? (1871).

their wounds as they sought the shelter of their barracks in the old château of François I. Next day (Thursday) the gates of Paris were thrown open, and crowds of people, some as fast as their horses could carry them, some in carriages, some on foot, came rushing down from the capital, bringing the most frightful tidings of the bloodshed there.

The hotel was filled to overflowing : the salon for the *table d'hôte* had rows of whatever could be got to serve for beds. We were able to retain our sleeping-room, but after we had joined our children in the morning, were unable to re-enter our hotel till midnight, and established ourselves in a bower close to the cottage of which we had fortunately possessed ourselves, for the crowd which separated us from the hotel was so great we might have walked upon their heads. Till then I had believed myself a heroine ; but the noise, the fierce faces, the universal uproar, the terrifying details of what was going on in Paris, given by a thousand voices all round us, with the knowledge that we with our little ones were in the centre of a revolution, so shook me (especially as I had just been reading the volume of Lockhart's 'History of Napoleon' which gives the history of the revolution of '92) that my husband, having stumbled upon the surgeon of the Garde du Corps, who had been left behind, brought him to me in the bower. "Oh! madame, ce n'est rien, ce n'est qu'une petite émeute, ça passera bien vite : sans doute à ce moment tout est tranquille à Paris," he said to me with reassuring smiles. That evening he reappeared with a great tricolour conspicuous on his breast; there was no further allusion to tranquillity *à Paris.*

The heat in the garden, crowded with refugees from Paris, was so suffocating, and the air so sultry with thunder, that my husband, in spite of the prohibition, took the two elder children through the gates into the fresher air of the road leading to Paris, which was near at hand. It is a steep hill, and he had scarcely begun to descend it when with a tremendous uproar the whole mass of the population of St Germain, armed with every description of weapon, rushed like a torrent down the hill. He had but time to throw the children into the wayside vineyard and leap after them, or they would all have been swept before it. The cause was soon evident. A large body of cavalry was seen at full gallop at a very short distance on the white dusty road which led from the provinces to the capital. The armed vociferating crowd poured down the hill and reached the road while yet they were about two hundred yards distant. The cavalry pulled up. What was to happen? A pitched battle in the valley? The question was soon settled. They silently looked at each other for a brief space; then the soldiers turned their horses' heads and galloped back the way they came!

The red flag, the insignia of civil war, was floating from the old château, and the tricolour was mounted on the *mairie.* Next day Monsieur le Maire, with a party of the Garde Nationale, paraded the streets with a drum, stopping continually to read an address, the sense of which was but this—" Soyez tranquilles, vive la paix ! "—words easily said, but not so easily obeyed in the midst of a revolution. On Saturday news came down from Paris that the king had abdicated in favour of the Dauphin. By this time there was not an English family left in the town of St Germain but ourselves, and I was too ill for us to follow the example of the refugees from Paris, who were speeding to the coast in every direction. We

were joined by one family. A large carriage drove
into the hotel yard, from which descended three girls
and a young boy, who with their servant carefully
assisted an old gentleman to alight. This was General
Knollys and his family; he was paralytic, and had
been lifted over several dead bodies at his own door
in the Champs Elysées; it was impossible for him
to travel farther than St Germain, but that was safety
compared with Paris. We soon fraternised, our
mutual anxieties becoming a bond of friendship
between our families, which has resulted in a bloom-
ing group of grandchildren, the younger of the two
little boys at my side marrying the General's granddaughter, and the son of the elder brother, then seven
years old, becoming the husband of her youngest
sister,—the peaceful result of these stormy times.[1]

Every street now rang with the Marseillaise, a
sound that had been unheard for years. Though all
was jubilee it was impossible to dismiss anxiety, for
who could say into what shape the conflicting elements
might settle? Were they to gather into a tempest,
and reproduce the days of Marat and Robespierre?
Or were they to clear away the threatening clouds
of disorder, and so help forward the dawn of a glorious
day? A good providence prevailed over the counsels
of France, and in a few days Louis Philippe was
proclaimed king. The elder branch of the Bourbons
had proved their incapacity for change. Nothing
had been able to teach them the necessities of the
present era, and so they retired to Holyrood.

There was universal joy, and a sense of safety

---

[1] Emma Knollys became the wife of Sir Edward St Aubyn, Bart., and
their eldest daughter Emma married Charles Wake, afterwards Admiral,
R.N., and their youngest, Catherine, married his nephew, Sir Herewald
Wake, Bart.

changed the expression of countenance of every man
and woman in the crowds still collected everywhere.
We got into our charming house, the old part of the
Château Neuf; and so deeply did we share the feelings
of those around us that we gave the name of the
citizen king, Philip, to our little boy, born before we
were well settled in our new home, frightened into
the world by the events which freed France from
the absolutism and weakness of the reign of Charles X.
Nothing could be more enjoyable than the autumn
in the forest of St Germain-en-Laye, and when we
moved into Paris for the winter, into pleasant apartments in the Champs Elysées, we no longer regretted
the *contretemps* that had stopped our progress farther
south.

The stirring events of the time filled Paris with
vivid interest. Prince Poligniac's trial produced great
excitement. A counter-revolution was the secret hope
of the defeated party, and every pretext was laid
hold of to produce it. One night the tambour beat
to arms, groups began to gather in the streets,
troops were bivouacked in many of the "Places,"
and we were disturbed all night by the family above
us packing up for instant departure. We made up
our minds that come what would, we should stay
where we were. No harm came of it, and we had
the enjoyment of many picturesque and characteristic scenes consequent upon the alarm. We drove
about Paris for the purpose, and next day, towards
the winter evening, came upon the bivouac in front
of the Panthéon : it was a sight worthy of a painter
of the first class. The piled arms, the lounging
soldiers round the red fires throwing strange lights
and shadows over the venerable buildings round,
and here and there countenances strongly marked

with excited intelligence coming out in strong relief
from the dusky atmosphere as the glare caught them,
made altogether a picture that could not be forgotten. ·

Next morning there was another scene I would
not willingly have missed, it was so thoroughly
characteristic. Our coachman suddenly drew up,
explaining that it was not safe to proceed, — the
reason in a moment became evident. A band of
young men of the Faubourg St Antoine, linked
arm - in - arm many files deep, swept the streets.
Nothing could be more sternly threatening than
their knitted brows (for we were close up to them),
and their wild voices shouting the Marseillaise. We
remained immovable in the crowd, anxiously observ-
ant. They debouched from a narrow street opening
into the Place. Straight opposite, from the corresponding street, emerged a band of milkmaids with
their pails upon their heads. In one moment down
went every pail, Faubourg St Antoine dissolved as
though by magic ; each man had thrown his arm
round the waist of a milkmaid, the Marseillaise had
changed into a popular valse, and the whole party
went circling round the Place in a remarkably well-
ordered valse amidst the laughter of the crowd.
None laughed more merrily than ourselves as we
drove rapidly home.

Another picture has vividly kept its place in my
memory, cherished there not only as giving a sketch
of French life not much known to us, yet quite as
characteristic of the best part of the nation as the
barricades and the wild Marseillaise are of the
rougher and more excitable sons of France, but
as bringing back much pleasure and interesting
associations with a charming family belonging to old
France. Accidentally or incidentally we had made

acquaintance with the young Baron de Montigny, who speedily introduced us to his mother and sister. We found the trio just what we could desire,—intelligent and *prévenant* in their manners, highly cultivated, and altogether very superior to the usual style of young Frenchman and demoiselle and elderly lady. There was nothing stereotyped about him. Before we parted we agreed that Madame was to call on us next day in the Champs Elysées, and that we were to return the call as soon as possible.

On the afternoon of the third day, having been detained by the crowded state of the streets till it was nearly evening, we found our way to their house in Faubourg St Germain, a grand old building surrounding the court, into which we drove through a gloomy *porte-cochère*. Admitted, we found ourselves at once in a large old hall with roof reaching the whole height of the house, in the centre of which a large dining-table laid with many covers indicated that in an hour many guests would assemble round it. From this we were ushered into a large salon with polished floor that shone like a dark mirror. To English eyes it seemed half furnished, but at the farthest end there was as pretty a sight as ever met my eyes,—gathered round the large antique fireplace a group that united in itself all ages; close to the chimney sat, with the light from the blazing logs falling full upon her, beautiful as a fairy god-mother of the benevolent sort, a little old lady who might be any age, for her hair was of shining silver, her form slight and erect; she was dressed in some light material, and was of herself a picture. Playing on the ground near her were two bright-eyed children, who looked up in astonishment at our entrance, while the lady of the house and her son, our new-made acquaintances, advanced to meet us, and speedily presented us to the other members of the group—*la vieille Baronne,* the ancient lady seated by the fire; a young married daughter, the mother of the two pretty children, who now stood up at the knees of their great-grandmother; and her husband, the Comte de Villequier, a tall bright-looking young man with the polished manners of good society. Two more children emerged from the fire-light shadows, and, with the young sister we already had met, whose name we found was Eglée, completed the family party, now assembled together in dinner toilette to spend a pleasant half-hour round the fire.

We apologised for the lateness of our visit, and were met by the assurance that we could not have come at a better time, as they were all assembled together, which at an earlier hour they could not have been. We were delighted with them all. Evidently highly educated, there was throughout their conversation a deep tone of interest, while yet it was lively and amusing. It was easy to see that they were Carlist in their attachments, devoted to the old *régime* and to the family of Charles X., reminding me much of our own early romance for the Stuarts; while the love of their country, and their enlightened views of what ought to be the happiness of a nation, were equally evident, and formed a contradiction I could well understand, from our own English feeling that would have defended Charles Stuart, and yet acknowledged with joy the benefits brought by Cromwell. I believe there is no theory that can be fully carried out.

I was especially charmed by their courteous manner to each other—above all, by that of the young Baron to his mother, who I found had been early left a widow with this one son and two daughters. They explained that they all lived together during the winter months in this large old house, having their different servants, but dining together, and in the summer they all separated to their châteaux, which were in different parts of France. The dinner-table we had seen so decoratively laid out was for their own family party, usually joined by one or more intimate friends, often by some whose politics, talents, or adventures made them especially interesting. They did not receive much, but always had a pleasant little society gathered round them while in Paris. In the country they lived entirely their *vie de campagne,* which by their description seemed very delightful,—a sort of perpetual picnic, being almost entirely out of doors. It was in our after intercourse we gathered much of this information, as also that the husband of " la vieille grand'mère " had perished in the revolution of '92. We became exceedingly intimate with this family, and gained much by the friendship of the son, who made us thoroughly acquainted with Paris, not only as it is, or rather as it was, in 1830, but with historic Paris, seldom seen by English people.

From the old Roman ruins of imperial palace and baths, more entire than I have seen them elsewhere, step by step through every century, each event that had been was made to tell its own tale ; and that winter in Paris, thanks to the de Montignys, gave us more information than a whole library could have done without the actual scenes in which the characters had lived and moved.

I dwell upon this family because I believe that a like element of domestic worth, with all that education can do to refine and elevate, has always held its own among the fluctuations of French society. Two years spent in France, more or less in constant association with every class, making fast friends even with the picturesque old beggars, impressed us much with the affectionate nature and childlike disposition that seemed to us characteristic of the French people. Why is it that individually they are so charming, while collectively they have so often been "atroces"? They never seem to attain mature age.

CHAPTER XIV.

WHILE we were thus throwing off many of our national prejudices, what was the manner of life of the young scholar at home? He had finished his time in Glasgow on the 1st May 1830, when he had returned to his father's house in Park Place, spending the three succeeding months in energetic work. He also attended all manner of lectures, chemistry, &c., and read Greek Plays with the Rev. H. H. Marriott, a very eminent scholar, and one of the masters of the Edinburgh Academy. He had worked hard, and deserved a little rest and amusement. He found both, with many of the younger branches of his family, at Kinrara, one of the most beautiful places in the Highlands, situated on the banks of the Spey. Sir George Sitwell during the shooting months rented this charming place from the Duke of Gordon, whose property it was. Nothing could form a more delightful contrast to the absorbing months of study from which our Archie had emerged, more wearied than would have been good for him without the period of pleasant repose that followed. Endless expeditions towards the more distant glens and lochs, and saunter-

ing about on the banks of the rapid Spey, were the
daily pleasures of old and young as suited them
best, and here our dear old father, broken in health
and unable to undergo fatigue, found much enjoyment.
His daughter always filled her house, whether in
England or in Scotland, so that while the infirmities
of his age were lovingly cared for by her, he was
interested and amused by pleasant society as well as
gratified in his taste for beautiful scenery. Indeed,
it was not necessary to stir from the fireside to enjoy
this, for over the fireplace of his bedroom was a large
mirror which reflected the window immediately opposite,
and this window looked out upon the grandest of the
distant mountain-passes ; so that without stirring from
his arm-chair, and with his feet upon the fender, he
beheld a matchless picture, lighted by the rapid gleams
of sunshine battling with hurrying clouds, and alive
with wind and storm sweeping down the glens that
divided the mountains. Could there be anything more
charming for the dear old man who sat there, resting
from the rambles with his much-prized son, for which
he was in some degree still able ?

It was in the year 1831 that our youngest sister
Marion became the wife of Richard Wildman, second
son of Mr Wildman of Chilham in Kent,—a man who,
had his energy and steady perseverance equalled his
flashes of ability and insatiable love of reading, must
have risen to the highest of his profession at the bar.
He is the author of several valuable works on Law
and became Recorder of Nottingham.

The pleasant time at Kinrara ended, the university
life for the young undergraduate began in October.
From his dictation I write :—

"I took possession of my rooms in the top attics
of Balliol, as completely a garret as could be imagined.

L

I was at once introduced to Moberly, Tutor of Balliol. He asked me to breakfast with him next morning, which was Sunday: the party consisted of Herman Merivale, whom I had already begun to know, Manning, whom I never did know well, and Stephen Denison.

"Dr Jenkyns followed up his first kindness by giving me excellent advice, cautioning me as to the young Scotchmen from Glasgow, who formed a set by themselves, not of the most desirable or creditable description, and advising me to go in at once for the Balliol Scholarship, which was to be given in November. This advice I followed with success, and the having obtained it, after scarcely a month's residence, gave me an important standing in the College, and Jenkyns looked with increased benignity on the young undergraduate; notwithstanding that this young man had been led to his beloved Balliol by the helping hand of John Snell, to whom he bore no goodwill, looking upon his creation of the Glasgow scholarships more as an impertinence than as a good deed.

"The Scholars of Balliol when I joined them were Payne, son of Sir Peter Payne of Bedfordshire,—he had the first of the open scholarships; Grove, who became Principal of Brazenose; Whitaker Churton, afterwards Fellow of Brazenose; Charles Marriott, afterwards Fellow of Oriel; Sir John Eardley-Wilmot; Elder, afterwards Headmaster of the Charterhouse; and Herbert, a very clever man from Eton, strange and rough in his manner: he died young, and his death is sad to think of, for, making a walking tour in Switzerland alone, he fell into a well, over the edge of which he was supposed to be stooping to drink, it being one of those furnished with a cup fastened by a chain. All these I found at Balliol. Blackburn was elected with me; he gained the first scholarship, I the second. The next year came Lord Cardwell, and Father Tickell of the Jesuits. After them Vice-Chancellor Wickens, and Dr Holden (Headmaster of Durham). A little later, Arthur Stanley (Dean of Westminster), and Professor James Lonsdale; then Lake (Dean of Durham), and Goulburn (Dean of Norwich); Lord Coleridge (Chief Justice of England), and Seymour, who died early; Sir Stafford Northcote, Arthur Clough, and James Riddell,—all these were my friends and contemporaries. But the men with whom I so 'habitually lived that we acquired the name of 'the family party,' our rooms being on the same stairs, were Bence Jones, Joseph Salt, and dear old John William Pugh, a truly Christian friend, two years older than myself: this man, though never known in public life, was of most saintly character, and to me he was invaluable.

"I found my letters of introduction of the greatest use. One was to Mills, the Professor of Moral Philosophy, who introduced me to the acquaintance of Cramer, the Head of New Inn Hall. Both Whately (at that time Head of St Alban's Hall, to whom I had a letter from Sir William Hooker, Professor of Botany at Glasgow) and Shuttleworth, afterwards Bishop of Chichester, were in the habit of inviting me to their houses. No person of any eminence ever came to Oxford without dining with Shuttleworth; and from his intimate relations with Holland House, having been tutor of General Fox, Lord Holland's son, his acquaintance was most extensive with all the intellectual lights of the day. The invitations to his house were therefore very advantageous to a young undergraduate."

At the end of the short Christmas holiday he

allowed himself at Renishaw, determining to do all that man could do to win the higher rounds of life's ladder, Archie returned to Oxford, and with patient courage set himself to work in the empty College, for there was not one soul there but himself, and day after day he read alone and dined alone.

When the term recommenced, his Oxford life became exceedingly interesting to him. He belonged to the famous Union Debating Society, and there began to try his powers as a public speaker, with the greater ease that at Glasgow he had already gone through the experiences of the first essay.

Easter Monday, April 17, 1876, Addington Park.— Sitting this wet day in the library, after service in the chapel, the Archbishop tells me that the person to whom he owes more than to any one else during his early college life was Frederick Oakeley, Fellow and Tutor of Balliol, now unhappily Father Oakeley, a canon of the Roman Catholic Church living in Islington. He was not only his tutor but soon became also his attached personal friend, and seemed never weary of doing him acts of kindness. Oakeley was a man of great refinement of mind, the son of the late Governor of Madras and brother of Sir Herbert, who was Chaplain to Archbishop Howley. He had been a favourite pupil of Sumner, Bishop of Winchester, at Highclere, and having passed his own undergraduate days at Christ Church, had an extensive acquaintance with all the most eminent people of his own standing. He was nearly ten years older than his pupil, but seemed to have conceived an affection for him from the first day when he was present to listen to his construing of Lucan's "Pharsalia" in the Master's study.

Through the three years of his undergraduate life

the pupil was continually with his tutor, and was introduced by him to many of his friends.

"Oakeley paid a visit to Kinrara with me in one of the long vacations, and thus the friendship was extended to the rest of the family; and I also visited old Lady Oakeley in the Bishop's palace at Lichfield, which she rented. When I first knew him his mind was opening more than it had to religious impressions, and the influence of Bishop Sumner and his friends had given him a strong bias to the Evangelical school. This continued more or less during the three years of my undergraduate life, but gradually he succumbed to the then almost irresistible fascination. How I myself escaped I know not, unless it were by God's blessing on the Shorter Catechism, in which I had been well indoctrinated by old Betty." (And his biographer may add, by the possession of a fund of sound Scotch common-sense,—an inestimable gift, that has been of much value through all his career.)

Jeune, late Bishop of Peterborough, speaking afterwards of these times, used to say that the prevalence of Newmanism, as it was then called, was like the measles, nobody was safe from it in Oxford who had not had it already; and when asked how he himself had escaped, he answered that it was only through the good fortune of having been absent as tutor to some young man in America while the disease was at its height.

For good or for evil, the young Scotsman's constitution withstood the infection, not only when tried by all the softer influences of his friendship for Oakeley, but also when exposed afterwards to the overwhelming arguments of that strange incarnation of logic, who was elected to a Fellowship on the same day as himself, —William Ward, author of 'The Ideal of the Christian Church,' and now the wealthy proprietor of a beautiful place in the Isle of Wight, and ultramontane editor of the 'Dublin Review.' But to return. With Oakeley, as with many others, this playing with mediæval Christianity soon became a serious matter, and as time went on, it was impossible but that it should interfere even with the most sacred friendships.

"The kindly intercourse between us lasted, however, through all my undergraduate days, and on through years afterwards when we were brother Fellows and brother Tutors of the College; but Oakeley went to London, first as Whitehall preacher, and then as incumbent of what afterwards became All Saints', Margaret Street. In London he fell more and more under the influences to which he was yielding, and at last, like several others of the best and noblest spirits of the Oxford of that day, sacrificed all his prospects in life to become a Roman Catholic priest, without ever winning entirely the confidence of the rulers of that Church to which he had transferred his allegiance.

"The brilliant and refined Fellow of Balliol has spent his days ever since as a missionary priest amongst the wild uneducated Irish of Islington, a post for which of all others his university career and peculiar character seemed least to suit him. Strange! considering the character which the Roman Catholic Church enjoys of knowing how best to choose and use its instruments, but not more strange than its treatment of John Henry Newman.

"Oakeley, now almost blind, and worn out with repeated attacks of bronchitis, between seventy and eighty years of age, still drudges on uncomplaining, in Duncan Terrace, Islington; the only symptom that he shows of returning to former feelings is that now in his old age he is very fond of seeking opportunities of seeing old friends and scenes. It is not an uncommon thing now to find him visiting his old college, and wandering like the ghost of his former self amongst his former haunts, living with Woolcombe, who inhabits what were once my rooms. All through his Roman Catholic life he has sought opportunities of writing kindly letters, and making occasions for visits to me, which have always been most welcome, though calling up many sad thoughts. No one rejoiced more heartily than he had done at my election to a Fellowship in 1834."

`Rome has made many martyrs, but I doubt if there has been a martyrdom more complete or more sad than this long dreary waste of life in a highly educated man, whose very refinement of mind made him less fit for work among the coarse and wild Irish than would have been one cast in a rougher and stronger mould.

"At the same time with myself," continued the Archbishop, "was elected William George Ward of Christ Church : he was at this time a strong Radical, and great admirer of Arnold. Some years after he broke up the whole High Church party by worrying Newman into writing Tract No. 90, which brought down upon him a charge of all the Bishops.

"Ward was quite a character; it was worth something to dine with him at old Dr Achmet's, Fellow of All Souls', who had everything in perfect style around him, and to see Ward, with his most peculiar appearance, the size of a tub, and stockings that had once been white, kick off his shoes under the table, consulting then and at all times his own particular ease, in utter defiance of the decorums of life. His lectures, as everything else he did, were never to be reckoned upon ; devoted to reading, he liked to bury himself among his books, and could little endure the interruptions of everyday life,—his health, or rather his enormous tun of a body, always furnishing him with an excuse. He would on one pretext or another keep out of the way till the very hour of his lecture, when all of a sudden he would start off, trundling upstairs ahead of the undergraduates, who, anxious for their lecture, were in full pursuit; but he had the start of them, gained the door of his room, sported the oak against them by turning the key upon them, and quietly set himself down to read his novel, while supposed to be, or wishing it to be supposed that he was, under medical discipline. He was a ceaseless worry to Jenkyns, who had favoured his election to the Balliol Fellowship because he had a weakness for well-connected people, and Ward was a son of the M.P. for the city. His whole college career was most peculiar, ending with his trial for heresy and threatened deposition. The sudden announcement of his marriage whilst the trial was going on at once changed tragedy into comedy, for all the High Church party from every quarter had rushed up to Oxford, viewing him in the light of a martyr to the strictest High Church principles, including celibacy, and determined at all hazards to save for him his Fellowship. Behold, in one moment it was forfeited by his marriage. They returned as speedily as they had come.

"After his marriage he became Lecturer of St Edmund's College, Ware, went over to the Roman Catholic Church, and a great disturbance he made in it. Archbishop Errington, while acting for Wiseman in Westminster, suspended him for preaching heretical doctrine. He appealed to the Pope, and both Wiseman and the Pope decided in his favour, much to Errington's disgust. After this he succeeded to a fortune, and still carries on life in his own peculiar fashion.

"In November or December I took my degree, having won a first class in classics. I do not know how much this success was owing to my *vivâ voce* examination in Aristotle, which was conducted by William Sewell, but I know that Sewell, in consequence of the examination, recommended me to several pupils, and always had a friendly feeling towards me through his long, chequered, and sadly overclouded life. He was, at the time he examined me and first patronised me, certainly the most famous tutor in Oxford, and the man of whose success in life it would have been natural to prophesy with the greatest certainty. With a crowd of admirers both within and without the university, writing articles in the 'Quarterly Review' which were read with attention by friends and foes alike, preaching at Whitehall Sunday after Sunday against Sir Robert Peel and his temporising policy, who could have anticipated for him the melancholy collapse of fame and fortune and health, which reduced him for the last twenty years of his life to live almost on the bounty of his family, and withdraw altogether from all spheres of public usefulness ? "

CHAPTER XV.

WHILE Archie was carrying on his Oxford life the
health of our dear old father was rapidly failing.
He declined to look forward to the spring visit to
Harviestoun, which had always been to him the source
of sad yet sweet enjoyment, replying to the solicita-
tions of his eldest son to allow him to plan a journey
there, reminding him of the scenes in which he had
always taken so much delight—"No, I do not wish it;
I shall soon be walking in fairer gardens with your
beloved mother."

He was mercifully spared all increased suffering
of body, all pain of parting. For long his nights
had been nearly sleepless. In the evening of the
10th May 1832 he laid himself down as usual, but
he never rose again : if he slept, his sleep had no
awakening, for in the morning he was insensible,
and gently breathed his last.

The following summer Archie went home; and in
this summer we also went to Scotland, with the sad
feeling that we were just too late. We had planned

with my dear old father that we should spend some time in Edinburgh after we left France, and had gladly looked forward to the reunion. Now the old home had lost its deepest interest: never can I forget the desolation of the old library, with the empty arm-chair by the fireside. I sat down upon it, and gave myself up to thoughts of him. My eyes fell upon an object that in a moment seemed to place me in direct communication with himself; it was his well-known Memorandum Book, a long, thick book, closed at the end by a small silver clasp. There it lay where he had placed it three months before, just within reach of his right hand. Oh! it was so familiar to me that to lift it was, as it were, to touch him again; to open it, to enter once more into conversation with him. Every entry brought back well-remembered scenes; sorrows I knew of but had not shared, separated as we had been; words that implied a touching resignation; and aspirations that breathed into a future still remote.

Many pages were occupied by a detailed sketch of his views for his youngest son. It had been written immediately after the boy had left the Edinburgh Academy, having gained both the gold and silver medals. It took him to the College at Glasgow, from thence to Balliol, step by step through scholarships and first-class degree to a fellowship, with vague indications of literary honours, landing him safe, with highest repute, in a bishopric. Only two links in the chain were wanting, and these had not occurred to him. By a Scotsman of that period the headmastership of Rugby School was not likely to be considered as a literary honour, and to make him Archbishop of Canterbury had not entered his views. In fact, I doubt if the importance of the position was very clear to him, or I feel sure that he would have placed his Archie in it. Reverently I restored the precious memorandum to its place, feeling that I had no right to keep it; and very sorry I have since been that I did not, for the book disappeared, probably accounted of no importance by the servants, to whom its value was unknown.

We soon established ourselves in Atholl Crescent, happy to be restored to the enjoyment of the society of the numerous branches of our family, from which we had been so long separated. Various marriages had made many pleasant homes in which it was delightful to visit, but Archie we did not see again till quite the end of the next year—1833.

The midsummer of that year he joined a reading-party, having Johnson of Queen's, now Dean of Wells, for coach; his companions were Alexander Hall and Roundell Palmer, afterwards Lord Selborne, Chancellor of England. The place that had been selected for their studies was Seaton, a quiet village between Dorsetshire and Devonshire. It possessed among its rural inhabitants a poetic and dreamy schoolmaster, whose attention was attracted to the reading-party, and a curious circumstance related to me not long since by the Dean of Wells is worth recording. The young men, with the Dean, were reading in some quiet nook out of doors, when this man appeared among them and addressed them in lines of his own composition :—

> " He whom near yonder cliff we see recline,
> A mitred Prelate may hereafter shine ;
> That youth who seems explaining nature's laws,
> An ermined Judge, may win deserved applause."

It seemed as though he had been' gifted with the spirit of prophecy, looking from the future Lord

Chancellor to the future Archbishop. "But," said
the Dean, with the peculiar twinkle of dry humour
for which he is remarkable, "he did not look my
way."

At the close of the next term the undergraduate
took his degree, a first class in classics, and arranged
to give himself a holiday in Edinburgh with his family
at Christmas. It was a great blessing that he had
made this arrangement, for by it he was enabled to re-
pay in some measure the tender love and devotion
with which his old nurse Betty Morton had watched
over his childhood and infancy. The dear old woman,
finding herself no longer equal to the fatigue of the
long stairs in the Park Place house, had withdrawn
into lodgings, from which she constantly visited us :
towards the end of December she came to see us in
Atholl Crescent, a few days after the birth of one of
my children, well and happy, and as usual interested
in all our concerns ; the next day she was taken ill, not
seriously, as at first appeared, but being myself unable
to go to her we did not know the extent of her illness.
Archie arrived and went to her at once ; he found her
fever high, and her mind occasionally distressed ; he
never left her except to seek the assistance of a clergyman. All night he sat by her bed. Often had she
soothed him to sleep during the many troubles of his
childhood, and now with the blessed words of peace he
hushed her griefs to rest in Christ. She died with her
hand clasped in his on the first of the New Year, 1834.
It was a lasting source of gladness that his visit to
Scotland had been so ordered as just to meet her time
of greatest need.

Shortly after he returned to Oxford, his object now
being a Fellowship. In the summer of 1834 he worked
hard at Renishaw to obtain it. In September he went

with Oakeley up the Rhine, then back through France by
Rheims to Paris by diligence,—a very different manner
of travelling from the present ease and speed of railroads. He returned to Oxford, and November brought
on the election of the Fellowship so earnestly desired.
He had bent all his energies to win it, but he did
not think that he had succeeded, and while the bells
were ringing for the election he sat alone in his room
in sad and anxious thought. Suddenly the door flew
open, and in rushed Father Tickell[1] to drag him off
to the chapel to take his place as the newly elected
Fellow. A new life was now begun with a new set
of friends, for the old ones were all gone. John Carr,
whose rooms had been given up to him, became an
intimate friend though twenty years his senior. He
now began to take pupils, and, thoroughly occupied
during term-time, as thoroughly enjoyed the vacations.

The following summer he joined us at Powick, where
he found our eldest brother and his wife with their
one surviving child, their first-born, John, a fine boy
of ten or twelve years of age, and James, our next
brother; and, anxious to win them from their sorrows,
we arranged a series of tours. My husband and I,
with Emily, our eldest little girl, made up with them
a party to explore the beauties of the river Wye.

Very much we all enjoyed it, not only the daylight
rambles amid the beautiful scenery, but the evenings
at the different inns. Brothers and brother-in-law
were eager politicians, and of different ways of thinking,—my two Scottish brothers determined Tories, my
English husband and the young Oxonian as decided
Whigs. Some public question then before Parliament
was so warmly discussed between them that both parties
became excited to the utmost, with loud voices and

---

[1] Not then so called, as he had not then joined the Church of Rome.

much declamation maintaining their opposite opinions by demolishing each other's arguments. Mary and I, knowing them too well to dread a quarrel, looked on amused, when something suddenly drew our attention from the arena of combat towards the ceiling, and there, in a high gallery for an orchestra, we beheld a crowd of curious people—in fact, all the inhabitants of the hotel—gazing upon the scene, evidently drawn there by the loud and eager voices. Tea had been brought in, but nobody had observed it. Our exclamation caused the combatants to look up, and brother James, who had been specially engaged with my husband, suddenly lifted the teapot, and pointing to the steaming urn said in his dry terse way, "Now, Mr Wake, I remit you to your chemicals." The sudden drop of this from the thunder of oratory was ludicrous beyond description, and thus ended the battle of Chepstow.

During our rambles on the banks of the Wye an incident happened in which the quiet decision and quick immediate action of our brother Archie saved the life of the precious child that was with us. One of the sights was the view from the top of a tower rising so close to the river bank that it seemed as though it rose straight out of the water. I had followed the guide up the broken steps to the top. They were almost perpendicular, but accustomed from my childhood to look down over precipices, I had felt no sense of danger till a cry from below caused me to look down, when to my horror I saw my Emmie, midway, clinging helplessly to one of the broken stones, and in another moment she must have fallen straight down, for her uncles John and James below could not reach her. In an instant Archie, from the base of the tower, had passed them, picked her up,

and quietly and firmly carrying her to the summit,
set her down by my side, still keeping a firm hold of
her as she cowered down so that she could not see
anything round her. 'Never since then have I been
able to endure to look down any precipice, for through
all the long years that have passed the terror of that
moment has never been lessened. The same calmness
of spirit has given my brother Archie efficiency in
many an emergency when to stop or turn back would
have been destruction.

We all returned to Powick Court, and from thence
the three brothers proceeded through Wales to Ireland,
seeing whatever could be brought into the time in both
countries. On arriving at Dublin they found a letter
from Dr Jenkyns with the important information that
Moberly had been chosen Headmaster of Winchester,
and that Archibald Campbell Tait had been appointed
to succeed him as one of the Tutors of Balliol, and thus
he dictates : " I spent the next few months in Scotland,
partly at Garscube with Ramsay Campbell and partly
at Montague Cottage with John and Mary, preparing
for my lectures.

" With the beginning of the next term opened a
totally new field of interest in the Tutorship of the
most eminent College in Oxford. Of course I succeeded to some eminent pupils whose time was already
half over — as Arthur Stanley, James Lonsdale,
Wickens, and others ; but my own peculiar class
with which I began my lectures was certainly not
undistinguished, including Waldegrave, late Bishop
of Carlisle ; Goulburn, Dean of Norwich ; Lake, Dean
of Durham ; Sir Benjamin Brodie, Professor of Chemistry at Oxford ; Pearson, Canon of Windsor. I was
now established in Moberly's rooms, the best in Balliol,
and I am vain enough to think that my lectures were

at least as good as any others in the College, so that
for a young man of twenty-three I found myself in a
somewhat unusual position of importance and usefulness. I was ordained on Trinity Sunday 1836 by
Bishop Bagot of Oxford, and soon took charge of the
parish of Baldon in connection with the duties of my
tutorship.[1] Some part of this work was divided with
Golightly, and Johnson, Dean of Wells, then Tutor
of Queen's : the lifelong friendship with the latter
was then beginning to be established."

In this most rural parish, adjoining that which Goldsmith has immortalised as " Sweet Auburn, loveliest
village of the plain," Archie learned the art of cottage
visiting, making friends among the very poor, and
finding the way to the understanding of the uneducated. The parsonage house was like a toy, it
was embowered in roses. He usually brought his
provisions from Oxford, and occasionally slept in it;
his housekeeper, a certain Mrs Harris, was worthy of
having been described by Walter Scott with Morton's
domestic tyrant, Mrs Wilson, in ' Old Mortality.'

One summer, we—that is, my husband and myself,
with Emmie—visited Archie, spending two nights in
Oxford at the " Mitre," and two in this pretty little
abode, the whole of which might have been contained
in a good-sized drawing-room. We thus understood
his manner of life, spending the hours not given to
lionising in his capital rooms in Balliol, being introduced to his friends; and afterwards at Baldon in
enjoying beyond measure the wild beauties of the
common, covered with straggling, detached, and picturesque cottages. Goldsmith's word-painting had been
so true that, not in the least knowing what neighbour-

[1] It is scarcely necessary to say that the sole remuneration of this charge
was the experience it gave in parish work.

M

hood we were in, we remarked how extremely like the whole scene was to the deserted village of Sweet Auburn. The weather was lovely, which was fortunate, for in order to accommodate us Archie slept in a sort of verandah. We had a most pleasant dinner in the tiny dining-room with the triumvirate of Oxonians, and we spent there a very interesting Sunday; it was not like real life, and now comes back as a sunny dream. This little village of Baldon, with its simple and tender cares, —so very wild and unkempt, so to speak, that it was marvellous to think of its existence within a few miles of the great university, — must have had a happy influence on the mind of its young pastor. It rescued him from a too great devotion to books and to abstract ideas, showing him the ever-living cravings of the human heart. He remembers now with tenderness some of his old grey-haired friends.

He often came to Powick Court, and it was upon leaving us after one of these visits that a most absurd scene took place. He and our brother James, who also had been staying with us, took their places in the coach to Oxford. An old servant of ours deposited their luggage at the coach office. The time for starting arrived, and Archie, finding that he did not appear with their portmanteaux, hastened down to the office, but even before he entered it was aware of a tremendous scuffle, a loud altercation, followed by a violent assault upon the faithful Perry, whose demand for the boxes had been met by the grossest abuse from the men there. Feeling that there was no time to lose, he had endeavoured to possess himself of them, and was collared and cuffed by men and maids, a detachment of whom armed with brooms had suddenly from an inner room joined the fray. The Highland blood of the young Oxonian was aroused, and with one blow of

his fist he levelled with the ground a ruffian who was
in the act of striking Perry when down. A general engagement followed, under cover of which Perry picked
himself up, shouldered the luggage, and master and
man made good their retreat just in time to catch
the coach as it was starting. The explanation of the
scene was that, unaware of there being two coaches
to Oxford, between which a bitter rivalry existed,
they had taken their places at the office of one coach,
while their luggage had been deposited at the office
of the other.

The most amusing part of the adventure was that
next morning a well-dressed respectable-looking man
came to Powick Court asking to see Mr Wake, and
stating that the young gentleman who had the
evening before gone by coach to Oxford had left
part of his luggage at the office, he requested his
name and address that it might immediately be sent
to him. My husband, suspecting no evil, asked the
man to sit down in the housekeeper's room and have
some refreshment after his long walk, while he wrote
" Archibald Campbell Tait, Esq., Balliol College, Oxford."
The man, whose whole demeanour had been so remarkable for its bland politeness, took the address with a
civil bow, and immediately repairing to the nearest
magistrate demanded a summons to be served upon
the said Archibald Campbell Tait for assault with
violence. Happily the magistrate was a friend of
our own, and pictured to himself the horror of Dr
Jenkyns, the most punctiliously correct of men, at
such a scandal against a Fellow of his College,
in his eyes the model of the whole university. It
might in truth have been a most awkward affair,
for there were no witnesses except the hostlers
and chambermaids, who were prepared with any

amount of evidence in support of their master. How the friendly magistrate quashed the whole matter I know not, but years afterwards it was his great delight to remind us of it, always declaring that he had rescued the Bishop of London from a prosecution for assault and battery.

In taking leave of his Oxford life I must relate the means by which he ensured early rising. Being naturally of a sleepy disposition, and having no longer the faithful Betty Morton, as at Glasgow, to pull him out of bed, he, in the beginning of his college life, purchased a strong and able-bodied alarum-clock, which on the first morning made such a clatter as effectually dispelled his slumbers. In two or three days it might as well have been silent, the sleeper was not awakened. Determined to conquer, he adjusted the machinery in such sort that a cord attached to his pillow whisked it from under his head. After the third morning he slept on soundly, regardless of the dangers of apoplexy. That night the cord was fastened to his bedclothes; with a jerk they left him in the morning exposed to the perils of cold and rheumatism; it was in vain, even to this a day or two accustomed him. Driven to desperation he fastened the cord round his neck, and head and heels was dragged from his bed at the appointed hour. This was effectual.

CHAPTER XVI.

WORCESTERSHIRE is a charming county, and Powick
Court was a charming place. We were very happy
there, and had many neighbours we exceedingly liked.
Of these, Mrs Mann of Hallow Park was one we
especially valued : she had been, with all her family,
the O'Briens of Dromoland, for long years the attached
and much-prized friends of my husband's family, and
it was delightful to find oneself, on coming into a
strange county, welcomed with almost maternal love.
Mrs Mann reminded me of what our mother might
have been had she lived to grow old, for her
beautiful old face recalled her features, and in many
ways she was to me like a mother. Best of all, the
atmosphere of true religion was that in which she
lived and moved, and with her cheery Irish nature
made her a friend and companion to be delighted in.

But the reason she is mentioned here is that she
had a charming niece, a girl of fifteen with lovely
dark eyes, bright, loving, and truthful as herself, who
speedily became a favourite with all, young and old.
She was the daughter of Archdeacon Spooner of
Elmdon, one of the best representatives of the Evangelical School of that day, and had been carefully

brought up in her father's views. Her earnest mind
had received with deep conviction the blessed truths
of the Gospel of Christ, and this made her, though
scarcely more than a child, extremely interesting,
while her lively nature not the less responded to the
fun and frolic of our boys and their father, with whom
she was an especial favourite. She was staying with
us in the summer when Archie made one of his
pleasant visits, and little Kitty, as she was habitually
named, and the young Oxonian suited each other
exceedingly well, though his devotion to his books
sometimes interfered with his chivalry. My husband
then drove a mail phaeton with two very spirited
horses, and Archie on the box beside him, little Kitty
and myself behind, we were in the act of driving from
the door when a commotion was excited by Charles
(my husband) suddenly snatching a book from the
hands of his companion and pitching it yards from
the carriage with a shout of "Are these your Oxford
manners, to bury yourself in a book when you have
the chance of driving with a pretty girl quite willing
to talk to you?" Away flew the book, away flew
the horses, and very happy we were. And what is
more, this little episode stretched itself on into maturer
years—one of the many little links that weave an un-
thinking present into an unthought-of but thoughtful
future. I do not think they met again for years, but
the threads of their lives having been thus brought
together, it was impossible for them to meet as strangers
when their destiny should again place them side by
side. But there was no thought then of the fair picture
which should in God's good time be woven into the
tapestry of a united life.

Meantime each character had to ripen and strengthen
for the work that now lay undeveloped, yet preparing

by-and-by to ripen; but it was still spring-tide with them.

Powick—sweet, lovely Powick—I know not why the few years of my long life that it was our home should be the deepest marked, should have left the most glowing memories. Was it because till then no child had left us, nothing had broken in upon the enchanted circle? or was it rather that while there the realities of the inevitable school life opened upon us, and we had to send from us one boy after another, had to suffer that strange attraction to have its way which calls a child from the nursery and the schoolroom to the hardships of a sailor's life? or was it that while at Powick death came among us and gently carried from our sight two lovely little ones who had been born there, and laid them beneath the old yew-tree in the churchyard, leaving with us, instead of them, the solemn knowledge that we were no longer a family on earth, for two were already in heaven? More would assuredly follow, but these little ones were the first-fruits to God and the Lamb, and we never again had the same assured feeling of a settled home.

All these things deepened our life at Powick Court with a richness of colouring all its own. And now at seventy-six I like to tell of its foreground of flowers; of the snowy mespilus, large as a forest tree, that shed its blossoms on turf and gravel, covering them with a carpet of silver; of the honeysuckle-bound larch-tree in which the nightingales always built, so filling the night with song that on our knees we heard it through our prayers, and on our ·pillows mingled it with our dreams, waking in the morning with a vague feeling of wonder whether nightingales ever slept at all.

Once more my husband's health required a decided

change, and it was determined we should cross the Channel. But it was with the deepest regret we left Worcestershire and all our kind and pleasant neighbours. The last visit we made was to Westwood, grieved to think it *was* the last; our intercourse with the Pakingtons had been one of the pleasantest parts of our time in Worcestershire. Sir John[1] was then in the very prime of life, a regular boy in his powers of enjoyment, full of energy, and so kind and so reliable that during the years we were his tenants there never was a written line in the way of lease or anything of that nature between us. He had met us when we first went to see the place, readily agreed to do what we wanted done, and did it as quickly and as thoroughly as we could desire. Though Westwood Park was fully twelve miles distant we had frequently exchanged visits, and he had been with us when our little sailor first went to sea. How little did we then think that he was twice to become First Lord of the Admiralty, and materially assist the naval career which was just then beginning. He is the best illustration I have ever known of the man "born with the silver spoon," &c. He was the younger son of a man of moderate fortune, Mr Russell of Powick Court, with no expectations beyond those he could realise for himself by industry and talent. This necessitated a university education and the determination to benefit by it. He was called to the bar, and it was not till after their father's death that the eldest brother married, and after four years died without children, leaving him in possession of the family property, which he thoroughly enjoyed with his wife and their only child.

His mother having been one of the two sisters of

[1] Not then Sir John.

Sir Herbert Pakington of Westwood Park, he in process of time inherited from him the large estates and ancient house of Westwood, one of the most picturesque relics of olden times, the centre tower belonging to the days of Henry VII. Sir Herbert had never cared for his nephew, and had shown his ill-will in many small ways regarding the succession, one of which was having stripped the valuable library : this, to a man with the tastes of the heir, must have been exceedingly provoking ; but Providence was kind, and almost immediately so ordered it that, by the bequests of two uncles of his wife's, the library shelves were refilled to overflowing. His talents for business caused him to be elected Chairman of the Quarter Sessions, and he was member for the county, so that there was no want of business and of duties, to prevent habits of idleness ; while his musical talents added to the social pleasures of the neighbourhood, for he had a charming voice, and sang with much taste and feeling to his wife's accompaniment. Mrs Pakington was as amiable as her husband was agreeable.

Years have developed most unexpected changes in his life. In the last visit we made to Westwood we witnessed what, had I possessed the second sight of my native land, would have been startling as well as strange. Grouped at the piano were Pakington, his wife, Augusta Murray, and Mrs Davies (wife of the other member of the county, who was then staying in the house), and he literally was singing a beautiful duet with his second wife, to the accompaniment of his first wife, his third wife turning over the pages of the music-book ; for the three ladies were fast friends. How little could any one dream of the changes a few years were to bring about !

The wife of his youth not very long after this time fell into bad health, and after a protracted and suffering illness died. He tenderly watched over her and deeply mourned her loss, the circumstances of which drew him more closely to his friend and neighbour the Bishop of Rochester, who chiefly resided at Worcester, of which he was Dean, and he found a comforter in his daughter Augusta, a charming and accomplished girl, who deeply sympathised with him in his sorrow, having herself been much attached to Mrs Pakington. This union was short, for to his great grief she died after giving birth to a son, Herbert.

Time went on, and in the marriage of his eldest son with Lady Diana Boyle new interests arose; but his life had been too thoroughly domestic, notwithstanding the public duties he had even then to attend to, for him not to feel lonely. His friend and neighbour Colonel Davies, long an invalid, died, and his widow was also left in the oppressive loneliness of a large country house. It was not very long before the mutual blank in each other's lives drew the former friends together, and Mrs Davies, originally Miss de Crespigny, became the third wife of Sir John Pakington. He could not have chosen better. With a lively disposition, considerable powers of conversation, and an affectionate heart, the present Lady Hampton has not only well filled up the vacuum in his home, but has made herself beloved by the various branches of his family. Thus while undergoing heavy misfortunes he still was fortunate, and when on the advent of the Conservative ministry he became Secretary for the Colonies, his life hourly became more interesting. It is pleasant to remember he was the bestower of self-government on Australia, the originator of our liberal policy towards those colonies.

Our Worcestershire life was at an end, and having made arrangements with Archie to meet us at Bonn as soon as the Oxford vacation had begun, we all proceeded together, a large family party, up the Rhine into Switzerland, in the year 1840. At Lausanne we were joined by Stanley, on the road to Greece. He passed on his way, and after a short stay at Lausanne we established ourselves at Geneva, in one of those pleasant villas that are situated on the Pâquis side of the town, so close to the lake that our boys fished from the garden wall. Here the enjoyment of the whole party would have been complete, had not my husband's health been a source of anxiety. Archie's society was delightful to us. It was the first time that he had *ever* been free to enjoy himself without the burden of some object to be attained on his mind, and very thoroughly he did enjoy the life of freedom from care, amidst the lovely scenery of the lake.

From our windows we looked across the lake towards Mont Blanc, never wearying of the glorious scene. Who that has seen those sunsets can ever forget them? No words can picture them. There are grander scenes amid solemn and stupendous heights, or one may feel a greater elevation of mind gazing upon classic ruins; but for charm, for exquisite beauty, there is nothing like the sparkling blue of the waters of the Lake of Geneva, ever moving from the ripple of the current of the Rhone—nothing like Mont Blanc, flashing out from the distance its diadem of snow, kindling into rose and crimson as the evening sun dips towards the horizon; growing pale and ghostly as the rays forsake it, and when all seems over, life returning with one vivid flash, glorious and glowing; then calm lovely night with thousands of stars, a

double heaven, in the blue skies above and in the
blue lake below. Well might we never weary of the
sight.

The great and almost daily delight was the boating
expeditions on the lake, Archie in command, our boys,
the eldest of whom was but twelve, for crew ; we rowed
up and down, visiting every nook of interest within
reach.

Twice in these excursions we saw that which is often
not seen for years together. While lingering over the
blue depths of the lake we beheld close to us the pure
white form of Mont Blanc mirrored in the very centre
of its bosom. It is impossible to describe the effect of
that sight, with the knowledge that the mountain is so
distant that the reflection being formed seems an utter
impossibility. We were told the distance is sixty
miles.

On Sundays we rowed quite across to the chapel of
Cæsar Malan. With him the young Oxonian made
acquaintance. He had brought letters of introduction to
all the celebrities of the place, few of whom, however,
were then in Geneva, this being the season when all
who could withdrew to the mountains to avoid the
sultry heat of summer. Merle d'Aubigné's house was
on the opposite side of the lake, and Archie, hearing
that he was at home, took boat to visit him : like many
of the villas on the lake, there was an entrance from it
through wide gates which enclosed a portion of the
water, making it private property. Having entered, he
became aware of a strange appearance paddling and
swimming in the deep water in evident enjoyment.
At the first glance it seemed of the seal genus, large,
dark, and rounded in shape, with head upraised as it
swam; but the disturbance made by the entrance of the
boat caused a rapid retreat, during which it became

evident that it was a fat old lady who had been enjoying the pleasures of the bath.

Occasionally the young crew were mutinous, scarcely
acknowledging the right of command in an uncle whose
very youthful appearance made him look almost a boy
himself. On one occasion he had felt it necessary to
assert his authority for the safety of the party while
they in turns bathed from the boat. When he was in
the water the young villains in revenge rowed away
from him, knowing that there was no landing-place
except through a crowd of washerwomen busy on the
beach, and that they could make their own terms with
him before he could possibly get back into the boat :
he used to tell me that it was a great comfort that he
could knock down any of them.

After a short time, to Archie's great joy, Stanley
reappeared, and was quickly joined by their mutual
friend Goulburn, who had travelled with the *malle-
poste* from Paris. The weather was excessively hot,
and he, hearing that it was dangerous to eat on a rapid
journey in hot weather, had provided himself only with
a bottle of wine, on which he subsisted, tasting nothing
else as he travelled night and day till he reached
Geneva ! It was not wonderful that as soon as he got
there he was attacked by fever.

The two newcomers were in the Hôtel des Etrangers
close to us, and it was intended that they should sleep
there and live with us, but of Goulburn we saw nothing
after the first day. The reports of his condition were
the more alarming in that, from dread of foreign practi-
tioners, the two friends were determined to weather
the storm by themselves as best they could. It is a
wonder the poor patient was not utterly wrecked, for
Stanley, who considered medicine simply as medicine,
and good for all cases alike, kept giving him what he

had, and as every Englishman travels with a medicine-
chest there was an alarming variety of choice. Archie,
doubtful of this treatment, begged my husband, whose
own experience had necessarily given him considerable
knowledge, to see the sick man. He did so just in
time to prevent his being subjected to a process of
blue-pill which would probably have sunk him entirely.
"I have given him two," said Stanley. "Two blue-
pills!" exclaimed my husband, who was in the habit of
speaking out his opinion without favour or affection,—
"two blue-pills! you have probably killed him." Poor
Stanley, the shock nearly made him ill himself. The
fever having left him, the sick man required all that
could be done to reinvigorate. It was clear that he
was safer in less scholarly hands. In a short time he
came among us to thank the amateur physician, who
had probably saved his life, and the two friends went
on their way.

Some time after their departure it was found that
the immediate vicinity of the lake was hurtful to our
own invalid, who, though he was able to doctor another,
could do nothing for himself; and we were advised,
before we decided on remaining for the winter at
Geneva, to try the atmosphere farther from the lake.
We therefore took a cottage in a beautiful garden a
mile farther inland : there was but one bedroom and
one sitting-room, and these were reached by an ascent
more like a ladder than a staircase from the corner of
the *rez-de-chaussée*, of which the possibilities were—
the means of making coffee and such light refection,
and of accommodating the one servant we had with
us. Archie, therefore, remained in our house by the
lake with the rest of the family, but spent the greater
part of the day and most of the evenings with us.
Between reading aloud and the enjoyment we found

in the strangeness of our life and accommodations—
being obliged to do everything for ourselves—we all
three found these evenings very pleasant.

He had undertaken to cater for us at the circulating
library, and the second evening he arrived with a book
which, with animated pleasure, he laid on the table,
saying, "We shall be sure to like this; I have heard
of it all my life, but have never seen it till now. It
is 'The Monk,' by Lewis, and it must be good, for he
was always called 'Monk Lewis' after having written
it." As soon as the tea was over we drew our chairs
round the cottage chimney, the advancing autumn
making the blazing faggots most welcome, and in
great contentment gave ourselves up to the full enjoyment of a real good romance. The book began, I
forget how, but with great interest; by-and-by some
hesitation disturbed the flow of the reader's voice. I
looked up from my work and saw Archie's face becoming redder and redder, while he hastily turned
over some pages. After a moment or two of silence
he threw the book across the table to me, saying,
"Take it and look it over; what I see of it is not fit
to read; judge for yourself." Happily he had come
armed with another, for that certainly was not fit to
be read by man or woman—a conclusion at which I
arrived upon examining it next day. The terrible
interest was so intense that I could not help reading
when I once had taken it in hand, but it was so
horrid that I put it in the fire and raked the red
embers over it. I would not for worlds have had
the pure mind of my young brother disturbed by its
dreadful scenes, and very sorry I was to have them
for a time recurring to my memory. To write such
books is deliberate wickedness.

While Archie was travelling back to Oxford we

began our journey southwards, to winter at Nice. Again the Duke of Wellington's coach was packed with all the necessaries for many days and nights. My husband and myself occupied the seat behind the carriage; our faithful man-servant Perry, with two boys, in front; our dear old nurse Keightley, a new Swiss maid, and four children inside the carriage : a goodly company we made, and right merrily we enjoyed our travels.

It was indeed most enjoyable, for nothing could exceed the beauty of both weather and scenery. It was the time of the vintage, and the country was alive with groups of peasants treading the grapes in the corners of the fields, now and then crossing the road with naked legs dyed crimson up to the knees with the blood of the grape, the whole scene recalling passages in the Old Testament. Never can I forget the beauty of an early morning as we coasted the lovely Lake of Annecy. A large boat had just left the shore, laden with grapes piled high on its deck, the level rays of the rising sun shining through the heaped clusters of green and purple grapes looking like jewels in their transparent beauty; the ripple of the waves as they parted before the boat; the glittering waters, half in sunshine, half in shadow from surrounding hills, —all made a scene like some dream of Fairyland.

Railways, no doubt, have been beneficial in bringing distant lands together, but they have utterly destroyed the picturesque delights of "travelling *vetturino*," with its necessity of sunrise and sunset scenes and the midday siesta. Delightful were our pauses when the horses were taken out of harness, and the whole party, under the shadow of some great rock, enjoyed luncheon and a mirthful repose.

Italy! The very name was suggestive of sunshine and warmth! Our imaginations filled with the description of the descent of Hannibal and his troops into the vine-clad valleys, we had no thought of cold *after* the passage of the Alps was safely accomplished and we were snugly established for the night in a little hotel at Susa, at the foot of Mont Cenis. We considered all difficulties at an end, and were therefore ill prepared for the storms which beset us towards the evening of the third day. The air began to get thick with snow, and when darkness closed round us we found to our consternation that our *vetturino* had never been there before and knew nothing of the way. The snow fell faster, the night grew darker, our four horses floundered along stumbling fearfully, then one of the wheelers fell — and we came to a standstill.

How well I remember the thrill of feeling when the silence was broken by the sound of the bells of a convent! It could not be far distant—at least we need not spend a night in the snow! Perry got down, and unscrewing a carriage lamp assured my husband he could make his way to the village that was sure to be near. We watched the light as it travelled, now up, now down, showing the uncertainty of the path. It disappeared altogether, and after a few faint attempts at conversation we subsided into complete silence. After about half an hour a young voice cried out, "Bells! bells! horses are coming!" and indeed the joyful tinkle quickly drew near, and in a few minutes a kindly face, gleaming in the light of a lantern, was thrust in at the carriage window with "Tout va bien; bon feu, bons lits, les chevaux sont ici." Then came

N

more lights, eager voices, six snorting horses, and several men with Perry in the midst of them. Our poor overdone team was soon taken out and the fresh one put in its place, and with tugs and pushes, accompanied by many uncouth sounds, for the wheels had sunk deep in the snow, after a tremendous jolt we were once more on our way, and very soon our troubles were forgotten in the most comfortable old-fashioned hotel that could be imagined. In every room blazing fires, bustle, and life, as the children ran about the house, establishing themselves as though we were there for the rest of the year; indeed, it soon became evident that it was the hope of the house that we should be storm-bound for any number of days, if not weeks.

After three days, during which the landlord protested that farther progress was impossible, the threat of writing to the English consul procured a fresh team of horses. We were once more on our way, and without further adventure arrived at Nice.

To our great joy we found there old friends and neighbours, Captain and Mrs Spencer,[1]—he the most reliable of men, and she so single-minded and so full of goodness and loving-kindness that to know her was to love her. It was most pleasant to find them living very near us, for somehow intimacy always increases in a foreign land faster than at home. We met other old friends and made several new ones. We had not known Baillie of Dochfour till then, but we speedily became friends. There were many interesting subjects in common between us; and his beautiful wife, Lady Georgina, and her pretty girls, about the age of our children, added much to the enjoyment of the time we were at Nice.

[1] Father and mother of the present Earl.

Under its sunny skies my husband's health rapidly improved.[1]

When the vacation was ended Archie had returned to his duties as Tutor of Balliol, and was sitting quietly in his rooms when the tub-like figure of Ward rolled in, with a pamphlet in his hand, exclaiming, "Here is something worth reading!" It was Tract No. 90!

Newman, and those who were of his opinion that the Thirty-nine Articles contained nothing that need prevent those who signed them from holding doctrines so nearly akin to those of Rome that a man might in fact be at one and the same time a Romish priest (only not acknowledging the authority of the Pope) and a clergyman of the Church of England, would have been well content to act upon that opinion without broadly stating it to the world; but Ward's restless mind and character would by no means be thus satisfied. He gave them neither rest nor peace till he had stirred them into publicity, and it was thus that Newman was induced to send forth the Tract which was indeed a declaration of war. The dangerous system advanced was immediately perceived by our young Tutor of Balliol, who sought his friends, and found their anxieties the same as his own. Then began a storm of excitement throughout the entire country,

---

[1] In talking of travelling *vetturino*, Lady Wake related how one day, in crossing a mountain-pass, they heard a slight noise, and looking down from his high seat at the back of the carriage, her husband beheld a ruffianly brigand coolly unstrapping a large valise hung on beneath, having so timed his theft that as it fell off on one side of the ascent, in another moment the carriage would have surmounted the summit and be rolling down the other side too rapidly to stop. Charles Wake could not reach him; he had no weapon handy; to his objurgations the man only looked up with an audacious grin. But the villain had reckoned too securely on an Englishman's lack of resource, for in the next second he had loosed his hold and was rolling helplessly in the dust, suddenly blinded by his victim spitting straight into his eyes. Away down the hill went the carriage—and the valise safely with it.

spreading over the land from Oxford like the bursting of a thunder-cloud, that has never since been equalled. Not even the disturbance caused at this moment (1877) by the efforts of the Ritualists and the Extreme Party, in what is called the High Church, can at all compare with the vehemence of feeling called forth by the first appearance of Tract 90.

It seemed a discovery of traitors in the camp, for that men could hold the sacred office of ministers in our Protestant Church, and yet disagree with the doctrines of the Reformation, did indeed seem like treason.

CHAPTER XVII.

OUR RETURN TO ENGLAND—HEADMASTERSHIP OF RUGBY—
DR BUTLER—ARCHIE'S MARRIAGE.

TOWARDS the end of May 1842 we returned to England,—not as we had left it, a joyous band. All things seemed changed around us: our brightest and our best had been taken from us, and to her father and me life had lost its charm when our Emmie died.

It was summer when we reached Courteenhall. The shadow of our grief was there, was everywhere; the very sunlight never seemed as bright again; but life went on, and it was fuller than ever with the varied needs and interests of the various ages round us.

Sir William, my husband's father, the kindest of old men, knowing well that in the companionship of our dear Archie there must be comfort, sent to him to beg him to come before he returned to Oxford. He was greatly needed, for the shock of sorrow had brought severe illness upon my husband; but the burden of grief was so heavy, that even as at the time everything seemed confused and unreal, so now, in looking back, I can remember but little, till a sort of strange light arising from a sudden call upon our interest seemed to break the cloud which darkened everything. Archie and I were at Blisworth station together; he was returning to Oxford. Our attention was riveted by the unusual sight of a multitude of boys filling the carriages of the up-train, all grave, silent, and sad. " Who were they ? " " The young gentlemen from Rugby," was the reply. Evidently it was no holiday. " What brought them there ? " " Arnold is dead," passed from mouth to mouth. Their hushed voices and subdued looks showed how suddenly the blow had fallen, and how it had told upon each one of them. Dr Arnold's character was one which acted more or less upon every boy in the school, and his sudden summons filled them with awe. They knew that the call of his Lord had not taken him by surprise.

Archie had known him well and valued him much. We parted in silence.

Not many days later a letter from him filled us with surprise and roused us into immediate action. It told how he had been advised by his friends at Oxford to become a candidate for the headmastership of Rugby School, vacant by Dr Arnold's death, and enclosed a list of the names of the gentlemen with whom the nomination lay, that they might be canvassed if personal friends of any of us. My astonishment was great. It seemed to my ignorance a retrograde movement instead of a literary honour that was sought. Many of the governors of Rugby School were personally known to Sir William, and many were the letters written by him and by all Archie's friends and connections. But it was the testimonials sent from Oxford that won the day, for as we afterwards heard, when the electors met, each having made his particular selection, there were so many candidates, and the votes were so divided, that it was impossible to arrive at any conclusion unless they came to an understanding

A. C. TAIT AS HEADMASTER OF RUGBY.

as to what was the best course to pursue. And this was the result of their consultation : having found that some of the electors had the name of the Rev. Archibald Campbell Tait first on their list, and that every one of the others had the same name as second, intending if they could not carry their own particular man to vote for him, they agreed unanimously to place him first on the list,—and so he was elected. This was in August 1842.

He spent the short time that intervened between his election and the meeting of the school with us at Courteenhall. The new life before him naturally occupied his thoughts and ours ; he was twenty-nine but did not look twenty-five, and a vast field of responsibility was opening up on his onward path, and curious were the differing views taken of his prospects by different persons. One near neighbour naturally took a deep interest in the whole affair. Dr Butler, Dean of Peterborough, having been for a long term of years Headmaster of Harrow, was eminently qualified to advise the young Oxonian, who had never himself been at a public school, and who therefore the more deeply felt how immense an undertaking it was to have the welfare of a whole army of boys at the most impressionable age committed to his charge. The Dean came to make him his farewell visit, and after much good counsel he wound up in an earnest voice,—so earnest that we (and we were a large party) all reverently bent our heads to hear his words,—"Remember, young man, in all you have to do, whatever may be your difficulty, remember never to lose sight of — church preferment." Every head went up with a jerk, and we all looked at each other with a violent desire to laugh : the conclusion of the address was so entirely different from what we expected that the effect was a sudden drop from the sublime to the ridiculous. Yet it would not be fair from this to assume that the old man had no value for the one thing needful : the manner in which he brought up his sons should refute any such idea. One of them had, some time after this, an illness in our house, and we were struck with his reverential conduct in all things that could show religious feeling : there could be no doubt of his religious training. But the Dean was so full of the prospects of the young Oxonian that his thoughts at that moment certainly rose no higher than his advancement in life.

He was a wonderful old man. Not long before this he was riding across a bridge, in the depth of winter ; the river below flowed in a swollen stream, dark and turgid ; it was evening and bitterly cold. His attention was suddenly attracted by the figure of a young woman running wildly down the bank. In a moment she had thrown herself into the torrent, and would have been swept away had not a strong hand seized her and dragged her to the shore. It was the Dean's, and he was seventy years old.

In October 1842 we were established at Pitsford, near enough to Rugby to ensure much communication between us ; and in November, about a month after the birth of my youngest child, we made our first visit to Archie (after whom our new-born was named), in his new home at the School-house at Rugby.

Nothing could exceed the comfort of the house, and as two of our own boys were living in it, being pupils, we felt much at home, and interested in the lively scenes in the playground, &c. This prevented our observing the one very decided want—that of a lady of the house, which would be the more felt when we were gone ; and I listened without much interest to Archie's

account of a dinner-party in the neighbourhood, at
which he said he had met an old friend, having taken
in to dinner a very pretty girl, whom he did not
recognise till she began to talk about Drury and
Herwald Wake,—"then all at once it dawned upon
me that the charming young lady sitting next me
was no other than my little friend Kitty Spooner,
quite grown up into a most agreeable and extremely
pretty woman. We talked of Powick days, and we
were friends in a few minutes." I heard him without hearing,—this was in the November the same
year, the spring time of which had brought so great
a sorrow that it seemed to have stupefied me; but the
words returned in full force when, a short time afterwards, our old Worcestershire neighbour, Mrs Mann,
having come to visit us at Pitsford, the conversation
turned upon Powick Court, and she naturally spoke
of her niece whom we had been so fond of. All at
once a light like a revelation shot through my mind,
and I exclaimed, "Kitty! is she not going to be
married, or is there not some engagement of that
sort?" "Certainly not," was the answer; "what
makes you think so?" "Nothing, nothing," I replied,
"I only wanted to know, for what a wife she would
make for Archie : he met her the other day at the Sand-
fords and admired her very much. Sit down directly,
and write to the Archdeacon that I send him my love,
and that for the sake of old friendship I depend upon
his inviting my brother to Elmdon soon; the Christmas vacation will shortly enable him to visit his
friends."

The old lady did as I desired her, and I wrote
to my brother to the effect that if Archdeacon
Spooner invited him to Elmdon Rectory he was
certainly to accept; adding that if he chanced to

fall in love with Kitty, he need not fear that she
would turn out to be a dragon with teeth and claws,
—alluding to the sympathy he used to express with
the fate of deluded bridegrooms. "Unhappy man,"
he used to say, "too often believing that he has
taken an angel to his bosom, he finds too late he
has united himself to a dragon with teeth and claws,
who has a right to pursue him to his very bed."
By return of post I received a brief reply — "I have
received your testimonial in favour of Miss Catharine
Spooner, which shall receive due consideration." After
this I had no letter from him for a long time, but
heard by side winds that he had been at Elmdon,
and that the Archdeacon's family had been visiting
in the neighbourhood of Rugby, where after a short
visit to the Sitwells at Renishaw he had returned,
though he had been due in Scotland for some
time. From all this the conclusion was inevitable
that a powerful attraction detained him there. At
length a letter from him dated Elmdon Rectory
reached me; it contained but a line, "Hurrah! I
have proposed and have been accepted."

Shortly afterwards he joined us at Pitsford, and
then he told that he had found the little Kitty
of five or six years ago as charming as she had
been at sixteen, but come out in a new character,
—a sort of mediæval saint blent with her energetic
lively old self. Catharine—no longer Kitty. They
held, opposite opinions, he said, on almost every
subject, and had fallen in love with each other in
a series of combats over the comparative merits of
the Christianity of the middle ages as contrasted
with that of the times in which they were living.
He had been nearly floored, he said, by his lack
of enthusiasm, especially in regard to 'Sintram,'

a book lately published, which she held in such high estimation that she had made its appreciation a sort of test of the value of the character of those with whom she came into intimate association : unhappily he neither understood nor appreciated it. Her romance on the subject was both interesting and amusing, and through it he could discern the depth of character which belonged to her.

The wedding took place in the summer at Elmdon Rectory, June 22, 1843. They went down to Scotland, where the young bride was as much delighted by the beauties of Loch Katrine and the mountain-ranges within reach of Glen Devon (in which the family still gathered itself together, though beautiful Harviestoun stood empty and still) as she was shocked and pained by the little barn-like kirks and Presbyterian observances, which she looked upon with a sort of holy horror.[1]

When settled in their home at Rugby the really practical character of the young wife shone out, for she at once with all her energy adopted the new life, taking the deepest interest in the welfare of the boys, seventy of whom dwelt under her roof. She had, indeed, no part in the management of the boarding-house, though it was in the same building ; but it was part of her husband's plan to keep up a friendly association as much as possible with his pupils, and no week passed without some of the sixth form, whether belonging to the School-house or to those of the other masters, being invited to dine and to spend the evening in her drawing-room,—a kindness greatly appreciated, for they were quite old

---

[1] The Free Church movement had not then filled Scotland with beautiful edifices Whatever else has been the result, the improvement in church architecture throughout the country has been evident.

enough to value doubly the trouble taken for their amusement by the Doctor's young wife because she was fair to look upon.

She was a great help in graver matters of business, keeping for him all his money accounts, to which he had neither time nor inclination to attend. She lightened his cares, and by her presence enabled him to get rid of a custom which had caused him much worry and loss of time. Arnold had accustomed the under-masters to come to him in the library in the mornings whenever it suited them to do so, bringing with them no end of discussion. To him this habit had had many advantages; to the new Headmaster it was simply intolerable, though an alteration was difficult.

It was achieved in a manner as simple as decided. The first morning after the return of the newly married pair from the Highlands a tap-tap came to the library door, which instantly opening, a figure with cap and gown was revealed standing transfixed with astonishment. No wonder, for in that apartment, hitherto sacred to study and to men, between the window and the fireplace, instead of piles of books and papers, there stood a charming little breakfast-table, at which Dr Tait and his bride were happily engaged with tea and coffee, eggs and hot rolls. It need scarcely be added that no figure in cap and gown ever again appeared in the doorway in the morning.

An amusing circumstance showed how little he looked the character he had to sustain. He was one day busy in this same library when General MacInnes was announced, and an elderly, bright-looking man immediately entered into conversation with him on all sorts of subjects. This was pleasant, but time was precious, and after a few minutes Archie inquired, "Is there anything in which I can be of use to you?" "Yes indeed," was the reply, "I am very anxious to have an interview with Dr Tait." "I am Dr Tait." "You!" shouted the General; "I took you for his son." There was naturally a laugh on both sides, followed by the earnest conversation for which he had come to Rugby, speedily convincing him that a profusion of curly hair might cover plenty of brains, and a young countenance be expressive of wisdom.

The summer vacation of 1844 was devoted to a tour through Belgium and up the Rhine. Their return to Rugby was saddened by the intelligence from Scotland that a heavy cloud of sorrow was gathering over the happy home in the valley of the Devon. Mary, the beloved cousin,—wife of our eldest brother,—had been stricken with illness, which all now knew to be hopeless. With cheerful patience and unfailing courage she had struggled against the malady that had for some time been slowly loosening her hold on life, but as the winter advanced it became too evident that her days were numbered, and as early as possible in the Christmas holidays Archie and Mrs Tait went down to Edinburgh to sustain the husband under the coming blow. They remained with him throughout the vacation. That winter (1845) she died, and thus was wound up the long love-story that had begun in early childhood. Never was there a union more fully blessed : death had no power to end it.

In the June of that same year the desolate husband was persuaded by Archie and Catharine to accompany them to the Continent; and taking with him his only son, then a youth of twenty, and brother

James, he joined them, and they proceeded together
to Rome and Naples. The pleasures of this tour,
which included everything worth seeing on the way,
were increased to the brothers by their mutual companionship, for the genial temperament of our family
always found enjoyment doubled by sharing it with
each other, but I doubt if Catharine would not
have found it pleasanter to have been alone with
her husband.

In March 1846 the happiness of the Rugby home
was completed by the safe possession of a greatly
prized daughter.

The following summer was spent at the cottage at
the foot of Dumyet, which now represented the family
home among the Ochills. Harviestoun was tenant-
less, John having made the wise decision that it was
best to decline an inheritance which, had it been kept
in the family, would have burdened him with debt and
crippled every movement. It was during this time
that Sir Archibald Campbell died, and the three
brothers, in the funeral at Garscube, saw the final
close of the well-remembered drama of the first part
of their lives. A new era had begun ; the old generation was passed away. Young Sir Archibald, who
succeeded his grandfather, belonged to a time of
different thought and feelings.

CHAPTER XVIII.

SIR WILLIAM WAKE'S DEATH — COURTEENHALL — ARCHIE'S ILLNESS
AT RUGBY — HIS APPOINTMENT AS DEAN OF CARLISLE — LORD
BROUGHAM.

IN the early part of the same year (1846), Sir
William Wake, my husband's father, had died, and we
shortly after removed to Courteenhall, thenceforward
to be our home. The short distance which separated
Courteenhall from Rugby allowed a continual intercourse, delightful to us in every way, for my husband
had loved Archie as a child, and every stage of his
life had ripened the feeling into the highest esteem
as well as affection : in his society he always found
unfailing pleasure.

After Christmas (1847) Archie and Catharine
joined us at St Leonard's-on-Sea, where we had
taken a house for the winter for the sake of the
milder climate. They were both there in perfect
health and in the highest spirits. I can see them
now at the close of a little dance we had given for
our children and their friends, all the guests being
gone, pirouetting round the room in a valse, Catharine (never having in all her life witnessed anything
approaching to a dance before) saying this was her
first ball. We little guessed what a change was at
hand.

In the first week of March we were startled by the intelligence that dear Archie was seriously ill. The letter that gave the alarm was immediately followed by a telegram. I was off by the next train with the bare possibility of catching the Euston train, escorted by man and maid; both were left behind on the way, and I rushed through Smithfield market under the protection of a farmer who in the train had spoken of the immense importance it was to him that he should catch the train to Birmingham. I had begged to share his cab, and we got through the market, so crowded with men and beasts as to be nearly impassable, just in time. Thankful I was when my farmer shut me into an empty carriage. I could scarcely breathe with anxiety when we rushed into the well-known station, with the shout of "Rugby" in my ears. The first words I heard were, "He is better": it was one of the porters who thus saluted me. He could tell nothing more, but they heard that the medical report was rather less alarming. I blessed the man for his kindness, for the word "better" gave me new life after the long strain of fear, and in a few minutes, at the entrance of the School-house, Marion confirmed the report: it was not very hopeful, but only this—"No worse symptoms have occurred."

.   .   .   .

After three weeks of serious illness, anxiety for present danger ceased; his permanent recovery depended much upon skilful management and care; if these were fully carried out, with God's blessing, there was every hope that he might soon be able to be removed from Rugby to Courteenhall. Meanwhile perfect quiet and repose of mind were strictly enjoined, and no conversation was permitted during the hours we spent by turns in his room. This was a rule most difficult to carry out, for during his illness all Europe was rocking in the throes of political earthquake : thrones were falling, nations seething in the boiling-over of long-suppressed discontent.

When Archie was taken ill in the first days of March, 1848, tranquillity everywhere prevailed,—" and will prevail," men said to each other, " so long as Louis Philippe, the citizen king, lives. What will happen when he dies, no man can say." One month after, when returning health made it safe for him to hear what was going on in the world, behold Louis Philippe was living a country gentleman's life at Claremont, and the world was going on tolerably well without him. Republican France had the disposal of his abdicated throne, and the nations of Europe were resettling themselves as best they could.

It was a difficult time in which to maintain the calm of look and word necessary for the wellbeing of a patient who was not even allowed to think. We, the brothers and sisters, when the first period of convalescence had begun, therefore dispersed to our different homes, leaving it to Catharine to adjust the balance with the patient between knowing nothing and the reception of the fact that the political world in Europe had turned upside down while he had been lying in his bed. He has often since expressed how great was his amazement.

We were scarcely re-established at Courteenhall before we heard, to our great joy, that Archie could be brought there. He was not able to walk, and he was lifted from the railway carriage to ours, waiting for him.

How we all enjoyed those weeks of slow, gradual recovery !

However, as health returned, the anxiety to retake his work came strongly upon him. He felt the need of occupation for his mental powers, and dreaded the tendency to hypochondriasis which he detected in himself. "My dear," he said to me one day in answer to an expostulation of mine on the subject, "I must return to my work, or soon I shall think there is nothing in the world so interesting as the beating of my own heart."

The experiment was tried. The work of the school had been carried on for him, but he now returned to Rugby to close the school for the midsummer holidays, from thence spending a few days with Archdeacon Sandford at Dunchurch. They proceeded to Elmdon, where Catharine hoped to spend a happy time with her father and mother. But anxiety and fear were still before her. The morning after their arrival in her old home, while she was still dressing and chatting merrily with her husband through the open door, there was a sudden stop, an exclamation of "Oh, Catharine!" and he staggered towards her with blood staining his lips.

She flew to him and tried to support him in her arms, but as she strove to open the door to call for help, he sank from them on to the floor. It was some time before she could make any one hear. They raised him, quite insensible, and laid him on the bed. Then, indeed, she looked upon him as a dying man.

A messenger had been instantly despatched for Dr Hodson from Birmingham, and Catharine telegraphed for Babington, who had so thoroughly understood his former attack. Dr Hodson's view of the case was all but hopeless; he looked for nothing short of rapid decline, and recommended the soft air of

Beaumaris as the atmosphere most suited to his condition, and the most easily reached. The verdict given, he departed, leaving Catharine too down-hearted to dwell upon the possibilities of his being mistaken; nevertheless, it was with a cry of joy that she discerned a little man coming hurriedly across the fields. Intuitively she felt that it was Babington, though it seemed impossible that he could have arrived in so short a time.

It was Babington: carefully he examined his patient, with the advantage of a perfect remembrance of all the details of his former illness, and of the opinion he had then formed. The view he took was totally different from Dr Hodson's. He had no thought of decline, and instead of the enervating air of Beaumaris he insisted upon the most bracing that could be had, and recommended Broadstairs.

The remaining weeks of the holidays were spent there with the two little ones, in a small and not very comfortable lodging. But what were inconveniences in comparison with the glad feeling of returning health?

In the end of August Dr Tait was able to return to his duties at Rugby, resuming the whole work with the exception of the morning school. The bracing system was successfully carried on, and the winter vacation was spent at Brighton, where they were visited by Ramsay Campbell, the cherished playmate of early days, college companion, cousin, and friend. He had lately married Miss Anstruther Thomson, a very charming woman, as good as she was fair to look upon, and a very pleasant time they all had together.

In due time they returned to Rugby, and on their sixth wedding day (1849) Craufurd, their only son, was born to them. The next summer vacation they spent in Scotland, and on their return home, for the first time they took the route through Carlisle. The impression made on Catharine's mind by this first view of Carlisle was very much the reverse of pleasant.

Health had been in a measure restored, but anxious feelings still pervaded the whole family. Archie was clearly not able for much exertion; notwithstanding that the bracing air of Broadstairs had much invigorated him, still many traces of his illness remained. It was evident to every one but himself that the attempt to carry on the work of the school for any length of time would be at the risk of his life.

The Deanery of Carlisle becoming vacant in October 1849, it was offered to Dr Tait, and immediately though not very willingly accepted.

But Babington would not hear of any hesitation. And so the die was cast, and Rugby was to be given up at Easter. Meanwhile, during the Christmas holidays they spent a dreary month at the Deanery, having left the children at Rugby: John and James bore them company, and the whole party disliked it so much that they almost repented the acceptance of the appointment. It is not wonderful, for the Deanery is in the heart of the town, and close to it were extensive premises belonging to the railway, in which the young engines were put through their paces, uttering shrieks and groans of the most lamentable nature all day long and far into the night. It was impossible to divest oneself of the idea that they were being most barbarously treated. To leave Rugby was a great trial to Catharine; the life there had been full of interest to her, and had the additional charm of being near Elmdon and many friends in whose society she had grown up.

The leave-taking was quite an ovation. There was a grand assemblage in the great hall of the school, and the inhabitants of the town, the school, the masters, the sixth form, the School-house, each presented splendid memorial offerings, and a touching one was made to Mrs Tait by those pupils who had been, but were no longer, at Rugby, who now sent a deputation to present to her a picture of her husband by Richmond. The scene on the day of departure was almost overwhelming, Archie still so delicate, the whole school, five hundred boys with all the masters, and many people of the town with Moultrie at their head, surrounded the carriage; the horses were not allowed to remain, and the boys drew it through the streets down the hill to the station. The occasion was sad, yet the excitement of the boys vented itself, boylike, in loud hurrahs while yet they crowded round him to express their sorrow at his departure.

On the first of the following September (1850) their third little girl was born, and it was this which first caused them to realise how complete was the isolation of their new position, for there was no one near to sympathise either in the anxiety or in the joy of her birth. But this feeling passed away, for once settled at Carlisle the Dean soon inaugurated a system of useful work which showed what might be done in these cathedral brotherhoods which common consent had given over to sleepy learning.

In a short time he found his way and made his influence felt everywhere; nothing was taken in hand that was not thoroughly carried out. He visited in the hospitals, the Union, the schools.

The men of the north are full of intelligence, and he found a workman's institute in full career, but was told that from the spirit of irreligion prevailing among the men they were more likely to derive harm than good from their meetings. This was enough to draw him towards them. He proposed himself as a member. They were flattered, and agreed. The first night he attended he found that the subjects given for discussion were "The character of Oliver Cromwell," and the question "Whether poetry or prose was best calculated to move and guide the minds of men?" This was encouraging, and he threw himself into the proceedings with so much zeal, bringing with him so much interesting knowledge, that he was soon elected President of the Society. His earnest desire was to win their confidence and acquire a beneficial influence over them. In these objects he succeeded, and soon induced them to weed from their library several pernicious books, and to discourage irreligious and radical tendencies. This was chiefly done by filling their minds with subjects of wholesome living interest, and by conversing with them with kindly familiarity so as insensibly to guide their opinions. By these means the influence he acquired in Carlisle was immense, and his position in the institute was by one of themselves, at one of their meetings, aptly described by a happy quotation from Æsop's fable of the wild horse, who having once allowed the man to get upon his back, not only could never get him off again, but found himself guided into good behaviour.

To sum up all, the Dean of Carlisle soon found himself abundance to do; and not only so, but in an article in one of the Reviews he ably put forward what ought to be the position and duties of those dignified ecclesiastics who formed, as it were, the staff of every bishop. He demonstrated that each cathedral body ought to be the nucleus of educational progress throughout the diocese, that every good work therein ought to be associated with and aided by the counsel and assistance of the bishop and his staff,—in short, that each cathedral body

should be the heart of the diocese, from which should
irradiate spiritual life and work, carrying with them
in free circulation health and vigour to its most distant
members. The article bore no name, and it created a
considerable stir among those whose learned and rather
languid ease it disturbed. It was, as it were, a call to
arms throughout a drowsy city with apparently no
enemy at the gate.[1]

"Wherefore the disturbance?" Who was it that
had blown the unwelcome blast? The article was
the subject of conversation at Rose Castle. "Do you
know, Mr Dean," asked, probably with some lurking
suspicion, the good and tranquil Hugh Percy, Bishop
of Carlisle, from the head of his dinner-table,—" do you
know who is the author of this article upon deaneries?"
"I do," replied the quick-witted Scot, "but it is a
secret,"— thus avoiding the being surprised into a
denial, or bringing upon himself from many a hive
throughout the land the angry hum of those who
preferred dignified leisure to labour.

The spring of this same year, walking home from
St Paul's, I had found myself between Wilberforce,
Bishop of Oxford, and the Dean of Carlisle, listening
to a conversation on the subject of cathedrals, which
possibly suggested the article in the Review. The
Bishop of Oxford asserted that every deanery was a
useless appendage to the Church, and that it would
be a great advantage to the country if they were done
away with altogether, because there was nothing for
a dean to do. I ventured to say that need not be,
and that I thought if he went to Carlisle and saw
the amount of useful work accomplished by its Dean,

---

[1] The same views were expressed later in the Archbishop of Canterbury's
third Charge, in which he urged them in like manner upon the clergy of
the diocese.

he would change his opinion. "No, I should not,"
he replied. "If one man perched upon a lamp-post
produced a great effect by haranguing from it to the
people, should I be justified in thinking that in every
street there should be a man perched upon a lamp-
post?" I was amused but not convinced, for I felt
there was a fallacy in the comparison and argument.

Certainly the Dean of Carlisle fully proved in his
own person the amount of usefulness that could be
accomplished. Not only was the cathedral restored
(that was a work in which he found many willing
coadjutors), but with true missionary spirit he
awakened the dormant energies of the place, securing
a better care for the poor, both in additional pulpit
teaching and in private visiting and instruction.
Through his exertions the Grammar School of Carlisle
was rebuilt and its system of education extended and
improved. When we reflect that at the same time
the Dean was carrying on the labours of the Oxford
University Commission, we may well acknowledge
that the energy of his nature was not affected by
his weakened health. Yet the life at Carlisle was
scarcely sufficient for the intellectual part of his
character. Too seldom he enjoyed the society to
which he had been always accustomed,—that of men
of letters,—but he was happy in his work, most happy
in his home, which was conveniently situated for
both his Scotch and English friends, and he saw
more of them than he would probably have done in
any other cathedral town. His brothers often visited
him; on one occasion they were accompanied by a
confidential servant, a Scotsman and a Presbyterian.
"What do you think, Daniel, of the cathedral service?" asked his master the first Sunday evening.
"I think, sir," he replied, "there are ower mony

manœuvres; I was quite in a maze, an' couldna follow it ava. At last the Dean got into the pulpit and said, 'Let us pray.' Now, I thocht, I understand that, it's a' richt, and got up on my feet to pray, when a man pulled at my coat-tails and said, 'You mustna stand to pray.'"

The passing to and fro of his friends and occasional visits in the neighbourhood made a pleasant variety in the Dean's working life. Brougham Hall was the home of his old friend, William Brougham, who with his family resided there, Lord Brougham, the proprietor, joining them with Lady Brougham when it suited them to do so. The Dean remembered well his visit there in his boyish days, and no doubt anticipated much amusement and intellectual enjoyment from the society of the great statesman, whose conversational powers he knew well how to appreciate. He was not aware of the extraordinary changes that used to come over the man, and had he known of the taciturn mood that was then upon him, I think he would have declined the invitation that he and Mrs Tait had gladly accepted.

Lord Brougham did not appear till the bell rang for dinner, when he suddenly rushed into the drawing-room with peering eyes and knitted brows, ran up to Mrs Tait, poked out his arm at her as though he were presenting a pistol, and without a word walked off with her to the dining-room. There he sat at the head of the table without uttering a syllable. Other guests there were none, pleasant converse was impossible, and very uncomfortable was the feeling that there sat the man whose conversational gifts made his presence so highly desired at the most distinguished dinner-parties in London, without a word, looking as black as night, with a countenance

full of snarl, as though he would have bitten them
all round if he could.   It was exactly as if he
had taken some deep offence and was possessed by
the desire to avenge it.   All the time that the Dean
and Mrs Tait were at Brougham Hall he remained
in this strange mood, abrupt and erratic in his movements, from time to time startling every one by suddenly opening the sitting-room door, poking in his
head with a rapid glance all round, and, if his eyes
fell upon Lady Brougham, as suddenly slamming the
door to and darting back to his den.

Only once during a visit of three days was his
voice heard.   His brother, with his wife and children
and their guests, with a number of servants, were
gathered round a pond which was being dragged.
The net when drawn to the side came up full of
fishes, which as they were thrown upon the bank
leaped and glittered in the sunshine amid joyous
shouts of " What shall we do with them? what can
we do with them all?"   A harsh loud voice like
the fall of a hammer broke in, " *Crimp them,*" and
Lord Brougham darted into the midst of the circle.

Never another word was uttered by the great orator
and statesman all the time his guests were in his
house.   He had shown no sign of interest in any
person or thing except his brother's youngest child,
whom they were told he called " Baby," though it
was two or three years old; and once when on the
terrace, the sound of young voices having drawn all
eyes to an upper window where sat two of the
children busily blowing soap-bubbles, he stood motionless, gazing up at them for many minutes.   He spoke
not a word, but his countenance was full of earnest
meaning, as though their employment spoke to him
of many things.   There was something pathetic in

the look with which the crabbed old statesman watched the children's play and the glittering bubbles that floated from them only to disappear.

It appeared upon inquiry that these fits of moody silence had not come with old age. William Marshall, his neighbour, told the Dean that they were quite as remarkable in his most brilliant days, when he used to come down like a wet blanket upon the family at Brougham. I never heard of their exhibition in London; probably when he felt the wild-beast demon coming upon him he withdrew himself to Brougham Hall, as to the inner den, where he might snarl or sulk as he pleased.

There are still some who can recall Lord Brougham's well-known figure,—the spare limbs with the never-failing morning costume of check trousers; and those who knew him well will readily acknowledge that his dark keen face, with its extraordinary nose,—which was to him exactly what a dog's tail is to its owner, a complete index of his state of mind, working up and down, backwards and forwards, with every change of feeling,—made him altogether a remarkable phenomenon. A very startling one when the moody fit was upon him, and the first experience left an impression not easily forgotten.

George Moore, the celebrated city man, wholly unaware of this occasional peculiarity, invited his distinguished neighbour to White Hall, his place in Cumberland, and being rather proud of his guest, took care to have a suitable party to meet him.

Not a word would Lord Brougham speak; his grim face was as a dark cloud over the breakfast-table. With a desperate attempt at general conversation, some one, as a safe topic, introduced the Emperor of the French, then a subject of universal interest;

and Mrs Moore, by way of saying something to her grim companion, ventured the question, " Did he think that Eugénie had much influence over her husband ? " Up went his hand, with his forefinger sticking straight up, and, darting his face almost into hers, with his nose working like a steam-engine, he cried in a voice for which there is no English word—nothing but the French one *rauque* can express it, — sounding as though his words had to scratch themselves up from the bottom of his throat, "Influence ! aye, nag, nag, nag ; yes, madam, the influence women have, nag, nag, over their husbands ! " He looked like nothing on earth, unless it might be Barnaby Rudge's raven, when, after sitting on his perch in sullen silence for hours, he suddenly, without any provocation, burst forth into " I'm a devil ! I'm a devil ! " to the consternation of all, and the terror of little boys around him. Poor Mrs Moore was quite as much terrified as they could have been, and made no further attempt at conversation.

Various were the experiences of his friends and acquaintances ; nor was it possible ever to calculate what might be from what had been. The year following the unfortunate visit to Brougham Hall that I have attempted to describe, the Dean of Carlisle and his wife, hoping for better fortune, again accepted an invitation, and found the ex-Chancellor all life, and overflowing with his own peculiar talents for conversation. Whatever of his naturally "thrawn" temper stirred within him he expended upon Lady Brougham, with whom he carried on a perpetual battle across the table whenever and wherever he met her. At a public dinner in London some friend, fearing that a silent fit was coming on, by way of rousing him turned the conversation upon the newly published memoir of Cornelia Knight, in which Lord Brougham had been mentioned with reference to the Princess Charlotte, saying, "It is written, I suppose, by Madame de Flahaut." The ex-Chancellor burst out with, "Eh! Madame de Flahaut, she would not speak well of me; she never forgave me for saying that she was at least three years older than I; but she *was*," he added in a determined incisive tone, "for when I was a boy I used, with several more young boys, to go to the dancing-school to dance with the boarding-school misses, and I used always to be set to dance with her, and she was a big girl then." For a moment he collapsed into silence, then burst out, and oh! the eloquence of that nose and forefinger as in accent of broadest Scotch he poured forth, "Old gurls were always allowed to dance with young boys, but who ever heard of old boys dancing with young gurls?"

The idea of Lord Brougham dancing at all, at any period of his life, is almost too like a joke to think of seriously.

It is useless attempting to describe these things, for without the biting tone of voice, the rapid and almost threatening gestures, and the keen face and eager eyes that seemed ready to skin you with a look, they are nothing. Many are yet living who may remember when, as would sometimes happen, allusion was made to Mr Spalding, Lady Brougham's first husband, he would repeat the name as if he sent it from his throat with a bark, adding, "That gentleman whose loss we have all so much reason to deplore!!!"

And yet there was a better nature in the man—a pathetic, yearning feeling after a higher good than the prizes of worldly ambition. It spoke in the gaze

he had bent on the children intent on their soap-
bubbles.   He suffered from an ambition which had
attained the goal for which it had striven, and yet
was disappointed.   The living soul which the breath
of God had kindled within him struggled for the
mastery amid the uncongenial atmosphere of a sceptical mind that was like a tossing sea, of a snarling
and sardonic temper, and of an indomitable self-will.
The affections that would have softened the evil and
fructified the good within him had been disappointed.
Between him and his wife there was the reverse of
sympathy.   One only child he had fondly loved, but
her early death had sent back the unsealed fountain
of tenderness upon a heart that had no gleam of
Christian sunshine to cheer its solitary depths, and
it had hardened there as stalactites in a cave.   But
the memory of this love, and the ever-returning voices
of the lessons of his childhood, when he had repeated
hymns at his mother's knee, by turns clouded his
brow and lent startling emphasis and intonations to
his very peculiarly harsh voice.

When years after this time the Archbishop of
Canterbury sought repose and restoration of health
in the Villa Eleanore at Cannes, built by Lord
Brougham in the vain hope of saving the life of the
child who did not live to reach it, he found many
traces of the depth of the tenderness which, amid
all the strange bitterness of his nature, stirred the
heart of the great statesman even to the end.

CHAPTER XIX.

TOM'S RETURN FROM INDIA—THE CRIMEAN WAR.

IN the spring of 1851 the hearts of his relations were gladdened by the return of dear old Tom from India, where he had been greatly distinguished in many a campaign. The boy who had left us at nineteen had for many years commanded the 3rd Bengal Irregular Cavalry, known as Tait's Horse. At their head he had formed part of the avenging army under Pollock in Afghanistan, and was foremost in the bloody struggle at Ferozeshah. A constant correspondence with his family had been kept up, so that every action, almost every thought, on either side had been known, shared, and sympathised with, but for twenty-six years his absence had been unbroken, and now we met face to face. Sir George Sitwell, who had returned with his family from the Continent a few months before, went to Southampton to meet him; and they came together to London, where, the Great Exhibition in Hyde Park being just opened, most of the family were assembled. When we drove up to the Wildmans' house in Lowndes Square Tom came to the carriage-door. I looked at him without any consciousness of having ever seen him before; he spoke, and in a moment the twenty-six years were gone; he stood there, the same smile lighting up the same countenance as when we had parted, only the boy of nineteen was now the man of forty-five, with hair slightly grey, magnificent moustache, and a soldierly bearing. The "ancient warrior," the name his father had given in early childhood, was fully developed now. Though thus changed in outward form, the manly simplicity of character, the impetuous feeling, and crystal truth that scorned every disguise, distinguished him now as at nineteen.

It was indeed a happy family gathering. The four brothers, the two elder from Scotland, John and James, and the two younger, Tom the Colonel and Archie the Dean, took a house together close to Lowndes Square. It may be imagined how great was the enjoyment, how deep the interest, of this reunion. The joy of the restoration of the long-absent brother added a vivid brightness to the whole colour of the family life; yet to us individually sadness accompanied it, for our own son Herwald was that summer to sail for India to take up a civil appointment. The evident pleasure with which Tom talked of his Indian life cheered us with the hope that he too would be happy there; and we were deeply grateful to him when he went down with our boy to Southampton and saw him safe on board, full of spirit, grieved indeed to leave us, but knowing that friends and schoolfellows were there before him. The destruction of Haileybury College has deprived our young civilians of that source of happiness.

In the autumn of the year following Tom's return from India, the Dean and his family joined him and his elder brothers in Scotland. They together took Alva, a large and beautiful country-house in Clackmannanshire belonging to the Johnstones. The proprietor was an old and valued friend who had been the playfellow of our early years, and the glens and the hills around it were all associated with our happy

COLONEL THOMAS TAIT, C.B., A.D.C.

childhood at Harviestoun in its near neighbourhood. The united households (with the exception of the servants, who quarrelled like cats and dogs) spent a delightful time together, and received many of their family friends.

In 1854 men's minds were agitated, as they are now in 1876, by the Eastern Question,—whether there was to be peace or war between Russia and the Turks, and whether or not we were to support our ancient but most evil-doing allies? Our brothers, John and James, were making us a visit at Courteenhall, and had brought us from London the various opinions at the clubs. During dinner we were conversing on the subject, speculating whether the next letter from our son Drury (then, as we supposed, at Constantinople) would throw any light on it, when the door opened and there entered—Drury !

What could have happened? Great was our astonishment when he told us that he had travelled night and day to bring despatches of great importance, which he had delivered the night before.

He related that he was dining at the Embassy at Constantinople, being the guest of Sir Hugh Rose (then acting for Sir Stratford Canning, who was spending some time in London, in perfect security that there would be no war), when the startling announcement was made that the Russian troops were about to cross the Pruth ! A war might yet be averted by England's acting with. instant decision and energy. How much evil might be prevented if only it were possible to get despatches to the Cabinet in London before the arrival of the steamer, which had just started carrying the report that all was quiet in the East.

Thus spoke Sir Hugh Rose, himself full of the vigour and energy required. Drury came forward. If Sir Hugh would provide him with the necessary guides

P

and relays of horses he would undertake to ride across the Balkans and, he felt sure, could reach London before the steamer; at all events, it was worth the trial.

The offer was accepted, the necessary orders given, and in an incredibly short time the young courier was off! It would occupy too much time to dwell upon the ride night and day, for seven nights and six days, with neither stop nor rest but to change horses and guides, snatching morsels of food meanwhile, till all things seemed to swim and reel around him. The only difficulty he experienced was with an irascible old governor of Peterwardein, whose signature was necessary to forward the bearer of the despatches, and whose dependants were in such awe of him that none dared disturb him before morning. After a few minutes of wasted expostulations Drury made them show him the door of the dreaded chief's sleeping apartment. Receiving no answer to his demand for admittance, he kicked and hammered against it without cessation, till at length it flew open and an infuriated old gentleman appeared in his shirt, almost too speechless with rage to utter numerous threats, and an absolute refusal to sign anything whatever before morning. Nevertheless it must be done, said the young Englishman, and producing his credentials, he had it done, then and there, and was told to go—a good deal farther than London!

When he reached a railway carriage it was to him as a bed of down, and on the eleventh night he found Lord Clarendon smoking a cigar in his dressing-room preparatory to going to bed. In great astonishment the Minister took and read the despatch. After a few minutes of thought he said, "And what is your opinion? You are come straight from Constantinople;

is peace or war intended?" "War, without doubt,"
Drury answered at once.

"Nonsense, young man," Lord Clarendon replied;
"we have Sir Stratford Canning with us in London,
and he declares that there is no real thought of war;
he knows the affairs of the East better than any one."
And so the despatch was burked, which had arrived
in full time for the taking of measures which, it is
still thought, might have prevented the Crimean War.
The Blue Book of that year contains the question and
its political bearings.

Which was right—Sir Hugh Rose or Lord Stratford
Canning? The fast-following events proved.[1]

Perhaps that which now moves our wonder in the
transaction most is, that it would certainly require
but a few minutes to procure that intelligence from
Constantinople which in 1854 necessitated seven days
and nights of hard riding, eleven of travelling, at the
expenditure of so much young strength.

During the Christmas of 1853-54 the country homes
of England had been bright with the presence of
their sons. We had had a merry party assembled
at Courteenhall; the Dean and the Colonel were
there, and young Guardsmen who looked with envying admiration on the "ancient warrior." "We have
no chance of being heroes, we have never heard a
shot fired in earnest, how can we have medals?" cried
Hugh Drummond, as he counted the Colonel's. In
fact, the long peace in Europe had caused the horrors
of war to be forgotten, and our young soldiers complained that they had never drawn their swords but
at reviews. Suddenly as a bugle-call, the first note
of war sounded through the land!

It was said that we had drifted into war through

[1] February 1885. Does not history repeat itself?

the blunders of the Cabinet. It may have been so, but the summons was responded to with enthusiasm, and the poor boys rushed with pleasurable excitement to join their regiments.

But grave faces were among their parents and older friends. The Queen's farewell to her Guards will be long remembered. Then came the long, sickening suspense. Then battle after battle. With the fresh memory of bright faces so lately assembled under our roof, we awaited with dread the lists of killed and wounded. Alas! in the very first was the name of young Harry Bouverie, he who, Northamptonshire fondly hoped, in spite of difficulties, would have been heir of Delapre. He fell at Alma, his father's only son.

Then Agar Cartwright,—then Hugh Drummond, universal favourite. They had been so lately with us that the echoes of their youthful voices still seemed to linger in the gardens around the spot where they had erected, attacked, and defended a fort of snow. They were utterly gone.

It was a troubled time throughout the British Empire; the flower of our youth was gathered to that dark harvest of death, the Crimea. How the old Scotch song after the battle of Flodden came to mind —" The flowers o' the Forest are a' wede away"! Yet as a family we had escaped well. It is true that George Campbell,[1] a grandson of the old days at Garscube and therefore very dear to us all, had been shot through the shoulder in the Balaclava charge; and the young Balgonie,[2] also a grandson of the house of Garscube, died of rapid decline, the

[1] Afterwards Sir George Campbell of Garscube.
[2] He was the only surviving son of the Earl of Leven and Melville, and of Elizabeth, youngest daughter of our uncle, Sir Archibald Campbell.

result of the long campaign. Yet Leveson Wildman, our sister's son, without harm or loss, won his lieutenancy at a very early age by his gallant conduct, under Pelham, in the Baltic, and his father and mother received him back safe and sound. Our own sailor, Charles, had been called to the Commandership of the *Hannibal*, under our kind and gallant friend Admiral Sir Houston Stewart, just as the war was coming to an end, and much to his disgust had no opportunity of distinguishing himself or — of being killed.

The Christmas of this year was necessarily a sad one, for the thoughts of all were with the sufferers in the trenches. Peace came at length, and families settled down as they could to the many changes the war had brought. The Crimean graves held those who had been the hope and pride of their homes, and their places were filled up as best they might be. Soon they lived only in the hearts of those who had most dearly loved them, but in many of those who survived the war came a change that did not pass away. Thoughtless boys had been brought face to face with death, not as in a dangerous illness for a few days only, but for weeks and months, and during that time of trial there had not been wanting voices, like those of the prophets of old, to speak of God's dealings with His people. Some who had gone out to the war with little feeling but that of pleasurable excitement had returned full of thought, to become good soldiers of Christ. I could give many names, but that of Stevenson Blackwood is sufficient.

CHAPTER XX.

IN the autumn of 1855 we, on our way north, spent
a delightful week at the Deanery, repeating the visit
a month later as we returned home, and by this means
had the opportunity of thoroughly understanding the
extent and variety of the Dean's work, while at the
same time we had the full enjoyment of his family life,
which was delightful. There were now six children,
—only one, the third, was a boy; the five little girls,
from the eldest to the youngest, were charming, full
of life, and had such a share in all that was done
that an additional spirit and animation was imparted
to everything.

It was a happy family. Christmas with its busy
joys passed over them. In February a new baby
was added to the flock, and we had scarcely finished
our glad congratulations when we were startled by
the astounding intelligence that the lovely little
Chattie had been, as it were, carried away from the
midst of them. She was taken ill on March 5,—
another day and she was gone. So sudden, so
quickly over was her illness, that the dreadful fear
that it was scarlet fever was scarce acknowledged,
though too likely to be true, for one maid had

sickened of what might have been it, and it was raging through Carlisle. .

Alas! there was soon no room for doubt; one after the other four more darlings were smitten with the fell disease, and in five weeks they were gone![1] The poor mother was still on the sofa when the first blow fell; she arose at once, and God gave her strength and power over the agony of heart with which she saw one child after another.laid low. She and their father tended their dying beds, aided by the nurse, the faithful Peachie, who had been of so much value during his illness at Rugby.

.   .   .   .

In the beautiful churchyard of Stanwix lie the five sisters.

.   .   .   .

Few appointments have ever given more general satisfaction than the one of Dean Tait as Bishop of London. At all times we should have been glad, but at this time his family rejoiced with a joy unspeakable; we were filled with thankfulness that he was to be taken from his Carlisle life, so changed from what it had been, and placed in a sphere which would call into action every power of mind and spirit.

The news spread like wildfire wherever any interest had been felt in him. The announcement produced some amusing scenes. Sir David Dundas described one of them thus: "I was in Edinburgh, sitting in the club quietly reading; the room was full of men, most of them busy with the newspaper. Being interested in what I was about, I gave no attention to what was going on, when suddenly I became aware that there was a great stir of excitement in the room. On

---

[1] A full account of these five weeks is given in the memoir, 'Catharine and Craufurd Tait,' published by Macmillan & Co. in 1879.

looking up, to my astonishment I saw all the members shaking hands with each other, their faces radiant with some very pleasurable emotion. They were handing newspapers to each other. 'What has happened?' I said. 'Here, here!' was the eager reply from many voices, while many fingers pointed to a particular column in the circulating papers. 'See here, Archie Tait is made Bishop of London.' It is singular how national Scotch people are, and how much attached to each other. 'You might have been,' said Sir David in relating this scene to the Archbishop,—'you might have been own brother to every man there, to judge by their joy at your appointment.' 'Yes,' said his Grace, 'and it is singular how many Scottish gentlemen have decided upon putting their sons into the Church of England. Till I was myself made Bishop of London, I had no idea of the progress Episcopacy was making among my countrymen.'"

I fear there is some satire in this last remark.

Be just, my brother; these Episcopal tendencies were an afterthought. The first burst of gladness was genuine, genial, and wholly disinterested.

That same day the news reached the two elder brothers in Blairlogie. They rode over to the early home, Harviestoun, where lived the old servant who had been about the place before any of them were born, and now in solitary state had the charge of the house. "What do you think, Annie," cried the first comer, "Mr Archie, the Dean, is made Bishop of London!" "Maister Archie made a Bishop! Ech, preserve us! Bishop o' London; atweel, it's a fell place to be bishop o'."

There had been no exclamation of delight, but on the contrary a pause of consternation as the old woman's mind travelled from the more than doubtful position of a bishop at all to the thought of the great Babylon,—in her idea the very centre and stronghold of Satan's kingdom.[1]

"Truly Maister Archie would need a double measure of grace to bear him through the dangers of such a position,"—and though one laughed at the quaintness of her speech, who could deny its truth?

A day or two later than this the morning sun shone brightly on the placid waters of the Lake of Thun, and the tourists of Interlaken were settling their arrangements for the day, while those who had received letters by the post just come in were silently busy with them in the balconies. The groups before the door of the principal hotel waited in patience for their associates to join them; suddenly they were startled by an outcry from above, and looking up they beheld to their astonishment the unusual spectacle of a respectable middle-aged gentleman dancing a sort of war-dance on the balcony, while flourishing 'The Times' newspaper over his head. "What is it? what is it?" flew from mouth to mouth; "has Wildman gone mad?" "No," said another proprietor of a 'Times,' "but the Dean of Carlisle has been made Bishop of London." There were many friendly voices to join in congratulation, and the new appointment furnished a pleasant subject during the expeditions of the day and at the *table d'hôte.* All agreed that the Queen could not have done better, for the heavy trial that had befallen the Dean secured the sympathies even of those who might secretly have thought that they would themselves have made ex-

[1] It was another old Scotswoman who, on hearing much good related of one on the Episcopal bench, replied after a pause of deep thought, "Weel, I'll no' say, tho' he be a Bishop, but he may be saved."

cellent bishops. In every group of tourists we may be sure that two-thirds belonged to the Church, and that therefore the interest excited by the news was extreme. The first thing the new Bishop did on arriving in London was to visit Fulham, where he and Mrs Tait had been asked to remain a week; and a most interesting week it was. Bishop Blomfield treated his successor with paternal kindness, giving him much information eminently useful to him on the subject of the diocese. He was suffering much at the time from pain and swelling in his limbs, but through all his quick humour never forsook him : Mrs Blomfield, doing her best to give him ease, remonstrated at the exclamations with which he rewarded her endeavour to make his legs more comfortable. "My dear," she said, "you really make a noise like a cow." "No wonder," he replied, "when you are hurting my calves!"

Here is the account given us by the newly made Bishop of the ceremony of doing homage and taking the oaths to the Queen as head of the Church :—

"We—that is, Longley, the new Bishop of Durham, and myself—were received by one of the Maids of Honour, who gave us an excellent luncheon, of which she partook with us. We were then taken to the ante-chamber, where we waited with all those who came in attendance at the Palace. I was then conducted by Sir George Grey into the Queen's closet (a very small room), where I found the Queen and Prince Albert. Having been presented by Sir George, I kneeled down on both knees before the Queen just like a little boy at his mother's knee; I placed my joined hands between hers, while she stooped her

head so as almost to bend over mine, and I repeated
slowly and solemnly the very impressive words of the
oath which constitutes the act of homage. After I
had risen from my knees the Queen said very kindly,
'I think this is the first time we have seen Dr Tait
here.'[1] Not knowing exactly what I ought to say,
I only replied by a very profound bow, and retired
to make way for the Bishop of Durham, who went
through the same ceremony. He had not escaped
so quietly from the ceremonial when he had been
consecrated Bishop of Ripon; his oath was then
taken to William IV., and no sooner had he risen
from his knees than the king suddenly addressed
him in a loud voice, thus: 'Bishop of Ripon! I
charge you, as you shall answer before Almighty
God, that you never by word or deed give aid or
encouragement to those d—d Whigs, who would
upset the Church of England.'[2]

"After I had left the Queen's closet I found myself
among all the Ministers of State—in fact, I was the
only man present who was not of the Cabinet. All
spoke to me very kindly. A short time after we
were joined by the Bishop of Durham.

"The doors at the end of the room were thrown
open, and discovered the Queen and the Prince
Consort seated at the head of a large table, round
which we were immediately gathered in council."

The new Bishop of London proceeded to form his
staff of chaplains, secretaries, &c., and considerable
alarm was excited among those who may be called
with propriety the Evangelical Alliance, by the ap-

---

[1] He had been more than once at the Queen's *levée*, but never before at
Windsor.

[2] The Bishop of Durham is himself the authority for this anecdote.

pearance of the name of Arthur Penrhyn Stanley
in the list of examining chaplains; but the Bishop
had known him intimately from his earliest college
days, and had formed a very high opinion not only
of his individual character but also of his great
knowledge of all the requisite subjects, and he felt
that he was thoroughly to be trusted.

CHAPTER XXI.

THE Bishop and Mrs Tait were in the following summer established in London House, which had meanwhile been undergoing extensive alterations, the chief of which gave a chapel to the house,—an important feature and a great blessing. Long vistas of work, ceaseless, unbounded, opened up before them, and gladly they obeyed the call "Come and help us," which to their quickened hearing seemed to sound from every quarter. Some one more cognisant of public affairs, with a mind of larger grasp and a more able pen, may relate the public duties into which the Bishop at once threw himself. I can but tell of what I saw and know; and this I know, that very soon, wherever she heard of sorrow or suffering, there Mrs Tait found admittance,—in the hospitals for old men and women, in the homes for sick or friendless children, in every place where suffering had a refuge, and in many quiet homes where sorrow reigned, she took with her the comfort wherewith she had herself been comforted.

How great is the wisdom of our God! He had passed the husband and the wife through the furnace of affliction that they might be better fitted for his own purposes of loving-kindness. Those darkened rooms at Carlisle, those dying children so meekly and trustfully resigning their innocent souls to the safe-keeping of their Redeemer, had formed a part of the mighty plan of love.

Christ came to destroy the works of the devil, whose work all misfortune surely is. Because of the evil sin has wrought, tears have watered the face of the earth, and sighs have mingled with the winds that blow over it; but Christ's own kingdom shall prevail notwithstanding; He fights and overcomes the foe with his own weapons wrested from him, and through misfortune had armed and equipped His servant before He placed him in the front of the battle.

Towards the end of the summer, that Sunday came round which is appointed for the service in St Paul's in behalf of all the charity school children in London. It is the metropolitan bishop who always preaches the sermon, and the desire to hear the new bishop naturally increased the usual interest. He took me with him in the carriage, together with Mrs Tait and Dean Hamilton. He told us not to speak to him, as he had had no time to write his sermon, and gave himself up to jotting down the various heads of the discourse that was in his mind.

The impression produced by the immense crowd that filled the body of the vast building, the galleries filled with myriads of· children winding round and round the dome, almost up to the vanishing point, is one that never can be forgotten. The long rows of childish faces, the little girls in their white tippets that looked like wings, seen through the dim, half-misty sunlight, were suggestive of the hosts of cherubim as represented by the old masters when they ventured in their pictures beyond the limits of human vision. I felt awestruck and overwhelmed, and then when my eyes fell upon my brother's single figure raised above the multitude below, with all those countless eyes bent upon him, I could have wept for sympathy and fear.

No need for fear; his thoughts were filled with his subject, and passed over the gazing crowds; but for sympathy! yes, there was room for that. The very subject, all that little children are, and are intended to become by Him who gathered them in His arms while He said, "of such is the kingdom of heaven," —that vibrated on the tenderest chords in the heart of the preacher, and his voice trembled a little as he dwelt upon those whose angels do always behold the face of their Father in heaven. But it was firm enough to plead their cause on earth, and to remind us how great is the responsibility of those who would leave to the withering canker of vice that early blossom of happiness which is natural to child-hood, and which drew from the Roman Empress Eudoxia that envying speech of hers that told how gladly she would have changed places with the little beggar girl who stood beside her chariot.

The Bishop was doing his best to awaken, or rather to restore, in the established Church the feeling of her true Evangelistic mission, not confining her teaching and her services to churches and cathedrals, but even as she gladly soothed the dying in their beds by carrying to them there the solemn rite of the Holy Communion, so under the canopy of heaven, in the streets, in the market-place, wherever her voice could be heard and listened to, to carry the Word of God. I had not heard of this idea of his, and was surprised, when one Sunday I looked in at St

James' Square, at being invited to accompany him to Covent Garden, where he was going to preach in the open air. Most gladly I went with him, first to the house of Mr Oakleey, where several friends interested in the movement were waiting for the Bishop; then very soon we were in the centre of the market-place in Covent Garden, where he at once stepped upon a sort of temporary pulpit just raised high enough to lift him above the crowd which quickly gathered round him. He chose for his text that passage of Scripture which describes the Apostles Andrew and Peter and the sons of Zebedee mending their nets, when the Lord Jesus called them to leave their work and follow Him for the new and more noble employment to which He destined them,—"I will make you fishers of men." The first sentence I distinctly heard as his voice rose above the listening crowd was, "The Apostles of the Lord Jesus Christ were nearly all—working men."

Closer and closer pressed the crowd, and most strangely varied were the countenances among them. The face of one man at no great distance quite fascinated me; never had I beheld so dark a scowl as that which gathered over him as with fixed gaze he looked at the preacher as though he would have liked to shoot him; gradually the scowl passed away and a look of deep interest took its place, softening into emotion. The message has reached that heart, I said to myself; "My word shall not return unto me void," was the promise that rose to my remembrance; he will carry it away with him.

Clear and sustained were the hymns that rose to the evening sky, many of the crowd lending their voices. Naturally there were books only with those who had accompanied the Bishop, and close to me was Lady Exeter, bending her tall figure over a small street boy that he might benefit by hers : the young urchin gave a quick glance into her face, and then with his little dirty finger followed the hymn line by line.

It is impossible to imagine a more striking or a more beautiful scene, for the slanting rays of the evening sun lit up faces and figures in the dense crowd and fell full upon the preacher, who, in his white episcopal robes, with his countenance so full of earnest feeling, and still so young, made a picture in himself. All who knew him then must remember the youthful appearance given by his curling hair and beardless face. I did not hear him elsewhere, but it was his open-air preaching which first established that bond of kindly relationship between him and the working classes that has never ceased.

Everywhere the Bishop was to be found with untiring energy, but as yet with marvellously sustained strength. From evening work at Bethnal Green, from all sorts of open-air meetings, with all sorts of audiences, he used to return faint and exhausted, unable to take the food necessary to sustain and to, as it were, rebuild him for the exertion of the morrow, — certain to have been settled beforehand ; some church to consecrate, some confirmations to hold, and the endless varieties of morning work in a diocese where the Bishop is willing to undertake it. Sometimes the amusing would blend itself with the gravity of extreme interest. At the consecration of one of the new churches a splendid procession moved through it, the Bishop of London in his robes at its head ; near him marched an official, the very personification of that species of dignity belonging to the Episcopal Church ; a turn at the corner of the building having

Q

brought him nearer, the solemn step quickened for a moment, and the Bishop heard in broadest Scotch a low whisper in his ear, "We've naething like this in *our* countrie, my lord,—I'm frae Dollar!"

Surely the wholesome smile this provoked, the very mention of Dollar calling up for an instant the vision of green hills and rushing waters, must have done him good, like the momentary unbending of an overstrained bow.

An amusing incident took place at Elmdon, Catharine's early home, which they visited about this time. It had been settled that the Bishop should preach in the old parish church of which his wife's father had been for so many years the incumbent, and the greatest interest was very naturally excited in the neighbourhood, vast numbers expressing their intention of coming to hear him. When lo! the day before, the clergyman of the parish, an out-and-out Calvinist, placed there by Mrs Lillingston, a Scotswoman of Elmdon Hall, intimated that he refused to allow the Bishop of London to preach in his church, as he did not consider him orthodox. Some amused wonder was naturally caused by this intimation, to which the Bishop replied that he should attend divine service in the parish church in the morning for the purpose of hearing the reverend gentleman preach, and that if he did not find anything to object to in his doctrine, he would certainly preach there himself in the afternoon. Accordingly, after morning service the Bishop went quietly into the vestry and said to the Vicar that, as he was happy to find nothing in the sermon he had just heard contrary to what he would himself have taught, he should keep his original intention and preach himself in the afternoon. To this turning of the tables the Vicar had nothing to reply, and accordingly the crowds who had assembled there to hear him were gratified.

His first Charge, made in November 1858, will be long remembered, at least by those who heard it, for it lasted five hours! and must have been very nearly the death of all concerned, from the terrible strain upon their attention, treating as it did of all the most important ecclesiastical questions that were at the time filling men's minds. "How did you get through it?" I afterwards asked the Bishop. "Did you not feel as though you were going to die?" "It gave me such a pain in my left leg that I thought it was coming off," was the absurd though true reply.

This Charge excited great attention in the country, through which it rapidly circulated. The earnest boldness with which it upheld Christ's Church as claiming the loving obedience of all, merging into one great eternal bond all futile questions which only disturbed men's minds, hindering the real advance of His kingdom, struck a responsive chord throughout the land, and everywhere for a short time it was the subject of conversation.

We were visiting one of our Northamptonshire neighbours, and at dinner I found by my side a young clergyman whom I did not know. Carrying on to him the conversation of my other neighbour, I asked him if he had been interested in the Bishop of London's Charge? "Extremely so," he replied, "and very much surprised to find so much that is good spoken by such a man." "Such a man," I repeated in great astonishment, "what do you mean? Do you know him?" "No, I do not; do you?" "Yes, I have known him intimately all my life." "Indeed!" said my clerical friend, becoming interested; "what, then, is the opinion you have formed of him? I should

have thought him a man whose religious views were
too wide to have any warmth in them,—that he cared
little for anything but the advancement of his own
ambitious views, in fact a mere University Commission
man; therefore I confess his Charge has taken me
by surprise." "It would not have done so had you
been better informed," I quietly replied, "for he is
a man whose one ambition is to forward the kingdom
of Christ; he is a man of no party, and of the deepest
feeling." Here I was interrupted by "He has, I have
heard, undergone great family affliction in the loss
of his children; that may have softened him." "He
has indeed suffered severely in the loss of five children
in a few weeks, but that was not needed to soften a
heart that was naturally full of kindness, though of
course the man who has suffered greatly himself will
always best know how to sympathise with and comfort
others. You may believe what I tell you, his character
is entirely and in every respect different from what
you have imagined." "I do believe it," he replied,
"and am glad to have met you to have heard all this."
Dinner was over. The ladies were about to retire,
and seeing Lord Bateman opposite us had been listening, much amused, to the conversation, I nodded to
him, saying, "I know that you will tell, so I will do it
myself," and turning to my neighbour said, "Before
we part, I must tell you, as you are certain to be told
the moment I have left the room, that the Bishop of
London is my brother; no one can know him as well
as I do." The poor man for a moment looked put
out, and then exclaimed, "Oh! what a shame to
have led me on to say all that; yet if I had not
been a fool I might have known it, for you are the
image of him, but it was too bad."

"It was quite right," I said very quietly; "it would

have been a great pity that you should have retained a totally wrong impression of him, and had I told you at once that I was his sister it would have been no good talking, for you would have received every word I said with suspicion; now I am sure you do not, for you must feel that no one can know him as I do, and that I have spoken only the simple truth."

And so we parted, all the better friends for the little scene.

There was compensation for the enormous work of the diocese in the charming life at Fulham, where the Bishop and his family always withdrew early in the London season. Thither resorted many whose talents and individual character made their society to be highly prized, while in the shade and coolness of the lovely garden they found a short and delightful repose from the bustle and din of London. They brought with them the various interests which occupied their thoughts, and nothing could be more delightful than the animated conversations which were the result. We often visited Fulham, and especially enjoyed their dinner-parties.

As a specimen, I remember finding myself placed between the then Bishop of Winchester, Sumner, a dear old man, still deserving in his looks and bearing the name given him in his youth, "the beauty of holiness," and Lord Auckland, the Bishop of Bath and Wells, whom, as he was an old friend of mine, I was glad to meet. He amused me by his observations on the other guests at table. My position, thus placed, was quiet enough, but on the other side of Bishop Sumner sat Mrs Tait, supported by Lord Campbell, our Scottish Chancellor, who, as he sat down, glancing round the table, exclaimed, "One, two, three, four—five—six—seven! bishops. What mischief is afoot to-day? There is something concocting we shall hear of by-

and-by." There was an infectious mirth in his lively conversation that was caught up all round; in fact, the presence of seven bishops was in itself a security for an amusing dinner-party, for I have observed that of all men there are none who more enjoy or are themselves more ready with good stories and lively conversation. I suppose the rebound from the pressure of grave care causes and requires this reaction. One of the guests was Macilvaine, Bishop of Ohio, who, with two really charming daughters, shone out as good specimens from far-off America. The two girls were, with their father, staying in the house, and thus gave an opportunity of rightly estimating the culture of their minds. I doubt if many of our own girls could have shown as varied and thorough a knowledge of our best authors; and our language did not suffer in their use of it, for only once or twice were we startled by one of those strange Americanisms which, though very expressive, are exceedingly like schoolboys' slang, and they did not speak through their noses. As for their father, there was in him so much refinement of manner that Lord Auckland at dinner drew my attention to it, adding, " He looks better than any of us."

Besides the bishops there was a good admixture of a different element, several of the political and literary characters of the day.

CHAPTER XXII.

THE INDIAN MUTINY—ARRAH—COLONEL TAIT'S DEATH.

IN the summer of 1857 our brother Tom (the "ancient warrior") had returned from his short essay to resume his military duties in India. Short as it was, it had wrought a greater change in him than all his campaigns had done before. He was so altered, so broken in health, that his brother James, who had come up from Scotland purposely to greet him on his arrival, met him and passed him without recognising him. In spite of his broken health, the life at Fulham was a great enjoyment to him. Notwithstanding the constant decrease of his bodily powers, his mind was as keen as ever in the interests of his profession and love of the Service to which the best years of his life had been devoted. It was with utter incredulity that he listened to the first tidings of the mutiny of the native troops in India. My son Baldwin had just been sent home, for the time incapable of service from serious illness; he and the Colonel, our two invalids, were to dine with us one evening. Our family party, with a few friends, were gathered round the table, but Baldwin's place was empty. He did not appear till ten o'clock, when, flushed and excited, he hurried into the drawing-room with the appalling news—all India was in revolt! "It is not true!"

thundered the Colonel; "there may be a rising among the natives, but there must be gross exaggeration about that, and the troops cannot have revolted. I pledge my life on the fidelity of my Irregulars, and the Sepoys are as true as steel." "It is too true," was the reply. "I heard it first at the Club in St James' Square; then I went off to the India House, found all there in a bustle and alarm, and there is no doubt about it." The Colonel was incredulous, and it was not till the arrival of mail after mail that he could be fully convinced of the extent of the calamity.

From this hour nothing else could be thought of: every family had ties in India, or sons that must forthwith be there. Anxiety filled every heart. Our son Herwald *was* there, could Baldwin go? The medical men laid hold of him, telling him that it was not a time for sick men to take the field, and that he would be utterly useless. For the Colonel it was out of the question, but both fretted at the bit that held them back.

We very soon returned to Courteenhall, our deepest interest in life being the arrival of the Indian mails. Horror after horror followed, as all may well remember who yet live to look back upon that time. By every mail we received most interesting letters from Herwald, whose situation, as magistrate of Arrah, was indeed most critical. Intelligence had been received that the three native regiments at Dinapore had mutinied, and it was hourly expected that they would be joined by all the rebels within reach and make a descent upon Arrah, where there was a prison and a treasure. The order had been given for the abandonment, as untenable, of the different stations by their civil officers; but Herwald remained, having had leave from the Commissioner to act according to his own judgment.

The suspense of each day was dreadful; and yet hope was stronger than fear. It is difficult from a distance to realise these things. One fine morning we drove to Northampton to secure the second delivery so soon as it arrived. The newspapers were eagerly scanned, and we took them on our way home to Delapre Abbey, to give our friends there the good tidings that so far no evil had happened in the Arrah district. Old General Bouverie, who had become blind, was sitting in his garden, and listened with much interest as we read the dreadful details of the progress of the mutiny. Thankful that at least it had not struck home, we left him, and went on our way to Courteenhall, and had nearly reached the gates when I heard my husband give a sudden exclamation and saw that he had dropped the newspapers. I picked them up, and read at the end of a long paragraph from the 'Homeward Mail' from India these words: "They have murdered all the Europeans in Arrah, and the worst of it is that the detachment from Buxar will fall into the trap too, for there is no way of warning them. Havelock will get no reinforcements, and will be driven back."

How we got home I know not. When the newspapers were further examined, it was found that the 'Indian Mail' stated: "It appears that the mutineers from Dinapore, after quitting that station, advanced against Arrah, a large civil station twenty-five miles west of Dinapore, the residents of which place were, unfortunately, sanguine of their ability to resist an attack for a time, and are said to have applied for a detachment of European troops, in place of adopting the more prudent course of retreat. The result was that the whole of the Europeans at the station, about fifty, were massacred. This disastrous event was succeeded by another. Two steamers had been despatched with troops for the relief of Arrah ; one of them grounded, and we have no further information respecting it. From the other a body of 200 European troops were landed, and fell into an ambush where nine officers and upwards of 100 men are said to have been cut off. The importance of these events, considering the command they gave to the mutineers of the line of communication between Calcutta and Benares, cannot but be obvious to every one."

How, after reading this, we could have any hope I know not, but the newspapers contained many contradictory rumours, and knowing that Herwald was full of resource, and had courage and ready wit to meet every emergency, I felt as though his energy and daring could not be overcome. Still,—but to look on the losing side after all the horrors we had read was too dreadful to be borne. Mr Wildman, who was with us, went to town next day to see if at the India House any reliable intelligence had reached them. He returned in the evening looking so worn and castdown that we dared not question him. In a sort of slow monotone he recapitulated all that had been said to him at the India House, the Horse Guards, the clubs, &c.,—not a ray of light, not a hope. At last he produced from his pocket a copy of the 'Morning Post,' saying as he opened it, "I found this at my Club, but no one gives it any attention, for they say it cannot be true." I darted upon the place to which he pointed, and read this blessed little paragraph :—

"'Morning Post,' *Sept.* 18*th.*—The 17th and 27th Madras Native Infantry were advancing up the Grand Trunk Road, and those besieged at Arrah were relieved by troops from Haggupore."[1]

[1] Sharupore.

"Saved! saved!" I cried aloud, and never had another fear. The words were few, but they seemed written in letters of light. I believe the others thought Matilda and myself mad, but we felt safe. Then letter after letter from friends of Herwald arrived giving us the glorious details. Paragraph after paragraph in 'The Times,' copied from the Indian mails, thrilled us through and through with the sense of escape from unheard-of dangers.

The best account of the whole affair is contained in the following official despatch :—

SIR,—I have the honour to forward for the information of the honourable the Lieutenant-Governor the following narrative of our extraordinary defence and providential escape. On the evening of Saturday, July 25th, I received an express from Dinapore warning us that a disturbance was apprehended on that day, but giving us no other information. On the morning of July 26th a Sowar whom I had posted at Koilwur Ghat on the Soane came in and reported that numbers of Sepoys had crossed, and that more were crossing. I found that Mr ——— had contented himself with sending over for the boats to the Arrah side the night before, but when leaving had failed to destroy them, as he had promised to do.

The police, I imagine, bolted at the first alarm. All efforts to ascertain the amount of the force of the rebels were unavailing, and the police left the city on Sunday the 26th. Thinking it highly inadvisable to abandon the station when the rebels might be few, and having fifty Sikhs on the spot, and finding the rest of the officers of the station of the same opinion, and the few residents of the district who had come in to us willing to remain, we, on the night of Sunday 26th, went into a small bungalow, previously fortified as much as possible by Mr Boyle, the district engineer of the railway company. . . . We had enough ottah and grain for some days of *short allowance,* and a good deal of water for ourselves, but owing to the shortness of the notice, nothing but the barest necessaries could be brought in, and the Sikhs had only a few days' water; but as we expected the rebels to be followed up immediately, we had not much anxiety on that score.

On Monday the 27th July, about eight A.M., the insurgent Sepoys—the whole of the 7th, 8th, and 40th Native Infantry —arrived in the station, and having first released the prisoners,

rushed to the collectorate, where they were at once joined by
the najebs, and looted the treasure amounting to 85,000 rs.
This did not take long, and they then charged our bungalow
from every side; but being met with a steady and well-directed
fire, they changed their tactics, and hiding behind the trees
with which the compound is filled, and occupying the outhouses and Mr Boyle's residence, which was unfortunately
within sixty yards of our fortification, they kept up an incessant and galling fire on us the whole day. They were joined
by numbers of Koor Singh's men, and the Sepoys repeatedly
declared that they were acting under his express orders; and
after a short time he was seen on the parade, and remained
during the siege. Every endeavour was made by the rebels
to induce the Sikhs to abandon us; heavy bribes were offered
to them, and their own countrymen employed as mediators.
they treated every offer with derision, showing perfect obedience and discipline. On the 28th two small cannon were
brought to play upon our bungalow, one throwing 4-lb. shot,
and these were daily shifted to what the rebels thought to be
our weakest points. Finally, the largest was placed on the
roof of Mr Boyle's dwelling-house, completely commanding the
inside of our bungalow and the smaller behind it, at a distance
of about twenty yards. The cowardice, want of unanimity, and
the ignorance of our enemies alone prevented our fortification
being brought down about our ears During the entire siege,
which lasted seven days, every possible stratagem was prac-
tised against us. The cannon were fired as frequently as they
could prepare shot, with which they were at first unprovided,
and incessant assaults were made upon the bungalow. Not
only did our Sikhs behave with perfect coolness and patience,
but their untiring labour met and prevented every threatened
disaster. Water began to run short,—a well 18 feet by 4 feet
was dug in less than twelve hours. The rebels raised barricades
on the top of the opposite house,—our own grew in the same
proportion. A shot shook a weak place in our defence,—the
place was made twice as strong as before. We began to feel
the want of animal food and short allowance of grain. A sally
was made at night, and four sheep brought in; and finally,
when we ascertained beyond a doubt that the enemy were
undermining us, a countermine was quickly dug.

On the 30th the troops sent to our relief from Dinapore were
attacked and beaten back close to the entrance of the town. On
the next day the rebels returned, telling us that they had anni- ·
hilated our relief, and offering the Sikhs and the women and
children (of which there were none with us) their lives and
liberty if they would give up the Government officers.

August 1st.—We were all offered our lives, and leave to go to Calcutta, if we would give up our arms. On the 2nd the greater part of the Sepoys went out to meet Major Eyre's field force, and on their being soundly thrashed, the rest of them deserted the station; and that night we went out and found that their mine had reached our foundations, and a canvas tube filled with gunpowder was lying handy to blow us up, in which, however, I do not think they would have succeeded, as their powder was bad, and another stroke of the pick would have broken into our countermine. We also brought in the one gun which they had left on the top of the opposite house. During the whole siege only one man, a Sikh, was severely wounded, though two or three got scratches and blows from splinters and bricks.

Everybody in our garrison behaved well: I should be neglecting a duty did I omit to mention specially Mr Boyle, to whose engineering skill and untiring exertions we, in a great measure, owe our preservation; and Mr Colvin, who rendered the most valuable assistance, and who rested neither night nor day, and took on himself far more than his share of every disagreeable duty. In conclusion, I must earnestly beg that his honour the Lieutenant-Governor will signally reward the whole of our gallant little detachment of Sikhs, whose service and fidelity cannot be overrated. The Jemadar should at once be made Soubadar, and many of the rest are fit for promotion, and when required I will submit a list with details.—I have the honour to be, your obedient servant, H. C. WAKE,
Officiating Magistrate, Shahabad.

This and the diary kept by Herwald upon the walls of the bungalow during the week of peril give the whole account of the matter.

DIARY

KEPT ON THE WALLS OF THE BUNGALOW AT ARRAH, BY H. C. WAKE, MAGISTRATE.

"We went into our fortified bungalow on the night of Sunday, the 26th July, one jemadar, two havildars, two naiks, and forty-five privates, and bhistie, and cook of Captain Rattray's Sikh Police Battalion; Mr

Littledale, judge ; Mr Combe, officiating collector ; Mr Wake, officiating magistrate ; Mr Colvin, assistant ; Dr Hall, civil assistant surgeon ; Mr Field, subdeputy opium agent ; Mr Anderson, his assistant ; Mr Boyle, district engineer to the railway company ; Synd Azeem Oodein Hosein, deputy collector ; Mr Dacosta, moonsiff ; Mr Godfrey, schoolmaster ; Mr Cook, officiating head clerk of the collectorate ; Mr Tait, secretary to Mr Boyle ; Messrs Delpeiron and Hoyle, railway inspectors ; and Mr David Souza.

"The police abandoned the town on the Sunday, and as we were wholly unable to estimate the force coming against us, we thought it right to remain in the station, trusting to Dinapore for relief.

"*July 27th.*—The insurgent Sepoys arrived in the morning, and all attacked us in force. They were joined by the najebs,[1] or some of them, and numbers of Koor Singh's men. The Sepoys have repeatedly declared that they were acting under Koor Singh's orders, and endeavoured to seduce to their side the Sikhs[2] who have hitherto behaved nobly, refusing to have anything to do with them, and showing perfect obedience and discipline.

"9 A.M. *same day.*—The najebs are firing on us with the rest.

"*July 28th.*—Two small cannons are brought to play upon the bungalow ; they load them with hammered iron balls and brass door-handles, and such-like, fired at us all day from behind their barricades, but could not get the range with the biggest, which seems to carry heavyish metal. The little one has done us no serious damage hitherto, only one man

---

[1] An armed police corps, furnishing jail and army guards to the civil station.

[2] Of Captain Rattray's Bengal Police Battalion.

(a Sikh) wounded, but seriously—a ball in the head. The scoundrels skulked behind trees and walls and Boyle's house, which, unfortunately, is within eighty yards (afterwards measured fifty), so we cannot tell how many are hit.

"*July 29th*, 7 A.M.—This morning they were up to something new; thousands are collected, probably the greater part villagers, and disbanded Sepoys, collected by Koor Singh.

" 5 P.M.—No harm done; they can't touch the bungalow with the big gun. The skulks won't come within shot, though now and then one is knocked over by rifle shots.

" 11½ P.M.—Heard commencement of engagement between troops sent to our relief and the rebels.

"*July 30th.*—About 5 A.M. one of the Sikhs sent to our relief came in and told us that only 300 Europeans and 90 Sikhs had been sent to our relief,—God aid them! Our well under the lower story is nearly finished. The relief has evidently had to retire, but we hear (from the Sikhs) that artillery is coming. There are four feet of water in the well! *N.B.*—The well is about eighteen feet deep, and was dug within twelve hours. In the afternoon made a sally into the compound and brought in some sheep, and two birds in cages that had neither food nor water for five days.

"*July 31st.*—The rebels have got the largest of the guns close up to the house, and fire on us protected by the garden wall (*N.B.*—through a hole). Several of the balls (round and cast-iron) have struck the lower story, but hitherto have done no serious damage. The balls are about four pounds, and how they do so little damage we cannot imagine. We have reason to apprehend that the Sepoys are mining us from the outhouses to the south. We have com-

menced a countermine. The Sikhs are offered their
lives and liberty if they hand over the judge, magistrate, and collectors.—The ladies and children, too !!!
are not to be injured !!!!

"*Saturday, August 1st.*—No cannonade till half-past
five P.M. Occasional small-arms firing all day. No
one injured, except one Sikh had the wind knocked
out of him by the bricks displaced by cannon-shot.
Several rebels supposed to have been killed by long
shots. They are raising strong barricades on the
roof of the opposite house, from which they are
likely to give us serious annoyance, as they can see
right into the upper verandah. The shaft of the
countermine has been sunk to the depth of about
seven feet, and the gallery carried off towards the
south, and there stopped under the outer face of the
wall. In the evening we were informed that it was
the Soubadar's wookum !!! that all our lives were to
be spared if we would give up our arms, and we
should be sent to Calcutta ! Firing from the big
gun, which they had placed on the roof of the big
house, kept on all night. Two alarms during the
night; but finding us prepared on both occasions, no
attack was made except with musketry.

"*Sunday, August 2nd.*—Guns fired three times
between daybreak and 11 A.M. Little musketry,
few rebels to be seen, gallery progressing.

"*Sunday, August 2nd.*—Major Eyre defeated the
rebels, and on the 3rd we came out.

Vivat Regina !

Written with the stump of a pencil on the wall at
any moment that could be snatched, in case we
should be scragged.

"·HERWALD WAKE."

The building was but a billiard-room built on open arches, which were filled up with loose bricks, white-washed over to look like solid wall. Had the mutineers persevered in any one of their plans, they must have succeeded in a few hours; or had they made up their minds to risk a hand-to-hand fight, they must have carried the place by assault. They tried to starve them out—to smoke them out by burning large quantities of red pepper to windward,—to drive them out by the stench of the decomposing bodies of their own horses which they had driven up and shot close to the bungalow. They strove to seduce the Sikhs by offering 500 rupees to each if they would deliver up the Europeans; but these gallant fellows only made game of their offers, calling to them to come a little nearer that they might hear better, and when they had tempted them within reach, sending an answer in the shape of a shower of bullets.

Herwald having, at the head of his fifty Sikhs, gone with Major Eyre in pursuit of Koor Singh and the retreating rebels, we did not hear from himself for some time. From the papers we learned that they had taken and destroyed Koor Singh's stronghold and scattered his troops.

It is permissible for his mother to add the following extract from Major Eyre's despatch, dated " Koor Singh's Palace, Jugdispore, August 13, 1857 ": "Mr Herwald Wake, of the Bengal Civil Service, nobly sustained the reputation already acquired by his heroic defence of the fortified house at Arrah against overwhelming odds; he was gallantly seconded by Mr J. C. Colvin, Civil Service."

In so united a family as ours, the anxiety, the alarm, changed into thankful joy, had been fully shared; but no one had so intensely felt all the

R

circumstances of the situation as the dear Colonel, for he alone thoroughly understood all its dangers. He had spent nearly a lifetime in India, and his affectionate heart was wrung by the horrors committed there. The whole history of that fearful time affected his enfeebled frame. When the measures for amalgamating the two services were brought forward, and he foresaw that there would be no more an Indian Army, he could not suppress his feelings, but strenuously opposed the project. Few ventured to express so vehement an opposition as he did at those meetings presided over by the Duke of Cambridge, the Commander-in-Chief, who saw nothing but advantage in the proposed measure. This opposition was founded upon his observation of the evil effects of what he used to call the red-tapeism of the Queen's Service : he felt convinced that in a country like India, where quickness of thought and promptness of action were needed at every turn, the official delays attending the movements of the British army would be fatal. It was natural for a man who had so long commanded his Irregular Cavalry so to think, and the kindly nature of the Duke took no offence at the violence of his opposition, but, sympathising with the feeling of the gallant old soldier, he soothed while he reasoned with him.

Alas! the agitations of those debates hurried on the end. We were together for a few days after Christmas, and it was evident to me that he no longer looked forward to any part he had to play in life's shifting scenes. The impression he gave me was that he considered his work as done.

When the Bishop and Mrs Tait came to town he was persuaded by them to leave his lodging close to his club and stay with them at London House.

It was a merciful Providence that suggested the kind thought, for he had scarcely been established there when Catharine observed symptoms of illness that alarmed her, and wrote to us at Courteenhall to come immediately. His throat was much affected, and before night diphtheria declared itself. John and James were telegraphed for from Edinburgh; our two sisters, Lady Sitwell and Mrs Wildman, were already close at hand. All were thoroughly alarmed. He could not swallow, and spoke with difficulty; he required constant help, and a nursing sister was sent for—a charming person, so gentle and refined in all her ways. She and I together watched by him during the night. He beckoned me to come close to him, and said in a low voice, "Dear Chattie, I am dying." I replied, "I do not know, my darling, but as it may be so it is well that you should think so. Dear Tom, I have a letter of yours that you wrote to me on the eve of the first of the three days' battle of Ferozeshah, at Nuzeerabad. You said in it that the army was ready for a great battle on the next day; that all were about to lie down to sleep with the certainty that it would be the last night for many; that in that thought you committed yourself to the Saviour in whom you trusted, and were calm and in peace. Dear Tom, it is just so to-night. If you have now to pass through life's last battle, Christ has beforehand secured the victory. Remember the night before Ferozeshah." He smiled and said, "I remember it well; Christ *is* indeed, as then, my only hope."

.   .   .   .

And thus—with his brothers and sisters round him, in the house of his youngest brother—passed away the man whose life had been one of peril. In many a

battlefield he had charged at the head of his brave
"Irregulars"; in their long marches they had swept
through deserts and camped in the jungle. He died
in peace, in a peaceful home, with loving voices mur-
muring over him the prayers of the Church.

There was alarm lest there should be infection from
the diphtheria of which he died, and at the instance of
the medical men the family dispersed, to meet again at
the funeral, which took place at Fulham. He was
buried there in the churchyard close to the private
door which leads to the Palace garden.

CHAPTER XXIII.

THE BISHOP'S VISIT TO RANNOCH—OFFER OF
ARCHBISHOPRIC OF YORK.

IN the summer of 1862 the Archbishopric of Canterbury became vacant by the death of Sumner, and the country, till Longley was appointed, was filled by speculations as to who should be his successor. Leaving these behind him, the Bishop of London went off with his family to Scotland; and having established his children at Seaview he, with Mrs Tait, made a charming visit to old Lady Menzies at Rannoch, the widow of Sir Neil Menzies, a Highland laird well known for his scientific management of trees, possessor of two beautiful places, Castle Menzies, and Rannoch on Loch Rannoch. She was a spirited old lady, residing on her estates, cultivating and improving in a manner of which few farmers were capable. At eighty years of age she took personal charge of her domain, was about everywhere in the early morning, and devoted the afternoon and evening to the pleasure and amusement of her guests, taking them over moor and mountain, wherever she considered they would be most interested. Some of the wildest scenery of the Highlands was within reach, and among other places one was of special interest—the cave wherein Prince Charlie lay so long concealed from the search of the Duke of Cumberland's soldiers. The day after the arrival of the Bishop and Mrs Tait an expedition was determined on, and a large party, well provided with attendants, left the house mounted on ponies, and taking with them a douce animal laden with panniers which contained everything necessary for food and comfort. Nothing could be more beautiful than the scene chosen for their halt on the shores of Loch Ericht. Absorbed in its beauty, before the luncheon party could persuade themselves to stir from the place the September sun was already low in the glorious sky, the loch glittering in his slanting beams, the deep shadows of the nearer rocks growing each moment deeper, and the amethyst colours gathering round the more distant mountains as ray after ray first caught and then vanished from their peaks: all told that evening was at hand.

"If we're to gang on to t'ither side, we munna bide here," said the gillie in charge, and forthwith the party mounted, old Lady Menzies leading the way,—not, as the others, upon a hill pony that might be trusted, but upon a spirited Arab, who feeling the soft sand beneath his feet was minded of his native deserts, and manifested a strong desire to roll, showing his displeasure at being prevented by violently kicking and plunging, to Mrs Tait's infinite terror. Glancing up the steep glen before them, she for the first time realised the dangers of the way. A friendly voice in her ear from one of the gentlemen gave warning, "That pony on which the Bishop is mounted is sure to come down." This was quite enough. "Stop! I insist upon it. The Bishop shall not ride that animal!" was the shrill command that arrested the company; and in the fast-growing darkness the obedient husband changed his steed. It was only in time; at once night closed in, the short Highland day was over, and darkness so complete fell upon them that no one could see the other.

A guide was at the bridle of each pony, but none of the guides knew exactly where they were; so suddenly had the utter darkness fallen, they only felt that it was now impossible to reach Prince Charlie's cave; that to return by the loch was equally out of the question, and that their only certainty was that when the top of the glen before them was reached the path lay along the edge of a dangerous precipice. They could but feel their way with hand and foot as they strove through the murky night to catch a gleam of the white pony that had purposely been placed first as leader of the band,—not that his rider knew the way better than any of them, but so far was certain, that where he had reached they might follow. The feeling of the visitors, complete strangers to the place, may be guessed; and from time to time the silence was broken by a plaintive voice, "Are you safe, my Bishop?" And so they rode on.

Suddenly through the midnight darkness the most terrific yell, the most horrible outcry, broke from the very midst of them, causing an indescribable panic. The whole band was thrown into confusion; nothing could be seen, but much was heard,—a rush through the darkness with violent clattering sounds. What was it?

The old Lady's Arab, impatient member of the slow procession, tired of thus poking his way in silence, and offended at being obliged to follow the sumpter pony, had relieved his feelings by a vicious bite, fastening his teeth in the poor beast's hindquarters. The atrocious pain and this sudden onslaught had so terrified the victim that, uttering that dreadful cry seldom heard, but like nothing else in the whole world, the yelling shriek of a horse in sudden agony, he broke away from his guide and dashed up the hill, scattering from his panniers as he went the whole luncheon paraphernalia, china, glass, knives, forks, and food. Where he fled up the rocks, as though pursued by demons, no mortal could follow. Loudly rose the plaintive cry, "Are you safe, my Bishop?" and the confusion subsiding, once more the party moved on in silence. At last there was a glad shout, "The sheepfold! we know where we are now"; and with assured steps the ponies clattered along, man and beast restored to life by the certainty of the way.

The sun had set at five. Seven hours they had toiled along their painful way, for it was past midnight when the house was reached, and the whole party descended at the doors thrown wide open to receive them. The Lady, passing into the well-lighted hall, gave the order to her butler as coolly as if nothing had happened, "Have dinner on the table as soon as possible,—we shall be ready in a few minutes." And at one o'clock, refreshed and benefited by a rapid toilet, they all sat down to dinner as though it had been the usual hour.

Right glad were our Bishop and his wife to find themselves safely in bed at 2 A.M. Soundly they slept, when at seven a tap at the door roused them to new efforts. "My Lady wishes to know whether you will prefer to ride or to go in the spring-cart to the hills this afternoon?" Yesterday's long ride had left them sufficiently tired to be thankful for the offer of the spring-cart; and as nothing could ever induce the old Lady to set out early enough to return home before sunset, they again had the glorious scene among the mountains, this time intensified by the really grand sight that broke upon them as they were sitting on the rocks finishing luncheon.

High up against the sky appeared on the top of the near hill a multitude of beautiful Highland cattle, a principal part of the property of the estate, their rich colouring burnished by the slanting rays. Led by a magnificent bull, down they poured into the pasture below, each one of them in itself a study for Rosa Bonheur. The very sight of the bull with his enormous curled head and chest was enough to have put the whole party to flight, but the Lady at once went in among them, called him by his name, patting his shaggy neck, and talking to each of them in motherly fashion well understood by them.

"Would you like to go to Glencoe?" was now her question. "What is the distance?" "Thirty miles." "And no possibility of food or rest," whispered the same friendly voice that had the day before given warning about the Bishop's pony. The offer was declined, and as they drove home the Lady amused her guests by the account of an expedition she had made with a large party some time before to Glencoe.

She related how on that occasion, on their return, night had closed upon them toiling on, weary, hungry, and spent, without the possibility of rest or refreshment. "For there is not anywhere an inn," some one had said dolefully, "and it is not far from midnight." "Never mind," had replied the spirited old Lady, "my brother's house is only two miles from the road; I will find you there everything you want,— follow me." And striking off the road, in a short time they found themselves approaching a large house, more to be guessed at than actually discerned through the darkness. "Hush!" said she, "not one word or sound; they are all asleep,—wait for me here."

She dismounted, and knowing every, yard of her way she went straight to a little window at the back, which she explained was always left open, in the scullery. Active as a cat, she climbed through it; in two minutes she reappeared at a small door, bringing with her the key of the stables, and with a renewed caution to silence led the way to them. The watch-dog knew her well and made no objection. Quickly the horses were comfortably disposed of and all their wants supplied. Back to the house and into it she led her party, and set them all to assist her arrangements for supper, which her perfect knowledge of every corner of kitchen, cupboard, pantry, and larder soon rendered very complete. The table was laid in the dining-room, and during an hour of complete enjoyment, much enhanced by the whispering mystery that was needed, the whole party refreshed themselves to their hearts' content, and between two and three in the morning departed as they had come, without having roused one person. Having seen the last of her guests out of the house, the Lady re-entered it in order to relock the door from the inside, and through the little back window she let herself out as she had let herself in, with a keen enjoyment of the joke, more like eighteen than eighty. The horses were led back to their starting-point, and the whole party, refreshed and highly amused, proceeded blithely on their homeward route. A few days afterwards Lady Menzies received a letter from her brother, who, having heard of her visiting Glencoe, expressed his regret that she had not taken him on her way, and then added that a most extraordinary thing had happened in his house.

It had been entered by burglars in the middle of the
night, apparently through the scullery window, who
had made free with everything in the house; but the
most extraordinary thing of it all was that they did
not seem to have committed any actual robbery
except having emptied the larder for their own benefit,
the remains of a plentiful supper having been left on
the dining-table, which had been found spread out in
the most orderly fashion.

The country people who dwelt in the glens and
mountains round were quite convinced that the
spirited old Lady was a witch, and that she was
greatly assisted in her various performances by a
friendly warlock, an old gentleman, Bob Cheape,
who used to make her long visits at Rannoch;
and they were confirmed in this latter opinion by
the fact that he had not died the death of other
men, but had disappeared in flames and smoke,—
the truth being that the poor old man had dropped
a lucifer-match on his bedclothes and was burnt
to death. They had little doubt that Lady Menzies
would follow in like manner. Meanwhile she lived
on for several years after this visit of the Archbishop's,
during which time she retained all her peculiarities,
among which was her style of dress. In the mornings
she always wore the same short plain black dress,
reserving her full splendour for the Assemblies and
balls of Edinburgh, at which she invariably appeared
in white satin, the petticoat very short, her bare neck
and arms adorned with pearls, and three ostrich
feathers nearly upright on her head. On minor
occasions she wore a still more girlish attire of
white muslin. She was an extremely good dancer,
particularly distinguishing herself in the Highland
reel. Animated and agreeable in her conversation

to every one, to young people she was peculiarly
kind and amiable,, unless they unhappily belonged
to her own family,—for, strange to say, she could
not keep the peace with any one of them, and
lived on bad terms with them all, with the exception of her second son, Fletcher Menzies: of
too kindly a disposition to live at enmity with
any of his family, he had taken pains to conciliate
his mother.

After leaving Loch Rannoch the Bishop and Mrs
Tait turned their steps south, but on their way
circumstances occurred which can be best explained
by Mrs Tait's letter :—

Private.   DRUMMOND CASTLE, CRIEFF,
                                              Oct 1.

MY DEAREST CHATTIE,—We have been living in deep retirement so as to escape the storm which raged in the ecclesiastical
world, and calmly to await God's will at this time for His Church
and for us. On Friday we heard that the dear Archbishop of
York was to go to Canterbury, and at once we prepared to return south for our own dear Bishop to resume his work of
intense interest in London. Having had a kind invitation here
we accepted it, intending to reach Cromer, where our children
are, on Saturday; but lo! just as we were going into church
at Weem on Sunday afternoon we met the post, saw a large
"Palmerston" outside a letter, and within as follows (note
inserted in the Bishop's hand, "which you are on no account
to read to any human being except Sir Charles") :—

"MY DEAR LORD,—I am authorised by the Queen to propose to you
to take charge of the Archbishopric of York, which will become vacant
by the transfer of the present Archbishop to the See of Canterbury, and
I hope that this proposal may be agreeable to you.—Yours faithfully,
                                              "PALMERSTON."

The Bishop has written to ask for a few days to consider, and
his dear heart is torn within him. To me, at first sight, it seems
a wonderful ordering of God, for the possibility never came into
our mind. I do not think his poor constitution would stand
many more years of London work, and yet I cannot say I
could, or did, for a moment covet for him the Archbishopric

of Canterbury. If it came clearly and unsought from the hand of God—well. Now this offer has come, what do you think? Ask Sir Charles to send the Bishop a line to meet us at the Station Hotel, York, by return of post, and be sure you earnestly seek that God will guide our dear Bishop to a right decision. Only those who know what he feels his work to be in London will know what it would be to him to give it up. And at present the duties and interests of the new post cannot find due place in his mind. I shall write to you at once when the decision is made. We go to the Cottage to-morrow, and on to York on Friday, where we shall expect our letters, &c., &c.

When they arrived at the Cottage, very naturally his health was his brothers' chief consideration. Their advice was that he should come to no decision till he and Catharine had seen Bishopthorpe, the residence of the Archbishops of York. They visited it on their way up, and wrote to the various members of his family asking for their ideas on the subject.

This was all very well; but I feel certain that his mind was made up from the first. His heart was in his London work, and he could not transfer his interest and his affections. My husband thought that the immense labour of the London diocese would kill him, and in reply to his letter counselled the acceptance of York, which, it appeared to him, would be comparatively a bed of rest.

I knew my brother better. Yorkshire!—containing the wolds with their half-educated inhabitants—a bed of rest to a man who would consider himself responsible for their souls if he suffered them to remain in ignorance!

My letter, I fear, was at utter variance with my husband's. I told him that if he gave up London for York he would be as a man forcibly separated from the wife he loved, and given in marriage to one who suited him not.

He decided for himself. In the second week of October we received the following letters :—

PALACE, NORWICH,
Oct. 6, 1862.

MY DEAREST CHATTIE,—After long and earnest consideration the Bishop has written to Lord Palmerston to say that he must decline the Archbishopric of York, and so I am thankful to say we remain in his beloved sphere of work, London. I have no doubt this decision is right; when we meet we can talk over all the matter. I do not think a northern home would have suited him even in health, and we must set that against the work of London. Our minds are now in a great calm after the storm. We did not get any letter from you or Sir Charles, so you will write to us to the Victoria Hotel, Cromer. We hope to reach our darlings there to-day. Craufurd has got into the Upper School at Eton, and seems quite happy there. . . .

CROMER, *Oct.* 10.

MY DEAREST CHATTIE,—Your letter made us laugh very much this morning, but is perfectly true. If you could only have seen the Bishop's long face those days of uncertainty! No smile came near it, but, with a look of distress as we neared York, he said, "Well, I suppose we shall have to go to this place." He is now as bright as ever, but wishes you to know it is six and not four years that he has been Bishop of London. I hope, dearest, that nothing will tempt us away from here till the end of the month; possibly in December, just after the Visitation is over, we may make a run to Folkestone for a few days and see you there, should all be well. This is a charming little place—such nice country and miles of sand, hard, and good for walking or riding. My darlings are so happy here. Our best love.—Your most loving sister,   CATHARINE TAIT.

No doubt since the Bishop had decided to remain, Lord Palmerston was glad he did so, for he was too acute not to feel satisfied that, if able to stand the tremendous pressure, there was no man more fitted to battle with the difficulties. He constantly consulted him on all sorts of affairs that had any reference to those subjects of which he considered him likely to be a better judge than himself. Not that he always approved his judgment. I remember an amusing and characteristic specimen of this.

"What do you think of the proposal that is now made of changing the order of baptism in our Church, and making the father to be sponsor of his own child?"

"I think," was the Bishop's reply, "that it would be well to do so when a proper person cannot be found to undertake the office."

"I don't agree with you at all, I don't agree with you at all," was the rapid rejoinder; "it is often so difficult to find them that it would be doing away with godfathers altogether. Where would Assheton Smith have been without his godfather? He left him £50,000."

CHAPTER XXIV.

DRURY'S ILLNESS — COURTEENHALL AND VILLAGE FEAST — SIR
CHARLES WAKE'S DEATH — MALVERN — THE SKATE ROCK —
WESTON-SUPER-MARE—CHARLIE AND H.M.S. *BULLDOG*.

1863 began for us in sorrow. We were at Dover
for the winter, hopeful of benefit to my husband's
rapidly failing health. Our poor Philip, again and
again thrown out of active employment by acute
suffering, was with us. Drury was gone down to
Northamptonshire to hunt. Suddenly we heard that
he was prostrated by illness. I went to him at once,
and found him paralysed from head to foot. So
suddenly had this come upon him that, in the house
of a kind friend[1] with whom he had intended to
remain two nights, he lay helpless for six weeks before he was able to be carried across his father's park
to Courteenhall, where Sir Charles and Philip and
Matilda joined us.

Shall I ever forget the procession when, as though
upon his bier, my bright active Drue was carried by
six men, with the kind ministering friend, Mr Gregory,
following, down the hill, across the park, into the
house through the windows of the saloon, and there
laid down motionless? And this, after so many years,
was the result of that unceasing ride across the

[1] The Rev. Maze Gregory, vicar of Roade.

Balkans, six days and seven nights in the saddle, in the vain hope of preventing, by means of the despatches he bore, the Crimean War. The unnaturally protracted fatigue had so weakened the attachments which join the head to the spine that each violent effort, each jump or fall, imperceptibly increased the evil, and this was the result! To himself the breakdown was not quite so sudden as to us, for he had been conscious of being unfit for so much exertion as usual during the previous autumn, which he had spent upon the Highland moors,—his gun had been too heavy for him.

The long winter lengthened into spring, spring into summer, and still he lay helpless; but his unfailing patience and good-humour helped us to bear the heavy burden. Dear Bishop Archie came again and again, and indeed we needed all the comfort that could be given. It was a lovely summer, we almost lived in the garden, and the family group looked like an Eastern encampment. Drury on his couch, sheltered from the fresh June wind by screens hung with shawls of every colour; his dear old father seated near him, bending forward on his staff, with his long white beard as white as snow, looking like some ancient patriarch in his latter days, surrounded with young men, maidens, and children, for every age was represented there; and among them all our Bishop, with his dark curled head showing distinctly against the bright green of the mighty wych elm, which might have canopied an army. His conversation was our greatest cheer, equally welcome to Sir Charles and his sons. Mercifully our sailor was with us, and was told by the medical men that he must not leave us; so he remained with his wife, the granddaughter of the old General Knollys whom the barricades of Paris had brought into our circle in the terrible "trois jours" of 1830. Her third child was born about this time, and named Drury.

In July the usual village *fête* went on, more beautiful than ever, with the tables spread before every cottage door for the different families and their guests, and we and the Rectory had each our table as usual. As the darkness fell, every window in every cottage was illuminated, as they always had been, by lights that shone bright upon the villagers as they danced down the village street,—if that can be called a street which has cottages covered with roses on one side and the green park on the other.

When it became late and the moon shone down in all her glory, the dancing ceased, and the voices, hushed for a moment, rose together with a wave of sound in "God save the Queen"; that died away; again a moment's silence, and then arose, solemn and sweet to the moonlit sky, the evening hymn, "Glory to Thee, my God, this night, for all the blessings of the light." When the last words had died away, the usual good-night was exchanged between the Hall and the Village, and all went to their homes, only I and one of my sons remaining to pace the little street till every light was out and we knew that those who were to our hearts as our children were all in bed and asleep, young and old. All was as usual; but every man and woman there knew that all was coming to an end.

We had been told that we must not remain in Northamptonshire for the long autumnal damps. So with foreboding hearts we left our loved and happy home for Brighton.

I will take one short sentence from Catharine's annual Memoranda to help me through. "In December 1863 Philip Wake died at Nice." "In February 1864 dear

SIR CHARLES WAKE. 1860.

Sir Charles was taken after a few hours of increased illness at Brighton. How much we shall miss him and that bright home in which he used to gather so many of us."

Our dear Bishop, our faithful friend, had been with us ; the affection between him and my husband had never varied from the childhood of the one to the old age of the other. He saw what was coming and made several suggestions, which were followed. The last letter that was written by Sir Charles was by his advice. It was to the Admiralty to ask for a ship for his son Charles, and the request was granted when one month later he had to hurry away to take the command of H.M.S. *Bulldog.* Could I at such a time be glad even thus to lose him ?

We went to Malvern in the hope that the beautiful air and the water cure would aid in the restoration of Drury's health. Dr Gully undertook the charge, and from this time we lived principally in a large tent pitched against our house, and under the shade of a large tree in our garden. At eight in the morning Drury's couch was wheeled into the open air, and only returned to the house for the actual night.

Our sky had indeed been clouded over, but through the gloom the love of God shone brightly down, enabling us to see our way and to do those things that were set before us. And that other light, surely a reflection from the sunshine of heaven, Family Love, that so often brings warmth, even cheerfulness, into desolated homes, came to our help.

We knew that from the very nature of Drury's attack all hope of cure depended upon entire calmness of nerve,—that if we were ever to see him better he must be spared all agitation ; that for his sake we must exert ourselves to be cheerful,—and we did, God

helping us ; and thus his helpless state, that very
evil which under the circumstances seemed the crown-
ing one, was changed into a good, for that which was
at first one long-sustained effort became in time the
real tone of our minds.   When now we look back
upon those days it is with amazement.   Sorrow after
sorrow had come upon us, but each one of us seemed
specially soothed and supported that we might not
only soothe and support but cheer the one amongst us
who might well have been crushed to the very earth.

Every hope of his young manhood seemed at an
end, yet he never ceased to hope, and no stranger
who came amongst us could have guessed the bewilder-
ing griefs that had gathered round us.

> "When all Thy mercies, O my God !
> My rising soul surveys,
> Transported with the view, I'm lost
> In wonder, love, and praise."

The Bishop and Catharine joined us at Malvern
on their way to the Highlands, where in August
they settled themselves at Bishopstone, the episcopal house of Ewing, Bishop of Argyle.   It stands
just above Loch Gilp, looking across Loch Fyne to
the Arran mountains.   A beautiful scene, and worthy
of the brightly genial and picturesque owner, whose
society we had so often enjoyed at Fulham.   The
combination of keen humour with earnest religious
feeling, that showed itself when least expected in
quick turns of thought, made him at all times a
delightful companion.   But he was not there ; he had
lent his house to his friend while he was himself
visiting his daughter in Sicily.   In this Highland
retreat the Bishop of London's family spent many
happy weeks. Craufurd was carrying on his studies

with his cousin, Max Spooner, two or three years his senior, who had already shown at college the ability and powers of mind that afterwards earned for him a Fellowship at an unusually early age. But it was his mother's delight steadily to carry on the system of private reading which she had never dropped from his earliest years. And while the afternoon hours were spent in all manner of out-of-door diversions by sea and land, the early morning hours from six o'clock were given by the mother and son to reading of deepest interest, thus strengthening a tie begun in childhood which death itself did not end.

It was a season of pleasant repose for the Bishop. But the shores of Loch Fyne are relaxing everywhere, and Bishopstone, enjoyable as it was, did not suit his health particularly well. It was during this time that an adventure occurred which had wellnigh closed for ever all plans of usefulness. It is best related in the Bishop's own words in a letter written by him immediately after.[1]

BISHOPSTONE, LOCHGILPHEAD,
September 2, 1864.

MY DEAREST CHATTIE,—You will probably like to know whether we are having sufficient change from the ordinary routine of Fulham and London House, and therefore I send you this account of our doings on Tuesday and Wednesday last, the last two days of August. On Tuesday at 10 A.M., by special invitation of the lieutenant commanding H.M. steamship on this station, we went with a large party to Arran,—a good day—its mountains and lake showing well, and all things most agreeable. Luncheon on deck—Brodick Bay and the Duke of Hamilton's castle and garden looking their best.

A little delay at Arran, for two of the party made us later than we expected. Still all was prosperous. Tea on deck, dancing—sailor's hornpipe, reels, quadrilles,—songs, guitar, and

---

[1] A few copies of this were printed at the time by Constable, the publisher, an old schoolfellow of the Bishop's, for private circulation.

then, as it got dark and set in, unfortunately, for a rainy night, we sat all together talking pleasantly under canvas, and scarcely noticed how dark and very wet it had become. All was very pleasant and snug when the clock struck (or the bell rang) eight. In a moment a cry, " Breakers ahead!" " Stop her!" " Back her!" then three tremendous bumps under our feet, a horrid scraping noise—the vessel was fast on the rocks, and to all appearance, if she ever got off them, would either swing over or would go down from the hole which we could not doubt was drilled in her bottom. " All hands astern!" a frightful rushing of seamen and marines, some of them half-dressed, turned out of their berths into which they had just turned in. The darkness intense, but breakers and land within a hundred yards dimly visible.

Every one behaved beautifully,—the ladies as composed as possible. Craufurd and Max took Catharine under their care. Craufurd only beseeching Catharine, " Dear mamma, promise me that you will lay hold of a table or anything that can float and cling by it." They then had a little prayer together; but in two minutes the captain had made up his mind. " Lower the boat; ladies and passengers on shore." One lady, who was very delicate, fainted, and the doctor determined for her and her husband that it was best to stay on board.

Two journeys of the boat took all the passengers and some six sailors ashore, but the landing was not very easy. The sea was now running very high; the boat could not come within some yards of the rocky beach. A middle-sized sailor, who was incautious enough to insist on taking Catharine on his back, came down like a shot in the water, and she waded from the boat. The same fate befell young Auchindarroch, who insisted on carrying me,—not from the same cause, but because he stumbled into a hole. But, providentially, some time before half-past eight, we—that is, seven ladies of all ages, myself, Craufurd and Max, Auchindarroch and his three sons, and three other gentlemen—found ourselves on what we supposed to be dry land—or at least land—without any accident.

The ladies, led by the gentlemen, stumbled up the rocks, which were not steep, and the tide rising rapidly, kept following them with a tremendous roaring. Ten minutes later no boat could have lived in the surf; and when we bethought ourselves that some covering would be desirable if it could be got, Archie Auchindarroch swam to the ship and had a tarpauling thrown to him, which proved in the event a godsend. And now Auchindarroch and another gentleman began to reconnoitre the land.

They soon returned, declaring it to be an island, and a very small one; whether covered by the sea at high water or no it was at first impossible to say, but after a little exploring they found a grassy spot at the top which looked as if the sea never reached it, and there a shed or large tent was erected with the tarpauling and another smaller tent. This, of course, took some time. Meanwhile I stayed with one sailor looking after the boat. The steamer was looming over our heads, apparently brought nearer and nearer to the shore by the tide, or seeming to get nearer from the wind blowing away the screen of the darkness and making the sight of the vessel easier. It seemed to me as if it was on the point of falling over as it rose in the darkness high above the sea. And now our own boat, hauled up on the rocky beach, was overtaken by the surge and filled with water, while it was tossed from side to side and was like to be shivered to atoms, the one sailor and I vainly tugging at the cable to draw it up the shore. The outcry we made soon summoned the other sailors who were ashore, and I shall never forget their wild chorus as they tugged at the cable, shouting a song very unsuited for such circumstances and keeping time by the chorus. At last their tugging hauled the boat up, and it seemed at last to be safe from the advancing tide.

Soon afterwards the steamboat moved, the captain (lieutenant) having, as we afterwards learned, sent out an anchor in the other boat and dropped it at some distance, and then hauled the vessel off by it. We heard their cheering as they got off the rocks, and saw no more of them that night, though from time to time our lookers-out reported that lights were to be seen which they supposed belonged to the vessel.

And now we all gathered under the tarpauling, every one wet to the skin excepting me. For my own part, the Colonel's excellent felt cloak, which I had fortunately brought with me, was a wonderful source of damp heat. It was obvious that, whatever was to become of us in the morning, we must stay where we were for seven hours till daybreak. All agreed that there was no house on the island. Some maintained they had seen two sheep in the darkness, but the existence of any living being but ourselves on its inhospitable shore was stoutly denied by others. Some thought we were on the Skate Rock, but a gentleman (Mr M'Kinnon) who had shot over the Skate (famous for otters) declared he was certain that it was not the said Skate. Some thought we were about Ardlamont Point, others that we were far higher up Loch Fyne. Meanwhile the pelting rain and utter darkness prevented any useful observations.

The foresight of the doctor, or some other kind genius, had sent in the boat a bottle of sherry and two bottles of rum; and we kept all as close together as we could—a strange group, as, lighted by the boat's lantern, we crouched under the canvas, lying on the damp boggy ground, or leaning against the rock. We had scarcely crawled into this place and begun to realise our position—some of us verging on in life, and most of us accustomed to all "the comforts of the Salt-Market," and therefore somewhat depressed—when a sailor proposed to keep up our spirits by singing a song. It was well enough in its way, and certainly better than the other which they had sung in hauling up the boat, but not very suitable for people who, through God's great mercy, had just escaped from imminent peril of death. I therefore proposed some hymns instead. We sang the evening hymn, both Keble's and the other, "Jerusalem the Golden," and others used in the chapel here, in which most of the party had been worshippers last Sunday. Then we had a short prayer commending ourselves to God's good keeping, and prepared to keep each other awake as best we could for the seven hours before us, as it was voted dangerous for any one to fall asleep in our soaking state. I pulled out of my pocket John Shairp's poem 'Kilmahoe,' and read aloud "The Sacramental Sabbath." The Presbyterian minister of Lochgilphead (who was one of the party) read the next canto when I was tired. However, it seemed that something livelier was needed to keep the party awake, and the wonderful spirits of Archy Auchindarroch (just come home from India with the 72nd Highlanders, as fine a specimen of a spirited young soldier as I ever saw, who had really done wonders for us on our leaving the vessel) were far more effectual than the grave attempts of the minister and myself. Auchindarroch, too, was a host in himself, keeping everybody's spirits up, and letting nobody fall asleep. His youngest son, ten years old, was the only one who could not be kept awake.

And thus passed the seven hours. There were endless speculations where we might be, anxious questionings as to the ship, much thankfulness that we had not all gone to the bottom, and somewhat fearful forebodings as to what might be the effect on elderly ladies and gentlemen, to say nothing of young ones, from so unexpected a conclusion of our pleasure-trip.

About three, some streaks of day were descried, and at last our scouts announced that the vessel was at anchor at no great distance. It was resolved that the indomitable Archy Auchindarroch, with two sailors and another gentleman, should row to the ship and ascertain how matters stood. About four, certain tidings were brought to us that the vessel was safe; that when she cleared the rocks, to the captain's surprise and great relief he found that, as she had struck on the keel, no hole had been made in her iron bottom—at least, she had not let in any more water, though at first she was reported to be letting it in, though slowly.

This intelligence put a happy end to our speculations as to the fate of our friends, and also solved for ourselves the question what we were to do. Before, opinions had been evenly balanced between landing on the Ardlamont shore, close to which we thought ourselves, where there is no road, and beating our way across country to the nearest point where we might be taken up by the *Iona* from Glasgow (this was one plan), and as the other alternative, rowing across to the Tarbet side of the loch and storming Stonefield House for breakfast. The easier course remained,—to row back to the steamboat. Very thankful were we all when the captain welcomed us back, and the doctor gave us mulled port to warm us. We all agreed that the captain was right in sending us at once ashore in the great uncertainty; and though those, no doubt, fared best who remained by the ship, still, for my own part, I confess I was glad to have escaped the great anxiety of hauling the vessel off the rocks, when the chances were that she might have sunk at once like a kettle with a hole in it, and none escaped but those who could swim. All seem to agree that the iron-bottomed vessels are more difficult to deal with than wooden in such circumstances.

Soon we were making progress for Ardrishaig. Before 6 A.M. on Wednesday we landed at the pier, thanking God; and for ourselves, were in bed at Bishopston before the little girls had even found out that we had not come home at eight the night before, as we expected.

Certainly you will agree that this is even more unlike a quiet Fulham evening than the night of which, with John and Lady Menzies, we spent six hours, two years ago, amongst the bogs of Rannoch and Loch Erichtside. But all is well that ends well. No one seems to have suffered; and it is not bad for any of us to be taught practically how near we may be to the greatest danger when we are least thinking of it.— Ever affectionately,   A. C. LONDON.

Not long after this adventure the Bishop of London, with his wife and children, joined us at Weston-super-Mare, and very pleasant it was to be together : greatly he needed all the benefit of the wonderfully restoring atmosphere of that place ; but his stay was short, for he could not long be spared from his diocese.

Having made mention of Drury's illness, it is well for the sake of any who may be in like manner mysteriously deprived of the use of their limbs to state that we were recommended to remove from Malvern for the winter months to Weston-super-Mare, the air there having wonderful powers of restoration in such cases as his. He spent the entire day out of doors in all weathers, though well protected in an invalid carriage, and there it was that he first gained the least improvement, a slight difference in some faint return of strength,—so slight, indeed, as to be imperceptible to others, but still it existed, and by very slow degrees led to complete recovery.[1]

The quiet of our lives was suddenly broken as with an electric shock by tidings from far-distant Hayti. My son's ship, H.M.S. *Bulldog*, was the only English man-of-war stationed there when the government was upset by the rebel Salnave and his ruffianly followers, who even ventured so far as attacking and insulting the British power.

The British Consulate was twice violated. Some Haytians who had taken refuge there were dragged out and shot upon the shore, and two ladies were captured who had sought protection under the British flag, which was torn down and trampled and spat on !

The *Voldrogue* and the three schooners belonging to Salnave chased and fired upon a steamer bearing English colours. All remonstrances were met only with insults. The honour of the flag and the main-

---

[1] It was seven years that Drury Wake spent upon his couch before his restoration was complete. But though he did not resume his practice at the Bar, he was able to fulfil all the duties of a country gentleman, and to hunt with the Pytchley Hounds, of which for some years he was the Secretary. In 1874 he married Louisa, younger daughter of H. O. Nethercote, Esq. He died in 1891, leaving a son, Drury, and three daughters.— ED.

tenance of England's authority had to be upheld. In
attempting to run the *Voldrogue* down, the *Bulldog*
grounded on one of the sunken coral reefs, and while
sustaining the whole fire of the batteries from the
town, she succeeded in silencing them and sinking
the *Voldrogue*. But no effort could get the *Bulldog*
off the reef. Was she to become the prize of Salnave
and the rebel negroes? Her captain and all under
him would rather die. There remained after the bom-
bardment but sufficient powder to blow her up. He
well knew he should be blamed for the loss of his ship,
but he remembered what happened to the *Tigris*,
sister ship to the *Bulldog*. She, in like manner, had
struck on a rock in the Crimean War; her captain
had been so severely wounded in the fight that his
lieutenant had to take the command, and not daring
to destroy her, saw her taken possession of by the
Russians, who triumphed over their prize as though
she had been taken in fair fight. She was long shown
as a trophy of their naval prowess. Charlie remembered this, and having seen all his men safe out of
her except the chief engineer, who remained with him,
with his own hand he sent her into the air. And thus,
come what would, the honour of his country was safe.
As he foresaw, the court-martial gave judgment
against him, but the universal feeling of the country
was expressed in 'The Times,'[1] when it said that
"he was evidently an officer of the right sort."

[1] And in 'Punch,' in which appeared a cartoon—"Admiral Punch does
justice to Captain Wake."

CHAPTER XXV.

In July 1866 we—that is, Drury, my daughter, and
myself—were invited to join the party at Fulham,
and I find these details written in a sort of journal
that I kept at that time :—

"*July* 17*th.*—Sat yesterday at dinner between the
Bishop of London and Sir William Maxwell Stirling
(Keir), and had most agreeable conversation with the
latter ; much amused by the former continually dashing
in to upset Keir's political talk, all verging to the new
point so anxiously desired by the Conservatives, a
broad basis—*i.e.,* to secure the support of the Whigs
against the Radicals. I think he is right, but Bishop
Archie calls me an Adullamite. Of course I showed
my colours, old Whig family, though I heartily join
in dislike of the Rads. ; yet if there must be extremes
America is better than Spain, but England should be
the happy *juste milieu.* Keir is a charming companion,
with a true countenance and genuine manners. Every
word is pleasant or wise, no nonsense. The party
besides is,—his dear and lovely wife,[1] whom it is good

[1] Lady Anna, daughter of Lord Leven and Melville.

to look upon; Earl Grey and his Countess; the Bishop
of Oxford, agreeable and amusing always; the Bishop
of Limerick;[1] Dean Stanley, the little man with such
large ideas, and with such powers of enlarging other
people's; young Shaw Stewart; Grant of Kilgraston;
Lady Lucy and her daughters; my son Herwald; and
Gray, the Bishop of Capetown; and the family party
in the house, besides the Rector of Fulham, Mr Baker,
the venerable bridegroom of over eighty, who last year
survived his wedding trip to Moscow, and was here
yesterday with his wife to tell the tale.

"Next day there was a still larger party, and to
my great pleasure I found myself in the drawing-room
in earnest conversation with Sir John Pakington, and
that he was to take me in to dinner. He is one of
those old friends whom I value most, and who in the
thirty years we have known him has always been the
same—clever, true-hearted, agreeable, and friendly. I
am glad that he is the new First Lord of the Admiralty, for he is very fond of Charlie, and was so indignant at the verdict of the court-martial on the
blowing-up of the *Bulldog* that he will be certain to
give him a ship—indeed, he told me that he would;
moreover, that the Duke of Somerset had left a note
to his successor stating that it had been his intention
to give early employment to Captain Wake, late
of the *Bulldog.* (Highly creditable this to the
Admiralty!)

"These dinner-parties at Fulham are charming.
There were many distinguished people both of the out-
going and in-coming Cabinet and party. Mr and Mrs
Gladstone and Miss Burdett-Coutts had been expected,
but had they come I can't imagine where they could
have been placed. I was too far from *my* Bishop

---

[1] I think it was Bishop Graves.—ED.

this time : conversation is always most pleasant when
he is within reach. I had Lord Houghton opposite,
and so many things of real interest to talk over with
Sir John Pakington that it was some time before I
discovered that the Bishop of Oxford was on my
other side, by whom I am always amused but never
interested, chiefly because he only lets me see what
lies on the surface; he knows instinctively that his
inner depths would not suit me, yet they suit dear
Catharine—so far superior to me in every way.

"We leave Fulham to - morrow after six most
pleasant weeks. At first the constant and varied
society and the continual bustle of business seemed
too much ; but very soon I learned to take my own
line, and spent my day in Porteous' Library, given
up to us because it was so convenient for Drury,
who could, through the window opening down to the
ground, be wheeled into the garden, where he spent
the greater part of the day. When I wished to be
even more private there was always the chapel. It
was a charming mixture of private and public life,
of books and flowers, of solitude and animated society.

"We have much enjoyed the Saturday gatherings
in the garden, rendered far more pleasant than the
regular routine of London Breakfasts by that very
mixture which would by some be thought to destroy
them. The size of the gardens gives people the power
of roaming about so that they can form their own
society, and it would be difficult indeed for any one
to be there without meeting some friend of his own.
The odd contrasts and the rival celebrities of all sorts
make the scene highly amusing,—the country curate
and his wife showing each other the different objects
of interest, and as they do so stumbling against political characters glad of the opportunity of talking

together at their ease, sometimes settling important
matters; fashionable groups amusing themselves at
the medley which would shock them in their own
domains, but which they allow to be quite right in
those of the Bishop of London; dark swarthy figures
with the red fez; Bishops, English and Colonial;
prettily dressed girls with a good sprinkling of
their partners and Park friends in attendance;
croquet parties; and above all an endless number
of children of every age, playing about with all
their hearts, riding by turns the two ponies given
up to them, and cantering in and out of the gay
groups. It is a pleasant sight, with the open
windows of the Palace through which the motley
crowd is continually moving in and out; the tables
with tea and ices among the flowers on the shady
side of the house; the long tables set out within
for the successive bands of children who seem always
to be there; and moving about continually, like a
personification of a kindly Providence, Catharine
herself, the very type of all motherliness, just
what the Bishop's wife should be, so lovely to
look upon in her matured beauty, in which the
graces of youth are replaced by those more real
and lasting,—beaming kindness and perfect content,
the sun so shining *in* upon her that she is a
moving Sunshine, warming all within her influence.
The Bishop, too, moving about among them all
with a kind word for every one, enjoying the
society of his friends, but looking worn and weary
as though Saturday would have been better for
him had it been a quieter day, anticipating the
rest he now takes (generally, not always) on Sunday,
—not always, for sometimes, in spite of his strength
failing before its time, he will respond to the cruel

entreaties of people who fancy the Bishop of London ought to preach for this or that, whether he is fit for it or not. However, he is enjoying himself now, looking around on the scene with evident amusement. Through the thickest part of the throng suddenly bursts the dear old Dean of St Paul's, his venerable bent figure running as a ship before the wind. 'Stop!' exclaimed our Bishop; 'you are going right into a holly-bush.' 'Let me go, let me go, don't stop me!' was the breathless reply; 'there is that dreadful woman in full pursuit.' In much surprise, we turned round and saw — whom? Miss Strickland, the Historian!!! What a blessing is the variety of tastes! How could the world go on without it? Later on in this same summer a young Earl (Lord Spencer) told me that they had so charming an addition to their usual party in the country that they had most thoroughly enjoyed it. 'Miss Strickland, the Celebrated Historian!' I was careful not to mention Dean Milman's flight at Fulham. Yet after all it was no disrespect to her; the difference was simply this, — Lord Spencer is young, thirsting for knowledge and information, while the Dean is old, weary of it all, and wanting no more; nevertheless he would very pleasantly and kindly impart some little bit of information himself. He told me this very day, while sitting on one of the garden-seats among the people and the flowers, a curious incident confirmatory of that sort of traditionary history which comes down to us in memoirs. Some necessary repairs having caused the vaults beneath Westminster Abbey to be opened, the Custodian informed the Dean that if he chose he could descend into that in which George II. and his queen, Caroline, reposed. He remembered in a moment all that had been related of the curious scene at Caroline's death-bed, when the king, bewailing his impending loss, expressed to her his determination to prove his fidelity to her memory by never taking to himself a second wife, and gave her for her comfort the extraordinary reason that has been recorded why she might depend upon his sincerity; adding that though she died first, death itself should not separate them, for he would take care they should be laid side by side in the same coffin. The Dean, remembering all this and also the directions given by the king at the time of his own death for carrying out this resolve, descended into the vault to examine into this post-mortem conjugal fidelity; and in very deed he found the inner sides of both coffins had been carefully and skilfully re-moved, so that Queen Caroline literally shared in death the last resting-place of the husband, who, though he had sense enough unconsciously to lean upon her, was in fact so little worthy of her. 'The vault,' said the Dean, 'had to be immediately closed up, so in great haste I summoned my wife that she also might see this most curious specimen of conjugal tenderness. She came, and thus Mrs Milman and myself are the only witnesses to the fact.' What a strange jumble of feelings must have possessed the mind of this George II., whose memory is only precious to us in that through him has been transmitted the royal line, at this hour our pride and our blessing.

"We shall carry away with us the remembrance of these garden-parties at Fulham, which have nothing like them anywhere."

In 1867 the Bishop attended some of the great

entertainments given in honour of the Sultan's visit :
happily he was not present at the great *fête* during
which Madame Musurus, the wife of the Turkish
Ambassador, died at the table. At the great entertainment at Guildhall, after the music was over, the
Sultan retired to a private apartment while the
banquet was in preparation ; but his absence lasted
so long that our Bishop, who had an Englishman's
value for time, waxed impatient, and suggested to
Lord Stratford de Redcliffe that he should go to him,
lest he should have fallen asleep, and rouse him up.
"It is what I have often had to do : both this Sultan
and his predecessor have had frequent need of rousing,
and I am happy to say I have never failed to do it,"
was the reply.

Catharine went to the great naval review, and saw
the meeting of the Sultan with the Queen, in a
tremendous storm. The Queen advancing in her
yacht from Osborne, the Sultan went on board from
his vessel, and she greeted him with a kiss. Some of
the duties of royalty are hard.

After this in Catharine's diary it is written : "*Sunday.*—Went down to Lavington with the Cardwells,
the Gladstones, and others,—the Bishop of Winchester [1]
the most charming of hosts, so agreeable and so friendly.
We visited with him the graves of his family (where
he now himself is laid). He preached. After the
second service we climbed a hill on the way from
church ; we gathered together at the top, where seats
were placed commanding a most splendid view, and the
Bishop read aloud to us 'The Dream of St Gerontius.'
This pleasure cost our Bishop dear, for climbing the
hill brought on a third attack, and he could work no
more." Nevertheless, after the brief rest of a month

[1] Wilberforce.

he had to attend the Pan-Anglican Conference at Lambeth, in which he took a prominent part. After that was over he attended the opening of the Church Congress at Wolverton. But these exertions so knocked him up that he was obliged to take another month of entire rest, which he spent in a villa near Broadstairs, where the wonderfully bracing air so restored his strength that he determined to purchase Stonehouse, then for sale, little dreaming of what importance the possession would afterwards be to him, as being in the diocese of Canterbury.

I was at Stonehouse in October 1868, when we received tidings of the unlooked-for death of Longley, Archbishop of Canterbury. Sympathy for his family was the pervading feeling which at first filled our minds. It was while listening to the funeral sermon preached by our Bishop at St Peter's Church that the importance of the office and position of the Primate of All England first dawned upon my mind. Many were the speculations as to who would be called upon to fill it, and on the morning of my departure for Folkestone the possibility was for the first time suggested of our Bishop being selected, as one in whom many of the necessary qualities were united, though it was probable the feelings of the present Cabinet would be against it. Catharine entered the room just in time to catch the words, "No, no; Dizzy is a clever fellow, but scarcely clever enough for that." It was but three days after this that I heard from my brother that he had just received a letter from Dean Wellesley containing a message from the Queen that the vacant Archbishopric would be offered him, and that it was her wish he should not refuse it. My brother accompanied this news with the injunction that

I should mention it to no one till I heard again. Very amusing it was to listen to the numerous speculations around me. When passing a knot of clergymen I heard one positively announcing that Bishop —— was to be the new Archbishop. I felt much tempted to touch his elbow and say, "No, he is not."

A week passed without another word to Stonehouse; then one morning the sound of wheels was heard, and in another moment Mr Fisher, the Bishop's chaplain, appeared, bringing a letter from the Prime Minister containing the expected appointment.

The importance of the charge was deeply felt by both the husband and the wife, and earnestly they sought from God the power to fulfil the solemn duties it imposed.

The Bishop, having immediately to meet several bishops at the consecration of the Bishop of Peterborough, wrote separately to each announcing his appointment, by which means all awkward observations and speculations were avoided.

CHAPTER XXVI.

THE family soon settled down in the full enjoyment of the lovely glades and woods of Addington, though the parting with Fulham was a great sorrow : the little girls nearly cried their eyes out at leaving the only home they had known, with all its brightness and all its associations. The Archbishop might almost have imagined himself to have returned to his native country, when he found himself among the pines and heather of the tangled wilderness embosomed in the park. Shortly after his arrival there we went out together in a little pony-carriage without a servant, and so completely lost ourselves that it was quite dark before we found our way back to the house. The park is a large one, but the walks and drives are so wonderfully managed that one may wander for miles always coming upon something new. Nothing could be more skilfully planned ; and the whole is due to the wonderful taste of Mrs Howley, who, in fact, with the assistance of a friend, completely made the place by means of enclosing a tract of common land, perfectly wild and covered with nothing but furze, heather, and the natural growth of those trees which thrive best where naught else would grow.

Some delightful days were passed together there ;
and the Archbishop found time to tell me some
incidents which I will give here in his own words as
I took them down in that charming library at
Addington :—

"The Dean of Wells is almost the oldest friend I
have now living. It was in the long vacation before
I took my degree that I first made his acquaintance,
becoming his private pupil, and our friendship has
remained steadfast ever since. No man ever distinguished himself more at the University. Going there
a mere boy from Shrewsbury, with very narrow means,
and to what was then an obscure College with indiffer-
ent tuition, he won the Ireland Scholarship, the blue-
ribbon of classical attainment ; and not long afterwards
he also won the Mathematical Scholarship, thereby
proving himself the best mathematician of his year.
Naturally there followed a first class both in Mathe-
matics and in Classics at his B.A. examination, and
later on he held the Professorships of Astronomy
and of Moral Philosophy.

"As soon as he could he began to take pupils, that
he might be able to support his mother and sisters ;
and the trials of that time, when besides all his other
reading and intense study he was occupied some hours
each day with his pupils, have ever since told upon
his health. This is probably the cause that he has
not risen to greater adventitious eminence, for a certain
amount of physical power is necessary for outward
success in the world. To him, as much as to any man,
I feel that I am indebted for widening the range of
my reading ; I look back to many an evening spent
in his rooms at Queen's after I had become a B.A.
and Fellow, when we used to read together Ecclesiastical History, Socrates, and Eusebius ; and to him I

owe it that I know something of the works of War-
burton, South, Berkeley, and other mines of thought.
We were drawn more together by the repulsion we
both felt, though in different ways, to the prevailing
theology of the Oxford of that day. Bishop Jeune
used to say that no man was safe from the Newman
fever till he had had it; nevertheless there were some
constitutions that were inaccessible to the infection,
and such was the case with us. Other things helped
our friendship. There were not many Liberals then in
Oxford among the resident Fellows; an Oxford Liberal,
mark well, was something very different from the con-
ceited philosopher and sciolist who goes by the name
nowadays. Arnold, with his deep appreciative vener-
ation for all that was great in the past, and strong
religious convictions, was the *ne plus ultra* of the
Liberal theologians of that day; or Whateley, in a
different line, still equally certain as to his Christian
standing, and the staunch opponent of a mere negative
and sceptical philosophy.

"I remember that Johnson and I, a little after this
time, were the only two tutors in Oxford who protested
against the absurd opposition to bringing the railway
to Oxford. The opposition was successful on the plea
that a station there would send all the undergraduates
to London, and destroy the discipline of the place.
The railway was accordingly kept at the respectful
distance of nine miles, the nearest station being Steventon, and the result, as might naturally have been
anticipated, was that fast undergraduates had the
delight of a double chance of breaking their necks in
the twofold journey to and from Steventon in a
tandem; while respectable Masters of Art and Doctors
of Divinity had to spend a weary hour and a half in
traversing by coach or omnibus a distance which, had

they been wiser, might have been accomplished in twenty minutes, much to the detriment of their pockets and their tempers. Our triumph was complete when after a few years, at great expense and much trouble, a branch railway was constructed to remedy the defect.

"Of course when a protest against the Tract No. 90 seemed necessary to save the University from going direct to Rome, I did not act without consulting so staunch a friend. But Johnson's line was not one of decided action, and though I believe he fully approved, his name was not appended to the protest. I think I have stated before how he and I were associated with Golightly in the charge of the parish of Baldon. It was only natural that when Lord Russell formed his Oxford Commission of Inquiry, after I had become Dean of Carlisle, he should place the two most eminent reforming tutors — *i.e.*, Johnson and myself — on the Commission, giving us Arthur Stanley as our secretary.

"Johnson had been from time to time much with us during the seven years of our life at Rugby, which was the especial scene of his love-passages with the charming Lucy O'Brien, whom certainly in those days no one ever expected to see united to a quiet Oxford don. According to his own declaration she spoiled the best monk that had ever established his quarters in Oxford. For two or three years they were engaged, with apparently small prospect of ever being able to marry. At last, weary of the delay, he accepted a College living in Devonshire, and set off to inspect it. His heart sank when he found a parish full of sheep-pens! Nor were his spirits much raised by his experiences in the Episcopal palace to which the Bishop of Exeter made a point of inviting the

clergy brought into his diocese. When he arrived
there, finding no one at home, he took a turn in
the Bishop's beautiful gardens; he had not been
there more than a minute when a footman hastened
after him to tell him they were not open to the
candidates for orders. Poor Johnson felt very small,
remembering his eight - and - thirty years and University honours; however, he did not choose to
assert his dignity, but retired to his room, where
his ruffled feathers were not smoothed by finding a
printed notice forbidding smoking and sitting up
late! However, the Bishop's kindness and civility
on his return soothed his wounded feelings, and
he told him he had invited to meet him a party
of those clergy who would be his future neighbours,
that he might make their acquaintance. Alas! the
dinner-party was worse than all; the conversation
of the agricultural divines dwelt chiefly on sheep
and turnips, and the refined and intellectual scholar
retired to his slumbers in a state of depression
over which not even the thought of Lucy could
shed a single ray.

"Early next morning he returned to town in any ·
thing but a rejoicing mood, and was pensively walking up a street when a man on the opposite side
suddenly made a signal to arrest his attention, and
rapidly crossing the street seized him by the hand,
pouring out congratulations. 'For what reason?'
said Johnson. 'Because I am to spend the rest of
my life among sheep and turnips?' 'My dear
fellow, I congratulate you on your appointment to
the Deanery of Wells; have you not received Lord
John Russell's letter?' It had been following him
about the country while he had been breaking
his heart in Devonshire.

"I have always felt astonishment that Johnson, with his prodigious powers, has not made more mark in life. This can only, I think, be explained by his want of physical power, which has prevented him turning his really great intellectual attainments to a profitable use. His Commentary on the Psalms in the Speaker's Book is probably the only literary work he will leave behind him. I think there is a warning in this to young men not to overtax their powers in early life, and to see that *bodily* keeps pace with *intellectual* development."

The justice of this observation Johnson himself was obliged to acknowledge, when after coaching my son Drury during a few pleasant weeks at the Lakes he expostulated with him for not going in for honours, saying that his abilities were quite sufficient to carry him through if he would only apply himself harder to work. "John and William Adams were both just such fellows as you, and they both got double firsts." "Really," was the answer, with awakened interest and a half-formed determination,— "really! and what are they doing now?" "Oh! well—they both died." "Thanks, I won't follow their example," was the inevitable rejoinder.

It was very well for the Archbishop to make these sage observations as to overwork, but unhappily he did not sufficiently lay them to heart for his own guidance. The interest of his new duties as Archbishop carried him on far beyond his strength. He always considered he had done enough to recruit his health by spending a few bright weeks with his friends in Scotland, finishing the autumn at Stonehouse. The exhilarating and bracing air there might have accomplished his restoration to strength had he not been overwhelmed by an ever - increasing correspondence, the fatigue of which both to body and mind culminated in a sudden and frightful attack of illness, by which his career was nearly ended.

At an early period of the Archbishop's illness Mrs Tait received the following letter from the Queen :—

WINDSOR CASTLE,
November 23, 1869.

DEAR MRS TAIT,—No words *can* express my *deep* feeling for you and my sincere anxiety for the dear Archbishop, who is so valuable to the country and to me! Many, many a prayer will be offered up for his restoration to health. But my heart especially feels most keenly for you, who have gone through so much anxiety and sorrow, and who are so kind and good to others in trouble. That our Heavenly Father may support and strengthen you, and that He may soon remove all cause for serious anxiety about the dear Archbishop, is the sincere prayer of your affectionate   V. R.

Our children wish to express their warm sympathy and inquiries after the Archbishop.

.   .   .   .

During the winter, spring, and summer that followed his recovery from this illness, of which for some time there had been little hope, the Archbishop made a gradual return to his usual work, much assisted by the appointment of a suffragan bishop, his old friend Archdeacon Parry being consecrated to this office as Bishop of Dover. He was able again to take his place in the House of Lords, and to conduct the summer ordination in Croydon Church, having previously addressed the candidates. He attended the great meeting at Canterbury held on the subject of the new Education Act, and, though little able for it, took his seat on the Judicial Committee of the Privy Council, helping to decide the intricate and distressing case of Mr Voysey.

But the effort was too much for his strength. It was never known how much it cost him and how serious was the attack that followed, though speedily overcome by the marvellous strength of his constitution.

But the warning was sufficient, and decided his medical attendants in insisting on his leaving England to pass the winter in some warm climate. This could not be done without the permission of Parliament and the Queen. Her Majesty's answer was conveyed by telegraph, and was in characteristic form,—" Go at once "

The journey was quickly arranged. That same day Catharine wrote to me at Folkestone—where I was preparing to cross the Channel with my daughter for the like reason of health—to say that if we would delay one week they would join us, and we should all go together. This was a pleasant arrangement. The war then raging through France made that coast out of the question. From Ostend we made our way through Germany, much interested on our route by the evidences of the war. For ourselves, our sympathies had been entirely with the Prussians, but when we constantly beheld long troops of miserable, ragged, pale, half-starved looking, disarmed Frenchmen plodding along almost barefooted in the piercing winter cold under charge of some two or three fat, comfortable Germans, well mounted and muffled up to their chins, we speedily went over to the enemy. We had abundant occasion to admire the admirable arrangements made for the sick and wounded of the German troops. At several of the stations drew up long trains entirely converted in the most marvellous manner into hospitals, and we found the patients glad of even the most hurried visits.

Neither the Archbishop nor myself was in sight-
seeing plight; therefore, while the others went forth
we made ourselves as comfortable in our hotel as
circumstances would permit. At Milan I was greatly
tempted to send a picture to 'Punch,' entitled "Our
Archbishop in a Warmer Climate." It would have
portrayed his Grace in his thickest greatcoat with a
cloak over it, and a purple episcopal-looking plaid on
the top of that, hat on head, and legs enveloped in
a carriage rug of fur; myself in bonnet, shawls, and
rugs to match; sitting opposite each other with our
knees as close to the stove as safety would permit;
against the window the snow falling thick and fast.

It would be the height of injustice not to acknowledge our obligations to Mr Cook, who, on hearing of
the projected journey, volunteered himself to act as
the Archbishop's courier. The effects were marvellous. From the first start we always found most
comfortable saloon carriages ready for us. As we
neared each halting-place for the night, the landlord
of our hotel met us a station in advance; and when
we arrived three carriages, beautifully appointed, were
in readiness to convey our party, sixteen in number,
to the hotel, where we found not only our rooms
prepared for us, but the names of each of our party
over the doors, including those of the ladies'-maids.
Cook knew by instinct exactly what would suit each
of us. Naturally, I felt great curiosity to see for
myself the magician who wrought these wonders, for
at the crowded stations I had not been able to distinguish him. My surprise was great when a quiet,
middle-aged man, very much like a home-staying,
retired tradesman, was pointed out to me, walking
up and down the platform with his hands in his
pockets seemingly taking notice of no one. He could

not speak a word of any language but his own. How, then, did he accomplish all these wonders? He had agents in every town, and one line from him could always settle every difficulty and arrange every convenience. On our first crossing to Ostend one of my boxes, not having been put under his care, disappeared. The circumstance was made known to Cook; his influence pursued it, so that after having performed a tour through Europe by itself, it joined us at San Remo, where the whole party in due time established themselves at the Hôtel de Londres; and there Cook left us.

We found a great difference on our return to England without his magic wand to clear the way; and it is due to him to state that the difference in the expense was hardly worth mentioning.

CHAPTER XXVII.

IT is with peculiar pleasure that I look back upon
the time we spent at the lovely Villa Eleanore at
Cannes, built by Lord Brougham in the fond hope
that the child whose name it bore might be saved
by being transplanted to the almost perfect climate
of the Riviera.

We were very happy there, living a truly family
life, my brother slowly but surely recovering health
and strength in the enjoyment of perfect repose
amidst the loveliest scenery that can be imagined,
in a climate that permitted an entire life in the
open air.

The house was full of tender and touching associations; for as its different apartments were pointed
out to us with the explanations given by Lord
Brougham's faithful servant, a sort of softening light,
as that of evening, seemed to be thrown upon the
closing years of the grim old statesman whom the
Archbishop had known under such different auspices.
Here was the room that was at first his bedroom,
looking towards the Esterels and the Mediterranean,

but which he insisted upon giving up to be made into the "Nursery" for his brother's children. There on the ground floor was the small turret, opening from the dining-room, in which he established himself till the remonstrances of his friends, backed up by the physician's opinion that the space was too confined for a sleeping apartment, sent him forth again. He then took possession of the dining-room, where he slept upon a small sofa-bed over which hung the picture of the only child, the daughter who never lived to benefit by the house built for her reception. His old servant showed us this corner in which he died, and pointed to the picture still hanging there. It was touching to be told that as the splendid talents of the old statesman subsided under the quieting touch of age, so also did the bitter sarcastic spirit that had been characteristic of the man. Advancing feebleness brought with it softening memories, and nothing soothed him as did the hymns he had learned in childhood from his mother. A verse or two of one of these is engraved upon his tomb; and while gazing upon it our thoughts travelled back to the scene at Brougham Hall, when he had stood with the pathetic expression, so unusual to his countenance, watching the soap-bubbles his brother's children sent up into the air, glimmering brightly in the sunshine, then disappearing in a moment. Still more arose a mournful picture of the lonely grave in the Temple churchyard where lies the young girl on whom all his affections were centred, with the unoccupied space at her side in which he had desired to be laid. Surrounded by whole generations of grave and learned men, the young Eleanore is the only one of her sex who is buried there: one cannot help the feeling that her father's wish ought to have been carried out, and yet it seems but right that his tomb should be in Cannes, which owes existence to his settlement there. It was not long before the report of his choice drew others to it ; and the munificent liberality of a kind old man, Mr Woolfield, in building a beautiful and most commodious Protestant church, gave stability to the little colony speedily established on that lovely coast. The name of Woolfield ought to be long remembered there, associated as it is with many deeds of kindness.

The Archbishop spent the entire day in the open air, beginning with early breakfast under the shade of flowering - plants that fell in clustering wreaths from the tree, at the foot of which was the seat where he passed the hours that were not given to long drives amid the lovely scenery of the place. It was below this tree that he dictated to me his reminiscences of his childish days when at Whitworth in the hands of the blacksmith doctors. He used to beckon me to his side, saying, " Bring your writing things and write what none now living know but myself, and other things which none but you can remember " ; and we used to pass hours of enchantment, the thought of those days mingling with the unspeakable beauty of the scene below us, looking over the Mediterranean glowing in the sunlight like a sea of melted jewels, every instant flashing up new colours, while the Esterels settled into mingled grey and lilac as the morning rays passed from them.

Each day the newspapers brought a tumult of interest with the terrible details of the war then raging between France and Germany, and changing into the worse storm raised by France herself as the Commune like a fiend rose into the skies where Peace should have spread her wings.

U

It was difficult to conceive that we were living in a part of the same country, for all around us was so peaceful, the peasants so occupied with their vineyards, their orange- and olive-groves, so happy with their abundant fruits, evidently caring so little for those public questions that convulsed their country; and yet Marseilles, where the storm raged with the infectious fury of Paris, was but a short distance from us, and the law of compulsory service had drawn from nearly every cottage at least one member of the otherwise peacefully minded family to take part in the strife.

"Vous êtes un beau garçon de ne pas avoir dix-huit ans," said I to our coachman, a broad-shouldered good-humoured young man of at least eight-and-twenty, whom I wondered to see so peacefully employed. "Ah, madame!" he replied, "quant à la guerre j'y ai été, j'en ai eu assez." He then related to me how he had been at Orleans with the army, had been taken prisoner and retaken, had been again engaged, badly wounded, and carried off by the Germans, how they had been kind to him, "assez braves garçons," till he recovered; that when they had left he had managed to remain behind, hiding himself in a barn; thought he had done quite enough "pour la guerre," and might return to his home in peace: "Ainsi, madame, me voici heureux de vous servir." I could not but agree with him.

Catharine's great object was to keep her husband's mind as tranquil as possible, always reducing us to silence when sudden and animated discussion arose, as frequently was the case when the newspapers brought us news of one startling event after another. My daughter and her nephew, Max Spooner, who was the Archbishop's chaplain, were forbidden to be within speaking distance of each other, being sure to plunge into amicable warfare whenever it was possible; and we were all under complete discipline, yielding willing and implicit obedience to our commander-in-chief. Much as I had admired and valued her before in the performance of her more public duties at Fulham and at Lambeth, the manner in which she devoted herself to the care of her husband and the talent she displayed in this quieter field of action raised her still higher in my estimation; and though it has been often said that travelling together and living together in a foreign land is the greatest trial, we, after six months between leaving and returning to England, were all bound together with yet stronger affection. Many new features of character we no doubt discovered, some amusing and some that explained the sources of hitherto hidden springs of action, so that we only understood each other the better. Now, looking back upon that time I am more and more impressed by the wonderful combination in Catharine's character of strong will with entire submission, never swerving from the decided opinions of her own inner mind even while she carried out with heart and soul the wishes of her husband, which were often at complete variance with them. I remember being particularly struck with this when during one of our long drives she wrote at his dictation his reply to the papers belonging to the Voysey case that had been sent to him for revision, his decision being absolutely necessary. "Those are not your opinions, Catharine, that you are writing," I could not help saying. "Certainly not," she replied, "but that is of no importance; his dear Grace is a wise man, and these are his opinions."

As the spring advanced the beauty of the country

round became indescribable; with its wealth of wild
flowers and orange-blossoms the air was really too
much perfumed for health, and it was time to return
home.   Craufurd, the dear and only son, had early
left us, with his cousin Max, for Rome, and was now
re-established at Oxford.   How were we to return?
Catharine much preferred the route through France,
and with her usual decision of character announced
that by that way they would all return.   I felt my
life to be of value at home, and having never forgotten the mortal terror of the revolution that de-
throned Charles X., I utterly declined again putting
ourselves within the possibility of being drawn within
the whirlpool of another, and decided upon returning
through Germany; and happily Catharine was convinced by the experience of a friend, who had to
escape by night from Marseilles or to consent to be
locked up in a cellar hidden away till the storm of
revolutionary feeling was passed.   The Archbishop
had drily remarked to her, while the subject was
under discussion, "If you persist on the route through
France, you will have the pleasure of seeing your
husband hanged in full canonicals in the Grande Place
of Marseilles; there is nothing they would like so
much as to catch an Archbishop."

After three most enchanting weeks among the lovely
Italian lakes and many amusing days of travel, we all
arrived in London, and in a very few more days all
had subsided into their own peculiar places, taking
up the threads of daily life and its duties, thankfully
conscious of renewed strength and of having brought
home our Archbishop in restored health and consequent power of action.

What his work was and how it was carried on there
is no need for me to dwell upon.   That history belongs

to his public life; but the dear domestic life still went
on as it had always done, Lambeth being the centre
where friends met, and family ties were strengthened
by the frequent meeting of those whose dwellings lay
far apart. Year after year we spent Easter at Addington, in full enjoyment of the happy circle, of the chapel
services, and all the spring-flower decorations that
gave so joyous a character to the whole. And year
after year at Lambeth, after Easter was over, the
work was carried on with renewed energy, extending
itself by a loving influence like the rays of the sun
to the far-distant corners of the earth. Men of every
shade of colour met there, seeking aid and counsel from
our Archbishop, to whom, if ever to mortal man, the
title of "Father in God" was well applied, and it
was deeply interesting to meet them there.

It was scarce more than a month after the death
of their only son Craufurd (in May 1878) when I
was summoned to Lambeth to help dear Catharine in
the arduous duty of receiving the assembled bishops,
who were to meet there for conference from every
part of the Protestant world; for neither she nor
the Archbishop would shrink from the work that had
been so gladly undertaken when all was bright around
them. There is no need of words to tell how great
was the trial; none could look upon them without
thought of the great grief that had befallen them.
There was that in look, word, and deed that showed
that, while moving among the courtesies and charities
of life, something had happened that raised them
above all. Beloved Catharine, her beautiful dark eyes
were ever seeming to look beyond, and in the tones
of her voice there was a soft echo of sorrow.

The morning before we all parted on our different
ways, we two sat together in her private room with

the Bishop of Louisiana, who had especially interested us, listening to him while he told us of an occurrence on board the steamer that had brought him over. He, the Bishop, had been deeply pained by the conduct and conversation of an otherwise gentlemanlike young man, a fellow-passenger, and he determined to try if he could not influence him to better things, but he was met with such insulting rudeness that he felt he could say no more. Nor did he try again; but the day before they reached England this man came up to him, and in a very quiet manner asked him if he would give him a few minutes in his cabin. Much surprised, the Bishop followed him there, when the young man said to him, "I repulsed you rudely when some time ago you would have spoken to me; now I ask you to repeat to me all you would then have said. I will be thankful now to learn all you can teach me." "First tell me," was the reply, "what has caused this change?" "That child," said he, half opening the door and pointing to a little girl playing outside. "Poor mite, her mother has been ill and confined to her cabin ever since they came on board. I am very fond of children, and it was so forlorn for her that I made friends with her; she gladly adopted me, but every day when perched on my knee she would repeat to me hymn after hymn. It was no use telling her that I did not want hymns; she would say, 'But you *must* want them; I have learned them from mamma, and I will say them to you because you are so kind to me.' The end of it has been that those hymns, whether I would or not, have sunk down into my heart; night and day I find myself repeating them,—they are most of them really prayers in verse, and I have learned to pray. I believe all I used to make game of, and I will be thankful to be taught." He spoke hurriedly, but it was easy to see that he was thoroughly, deeply in earnest.

It was a touching history, thoroughly appreciated by both the mothers who listened to it. Six months after this the good Bishop of Louisiana and Catharine on the same day passed into eternity. Did they meet on their way heavenward?—the one from Scotland, the other from his diocese in America; while I, so much older than either of them, live to write it down. I do so because I think it teaches so many things.

A month later Catharine wrote to me telling me that Edith's marriage was to take place at Lambeth late in the autumn; that it was to be as quiet as possible, with only those members of the family present who happened to be in town, but that she would be very thankful if I and Tilly would remain in Scotland at the Cottage, where we generally spent October, till she and the Archbishop, with Lucy and Agnes, came there, so that we should be there together. They had not been there since our eldest brother died, and Craufurd had been with them during their last visit. I well understood the wish, and felt deeply all it expressed.

In the first week of October we found ourselves once more at the dear old Cottage with dearest Jem. It was our second visit since John had departed, and every feeling was stirred among those well-known scenes,—the glens, the hills all the same, but we so altered! The Ochills I could fancy leaning their green heads together, whispering to each other that we used to ramble about their slopes full of fun, leaping from rock to rock, and making their echoes ring with our glad voices. "Look at them now," they seemed to say, "but we are still the same." Yes, they were still the same; there were our glens, all our favourite haunts on the hills behind Harviestoun, but Harviestoun itself had passed into other hands, and we—well, Jem was eighty, and I but eighteen months behind him. We drove over from the Cottage to visit the scenes of our early rambles, and then we went farther down to the family burial-place beside the Devon. Since the time our mother had been laid there it had always been visited with mournful feelings, continually deepening as the name of one and another was recorded on each new stone. But it had become gradually darker and more gloomy from the growth of the dense foliage that overshadowed it, and so rank was the vegetation that our eldest brother's grave, though little more than one year old, was scarcely visible. And near it stood the drooping figure of my brother James, showing me where he wished to lie—"Close beside my mother."

The words sent me back to the bright young days when she was among us, and turning to old Drysdale, the grand-nephew of the witch, I asked him where to find the "Canty Knowe," for that the woods were so grown I could not find my way to it though I had often tried. "Look up," he said; "yon place high up the brae wi' the sun shining on it is the Canty Knowe; they ca' it now by anither name, but yon's the Canty Knowe." And there indeed it was, bright in the sunshine as it had been when I was a little child, and there first learned that the great God was the God of love and kindness. It was well to look up to it from the gloom of that burial-place.

A few days later, when we were expecting the Archbishop and his party, he arrived with Lucy. Where were Catharine and Aggie? They had got

out of the carriage half-way between Stirling and the
Cottage for the benefit of a long walk in the lovely
evening. One hour, two hours passed, and they did
not appear. What could have become of them? We
were anxious; the Archbishop was not—he knew better.
At length they appeared. Catharine had been reading
aloud as they walked along, and they had taken the
wrong turn in the road and gone some miles out of
their way. It was so characteristic of dear Catharine
that she had to undergo some chaff from the Archbishop, whose opinion was that she might have
learned more from the sunset on the Ochills than
from her book.

We were together nearly a fortnight, and very
soothing it was. The beauty of that nest among the
hills, with all its rural sounds of running water and of
wind among the trees, is indescribable; and to them it
was a brief space of holy rest and quiet. We had
more of the enjoyment of their society than I had had
for years. The girls wandered with Tilly about the
hills and glens, often accompanied by Catharine, whose
powers of walking and of climbing were undiminished.
I had my two brothers to myself,—what that time was
is indescribable;—the long past, the mournful present,
the thought of the future, so full of those who were
gone before, that it was much more as of heaven than
of earth, and made the whole thing seem more vision-
ary than substantially real.

During the last week Anna Pitman had joined the
party now gathered together for the last time in this
the home of her childhood. One feeling united us
all. Yet there were bright gleams shining out upon
us from time to time. The day before we were to part,
at dinner I sat between my brothers, and Catharine
was opposite, with that strange beauty of hers that

years could not dim and to which sorrow had only given an expression that penetrated the very heart. My eyes could not but rest upon her, and as the Archbishop caught my look he said with an understanding smile, " Yes, it is not every man who has a wife like that."

Next morning we all stood together on the little platform before the Cottage door — to part. Both James and I felt that here we should meet no more —but Catharine . . . That day week she lay down to die ; it needs not for me to tell of the three days through which she passed from earth to heaven, for I never saw her more.

CHAPTER XXVIII.

1882.—During a short visit to Lambeth in the month
of May there was an earnest request made to me to
spend the month of July there, till they should leave
the Palace for Addington ; the very circumstance of
my being able to do very little causing me to form
a sort of standpoint in the family, for, as the dear
girls expressed it, they always knew where to find
me. Pleased that at eighty-two I could still be considered of use, it was so settled.

When July came, on our arrival both Tilly and I
were painfully struck by the change we could not but
observe in our beloved Archbishop. His usual work
went on, but evidently it was a burden he could scarcely
bear, and I am convinced that he suffered greatly while
he dragged himself through his various engagements.

We found that his daughters were aware of the
change, and were endeavouring in every way they
could to cheer and support him under it. The usual
influx of guests staying in the Palace had been brought
to an end, and we lived a perfectly quiet life, reading
aloud every evening some amusing book. But the
light was gone from his countenance, and there was
a look as if of pathetic appeal which went to my

heart. When I ventured to speak of the work being
too much for him, he replied, "Do you think I do not
feel that? But what can I do?" "Might you not
diminish the number of your public engagements, which
are so various, and must be so fatiguing to you in
hot, ill-ventilated rooms?" "They are nothing," he
answered hastily; "they are rest to me compared with
the persecution of those eternal letters; it is to my
secretaries, not to me, you must talk." I did speak
to them, especially to Randall Davidson, his son-in-law.
"It is too true," was the reply, "that his work is too
much for him, and I know it so well that we spare him
in every way we can; there are many, many letters
which now are never shown him. But where his advice
is absolutely wanted, or where he has to give a decisive
judgment, they must be submitted to him, and the
work of this sort has increased tenfold and is increasing every year,—we cannot help it. It grows daily,
and the more that men everywhere understand and
appreciate his character it will grow. It is his known
spirit of fair-play, his sympathy and readiness to help
in every case of difficulty in the Church, that doubles,
trebles his work. It is nearly the end of this session.
He must leave all behind him and remain for the
rest of the year in quiet, except one most important
subject—*most* important for the Church—which he
has undertaken and will have to carry through before
Christmas." I groaned in spirit at this reply, for I
saw that there was indeed no help.

Ill though he was, he would not allow those recep-
tions which he considered duties to be omitted.
Pleasant duties they had always been to his genial
nature, but none who now attended these could mistake the change that had come over him: kind and
courteous as ever, there was a languor over his move-

ments that painfully told of exhaustion, and if an
approach to a smile flitted across his countenance, it
was when his eyes rested on his girls moving among
the distinguished guests of this last dinner-party, and
no one who was at the last garden-party will, I think,
ever forget it. He came and went among the various
groups, exchanging kindly words with every one, but
there was a look, a something, which seemed to tell
that he no longer belonged to the life in which they
lived.

The end of July came, and the Archbishop went first
to spend at Fulham a few quiet days with the Bishop
of London, leaving us at Lambeth. When he bade
me farewell he said, " I shall never return here."

Early in August he went to Osborne to confirm the
two sons of the Prince of Wales, the Princes Albert
Victor and George. Though scarcely able to undergo
such fatigue, he said, " It is the last service I shall
render to the Queen, and I will not give it up."

The month of August was one of most distressing
trial. That which he most dreaded he felt was too
surely approaching,—so great a failure of his bodily
powers as would compel him to resign the work
which, to his mental vision, was ever stretching
onward in the extension of the kingdom of his Lord.
He feared the sectarian spirit which seems to belong
to our very nature, harnessing as it were the Illimit-
able Good to a peculiar set of ideas, cramping world-
wide benefits into the bounded space of party views.
" I feel that I should be so miserable," he would
often say, " in the knowledge that measures were being
taken which would hinder instead of help forward the
work of Christ's kingdom, and that *I could do nothing.*"
His great fear was not death, but thus to live. God
did not intend this. But the restless weakness of his

body and this distress upon his mind caused these weeks to be the most trying period of his whole life.

In the last days of August the accounts from Addington were so alarming that I decided to go there. In a few hours we arrived, and found to our consternation that every one, each one of the family, even every servant, had lost all hope. " Why ? " was the natural question ; " what had happened ? " " He sleeps so continually," was the reply, " scarcely can he be roused to take food ; he is asleep again in a moment, and both the doctors think that his brain is comatose, and that he will pass away in that sleep." Well may he sleep, I thought ; he has done the work of three men every day for years. It is nature's rest ; his brain needs it, and he will wake up refreshed. " It is possible," was Sir William Jenner's reply to this suggestion, " but not probable." It proved, however, to be true. After nearly a week the drowsiness passed away entirely, and he awoke to renewed powers of mind,—not of body, for he still remained feeble, unable for more than the society of his immediate family, out that contained in itself continual interest. He had said to me on my arrival, " I am glad you are come back, you are a sort of mother in the house."

But I observed that though even his physicians were no longer apprehensive of danger, his own opinion never varied that he should not recover. More than this, there were times when it was difficult to persuade him that he could live another day. Still he was calmly and placidly happy, enjoying the different books, some amusing and some grave, that were read to him.

There was besides an interesting set of friends who, as it were, naturally belonged to him, and their society was pleasant to him. Canon Knollys, bound to him in closest friendship since he was a boy ; the Bishop of

Dover; and Randall Davidson, his son-in-law, who entered into his every thought, almost supplying the place of the beloved and only son, grief for whose early loss had too surely helped forward the condition of health which had laid his father low. These, varied by visits from many of his intimate friends associated with his episcopal life, his girls, and his bright young chaplain John Ellison, kept round him just the sort of cheerfulness that was good for him.

Towards the end of September the Bishop of Truro, of whom he had the highest opinion, came by special invitation to spend a week at Addington with his wife and their young son and daughter. There was in this family a tone of kindliness, with so much evident information, making itself felt in lively talk, that it was impossible not to feel attracted by them : the son and daughter were quiet and retiring, the Bishop and Mrs Benson agreeable and amusing, with an undercurrent of genuine religious feeling that soothed and satisfied all the way through the various subjects of conversation that were continually cropping up. The Archbishop was so much better that we felt easy about him, and could enjoy the variety the Bensons had brought to the family circle. At the end of the week we decided that we might safely return home. He had become reconciled to the idea of a prolonged life. He gave us both a parting blessing, and I cannot express the various feelings with which I knelt beside his bed feeling the pressure of his hand on my head. So many thoughts of his childhood and youth mingled with the present scene.

As the weeks went on, each one being a gain, we were looking forward to the time when it would be possible for him to be moved to a warmer climate.

But towards the middle of November a change came

over the tone of the letters; soon it was plain that
a deep anxiety predominated. Sir William Gull was
again consulted, and his report was "that, though
whatever disease there had been was conquered, his
strength was gone—in fact, that he could not rally."
Clear and truthful accounts were sent to me, but they
did not say " Come," and I had to balance in my mind
whether in the state of the weather, dangerous to one
of my age and tendency to bronchitis, I should be
a comfort to my nieces or an additional anxiety. A
few days more of indecision, and I could bear it no
longer, so we started again for Addington.

Hope had died out, and when the next day we
found him supported by pillows in his arm-chair, and
heard him say, "You have come to help me to die,"
I could only bow down my head to kiss his hand, for
I felt that he was dying.

.   .   .   .   .   .

Advent Sunday, December 3rd, 1882. — At half-
past seven this morning he passed away from the
midst of his kneeling children and the few who
watched through these closing hours of prayer and
praise.

.   .   .   .   .   .

The nurse came to invite me to the room in which
he lay. I stood amazed as I gazed upon him. It was
impossible to identify the weary, suffering, dying man
with the soldier-like figure in calm and deep repose
before me ; far handsomer than he had ever been in
life, his features had settled into an expression of
manly peace, as that of a commander who had fallen
asleep after the fatigue of battle, in the hour of victory.
A cross of white flowers was upon his breast, and above
it his hands lay partially crossed ; in one of them—that
one which bore the archiepiscopal ring—was placed, as

though he held it, a lovely white flower that had been sent him by the Queen. It touched me to the heart to see it there, for I knew how he loved and reverenced his Sovereign Lady.

Day after day the many voices of the nation have joined together in loving testimony of their grateful affection for him who has been removed from amongst them, we trust to a yet higher sphere where the glory of God and the salvation of man is more fully accomplished.

When I read all that the different newspapers of every shade of opinion say of the Archbishop of Canterbury who has just been taken from us, I cannot help the foolish wish arising that our dear old father could read all that is written of his beloved boy whose training and education were the interest and solace of his saddened old age. The seventy years of this remarkable life seem now to pass before me partly as a series of pictures, partly as a written history unfolding the wonderful goodness and power of God; for what else could have given to the suffering child, as he was led step by step through many disadvantages and difficulties, the manly strength of mind and body which has enabled him to do so much in upholding and advancing the Church of Christ?

CHAPTER XXIX.

AFTER the death of Archbishop Tait the late Queen
Victoria expressed a wish to see the elder sister who
had helped to watch over his childhood; and when
next Lady Wake stayed with her niece and the
Dean of Windsor the summons to the Castle was
given, and on her return to Pitsford of course she
told her family all about her visit.

"I was received by a lady-in-waiting, who conducted
me through long corridors to a small room in which
were two chairs, where I was left. The lady-in-
waiting's impressive silence and gentle pressure of
my arm, as if to say, 'Don't be afraid,' made me
begin really to feel rather nervous, when the door
opened and a little lady advanced so quickly that
before I could struggle to my feet she had kindly
laid her hand on my arm, bidding me to be seated,
and had placed herself beside me.

"The Princess Beatrice accompanied her and stood
behind her chair. Knowing that childhood's rule,
'Speak when you are spoken to,' holds good for
intercourse with royalty, I only answered her Majesty's
questions, and we spoke of my brother and of my
family. Then, remembering that the Queen could

not know all I could tell her, I said, 'Please, ma'am, may I speak?' Her Majesty laughed as she assented, and was much interested to hear all about Balmoral as it was before she and the Prince Consort bought it, my brother-in-law, Sir George Sitwell, having rented it for shooting. There were no pauses in the conversation after that as we talked of life in the Highlands in those early days."

The next time Lady Wake was at Windsor, when she was still older and more infirm, her Majesty, with gracious thoughtfulness, said she would not trouble Lady Wake to come to the Castle, but would visit her at the Deanery, which she did, accompanied by the Princess Beatrice and one of the Princesses of Hesse. And on that occasion Lady Wake's daughter and other visitors at the Deanery shared in the interview.

Having, in obedience to the Queen's request, sent her photograph, Lady Wake received an autograph letter from her Majesty, accompanied by photographs of herself, Princess Beatrice, and Prince Henry of Battenburg.

This, and subsequent correspondence, are here given :—

OSBORNE, *Feb. 2nd*, 1885.

DEAR LADY WAKE,—I have to thank you for a very kind letter and for the charming photograph of yourself, which it gives me great pleasure to possess, and which I think very like. I hope you will accept one of me in return.

Let me also thank you for your kind congratulations on my dear daughter Beatrice's marriage. I could never have consented to it, nor would she ever have desired it, had it not been for her continued residence with me. You know what it is to have a devoted daughter always with you, and will understand how necessary it is for me.

Prince Henry of Battenburg is very amiable, and possesses

all the qualities I could wish for, combined with very good looks.

I think you may like to possess his photograph as well as Beatrice's also

Hoping that you have quite recovered from your indisposition and your accident—Believe me always, yours affectionately,   VICTORIA, R I.

We have the pleasure of a visit from the Dean and your dear niece.

PITSFORD

MADAM,—It is difficult for me to express how deeply I feel your Majesty's kindness in sending me not only your own photograph but those of the Princess Beatrice and her intended husband. I never saw a more charming countenance, so expressive of earnest feeling and of manly kindliness. It is full of promise of a happy future to the devoted daughter who has been so great a blessing to your Majesty, and will, I trust, live to be so to her husband.

I possess a dear little engraving of the little Princess Victoria, your Majesty's self at seven or eight years old, so calmly sweet in life's early morning, and it is deeply interesting to mark the touching sadness that *now* blends with the same expression and fills your subjects' hearts with sympathy for all the sorrows that time has brought. But God has been with you from the beginning to bless and to guide you, and will to your life's end.

Permit me once more to express my gratitude for your kindness, and believe me to be ever your loyal and devoted subject,   C. M. WAKE.

January 8th, 1887.

MOST DEAR AND GRACIOUS QUEEN,—It is difficult to express my deep sense of the kindness that prompted you to send me a Christmas and New Year's card, and to write with your own hand those gracious words.

It is my earnest prayer that our God may take your Majesty into His most holy keeping, and surround you and yours with an atmosphere of blessing.—Believe me, your Majesty's loyal and devoted subject,   C. M. WAKE.

PITSFORD, NORTHAMPTON,
July 4th, 1887.

MOST DEAR AND GRACIOUS QUEEN,—While the atmosphere of joyful congratulation and devoted loyalty surrounded your Majesty, causing so much fatigue and excitement, I would not venture to intrude even for a moment the expression of my own feelings; but *now* I cannot but give them utterance, trusting that in your great kindness you will pardon me. I am indeed thankful to have lived to see the day of your Majesty's jubilee.

The grand chorus of joyful loving voices from every land where Queen Victoria's influence is felt, harmonising with the outburst of loyalty and love at home, proves how truly she has reigned in the hearts of her people; and we cannot but feel that the Father above has set His seal upon the nation's joy in every blessing He has given during the momentous week.

Such a page of history unrolls itself in my memory, beginning with the well-remembered Jubilee of George III, when all were expecting the French to land,—a fear so real that my father had a large carriage made to carry us and my mother up to the hills,—the long war ending with Waterloo, and the dismay caused by the death of the Princess Charlotte, that I feel sure your Majesty will pardon my fervent "Thank God!" for the very different condition of the country now, for the family love surrounding the throne, for the true affection of your people spoken in the universal "God save Queen Victoria!" and that you will graciously accept the expression of devotion and of trust that every blessing will be continued to your Majesty and to those you so dearly love.

That you and they may be ever kept in the secret of God's presence is the constant prayer of your Majesty's devoted and loyal subject,   '   C. M. WAKE.

OSBORNE, *July 26th*, 1887.

DEAR LADY WAKE,—I am so touched and pleased by your very kind letter that I cannot let any one thank you for it but myself, which I now do. It is wonderful to be able to look back and remember so many great events, and to be blessed with such a memory to be able to remember them all.

I hope you will accept my Jubilee Medal in recollection of this memorable event. I can never sufficiently express my deep feelings of gratitude and gratification at the wonderful display of loyalty and attachment on the part of my vast Empire, from high and low, rich and poor. It has sunk deep into my heart. The respect and interest shown by so many foreign rulers and their people has also been very gratifying.

Trusting that you are well—Believe me always, yours affectionately,   V., R.I.

PITSFORD, NORTHAMPTON,
August 2nd, 1887.

MOST DEAR AND GRACIOUS QUEEN,—It is very difficult for me to express how deeply I feel your Majesty's kindness in sending me the Medal of your Jubilee, doubly valued as coming from your gracious self. Still more valuable is the letter expressing in your Majesty's own hand the feelings of your heart as you dwell upon the widespread affection and loyalty that has flowed like a river from every quarter of the globe. No conqueror in olden time or in modern days ever received such a tribute. May it not be said of our Queen that with an army fewer in number than those of the other great nations, she commands the greatest force in the world, the force that comes from the service of willing hearts far and near?

That your Majesty may, with God's blessing, long live the Mother of your people, to be their example in difficult times and their sympathising friend in all their troubles, is the earnest prayer of your loyal and devoted subject,

C. M. WAKE.

THE END.

PRINTED BY WILLIAM BLACKWOOD AND SONS.